BABYFACE GOES TO
HOLLYWOOD

ANDREW GALLIMORE was educated at the University of Wales College of Cardiff and the University of Oxford where he was part of the Reuter Foundation Fellowship Programme for International Journalism. A former print journalist, he became a television reporter working on several news and current affairs programmes in the United Kingdom. In 1996 Andrew set up an independent production house that produces documentary films for the international market. The company's programmes have been distributed to over forty countries. Andrew has directed *The Devil's Gardens* – a series on the history of landmines; *The War Detectives* – a history of war crimes trials, and *Journeys Into Genocide* – a series on the history of genocide. He recently directed a second series on war crimes investigations for the Discovery network in the United States. He is also the author of several books: *The Devil's Gardens*, a history of landmines, to accompany the landmines series, *Occupation Prizefighter: The Freddie Welsh Story* and *A Bloody Canvas*. A feature-length documentary based on *A Bloody Canvas* has been screened at film festivals in the United States and Europe, and a film to accompany *Babyface Goes to Hollywood* has also been completed.

BABYFACE

------ GOES TO ------

HOLLYWOOD

FIGHTERS, MOBSTERS
& FILM STARS

THE JIMMY McLARNIN STORY

ANDREW GALLIMORE

THE O'BRIEN PRESS

DUBLIN

First published 2009 by The O'Brien Press Ltd.
12 Terenure Road East, Rathgar, Dublin 6, Ireland.
Tel: +353 1 4923333;
Fax: +353 1 4922777
Email: books@obrien.ie
Website: www.obrien.ie

ISBN 978-1-84717-116-0

British Library Cataloguing-in-Publication Data
Gallimore, Andrew
Babyface goes to Hollywood : the Jimmy McLarnin story
1. McLarnin, Jimmy 2. Foster, Pop 3. Boxers (Sports) -
Ireland - Biography
I. Title 796.8'3'092

1 2 3 4 5 6 7 8
09 10 11 12 13

Editing, typesetting and design: The O'Brien Press Ltd
Printed and bound in the UK by J.H. Haynes & Co. Ltd

Picture Credits:
Photographs of Jimmy McLarnin courtesy of James J. Houlihan, Jimmy McLarnin Jr and
D4 Films. Photograph of star (front cover) © iStockphoto.com.

Acknowledgements

There just isn't anywhere else to start but with Lydia who was an integral part of everything to do with this book, from conception to completion. Thanks go as always to my mum and dad and also to John, Nanette, Peter and Paul for their hospitality and generosity once again. I'd also like to thank Patrick Myler, James J. Houlihan, and Patrick Fitzgerald and Brian Lambkin from the Centre For Migration Studies at the Ulster-American Folk Park. Thanks are also due to Jimmy McLarnin Jr and the Department of Special Collections of the University Libraries of Notre Dame for all their help sourcing pictures. Much of the research was carried out at the New York Public Library and this book could not have been written without the extraordinary body of work left behind by the sportswriters who sat at ringside in Jimmy McLarnin's fights in the late twenties and thirties.

CONTENTS

PROLOGUE

The old man, like a jeweller with his diamond, worked on the kid. He was small, even for twelve, weighing no better than 80 pounds and standing no more than four feet six inches high, but the old man, 230 pounds, six feet tall and nearly fifty knew the boy was going to be a world champion one day. Jimmy McLarnin was apprenticed to Charles Foster and money was the alpha and the omega of the McLarnin-Foster creed. The boy of twelve had already tired of the smell of poverty and every punch he threw was for the dollar. Prizefighting was a quick road to the wealth he craved. The ring is the refuge of the underprivileged and all the great fighters have been recruited from the ranks of the downtrodden. 'Once the bell rings they want their fighters to have no retreat, and a fighter with an education is a fighter who does not have to fight to live and he knows it,' commented *The Ring* magazine. 'Only for the hungry fighter is it a decent gamble.'

War wounds had ruined his legs, he had rheumatism and had trouble walking, but from the waist up the old man was quick and agile and he showed the boy how to block, feint and slip punches. They worked on the basis that perfection was not even remotely attainable. You had to try for it, but no matter how

hard you tried for it or how far you got you had no right to be satisfied. Jimmy boxed and punched the bag with a book balanced
on his head to learn how to move quickly without any jerky head
movements that could make a fighter lose sight momentarily of an
opponent's eyes or hands. Foster took a 12-pound weight off an
old butcher's scales and tied two leather straps to it. Jimmy sat on
the edge of a chair biting at the straps and swinging the weight
back and forth to build up neck and jaw muscles. 'Training camps
are small factories for the production of one rare psychological
item,' wrote Norman Mailer, 'an ego able to bear huge pain and
administer drastic punishment.'

This ego factory was built in the basement of a second-hand
furniture store. The floor was sanded and polished and sprinkled
with sawdust to speed it up and hour after hour, night after night
Foster bellowed after Jimmy, demanding speed and still more
speed until the sweat poured off the boy like jets of blood from
an artery. 'Faster with the hands, Jim. Faster with the feet. In
with the left now, Jim. All right, out again. And faster, Jimmy,
you've got to do it FASTER.' There were times when Jimmy
wondered if Foster really knew what he was doing. If he had anything at all to start with it was speed. Why wasn't this old guy
spending more time worrying about the things Jimmy didn't
have? But to Foster the unforgivable crime was to teach the letter
B before the letter A. And for a fighter who'd learned his trade
taking on all-comers on fairground booths the letter A was
defence and the essence of defence was speed with feet, with
hands and with the head. 'If they can't hit you, they can't hurt
you,' said Foster, about ten thousand times. There wasn't money
for the steaks, lamb chops, fresh vegetables and fruit that a

fighter was supposed to eat. Foster did make Jimmy give up the things that a fighter is not supposed to eat. 'I swore off candy and ice cream with a feeling of great nobility and terrible loss. Barring an occasional slip, I stayed off them too.'

Jimmy was the best athlete in the Methodist Mission flock of the Rev. A.E. Roberts and he was good at any game that the Reverend organised. But there was no time for other sports if you wanted to be a fighter so Foster made Jimmy give up baseball, football and swimming to concentrate on boxing. Baseball muscles and swimming muscles were worse than no good at all to a boxer so when the other kids went swimming Jimmy punched the bag and when the other kids were getting up a ball game he was doing roadwork. While they were playing, Jimmy was running through the forest in Vancouver's Stanley Park. Foster believed that fighters were made, not born, and to build the complete prizefighter, he worked on mind and body. Good-natured guys didn't make good prizefighters and the ego that Mailer wrote of, that state of unfeeling a boxer needs to demolish a man he knows nothing about, was an integral part of honing the diamond. Down in the basement 'babyface' became the angelic cherub from hell.

'I can't deny that I started out with, or soon acquired, things that are useful to a fighter, things that a lot of kids don't have to start,' said Jimmy. 'My father gave me the constitution of a ring-post. My mother gave me a Methodist upbringing and I never had to be told that wine, women and song could ruin a boxer because I'd already been told and believed that wine, women and song could ruin anybody.' The diamond took little personal credit for his success; instead he gave most of it to the jeweller. 'Work hard, but more important get yourself a good manager. I know I had an edge over all the boxers of my day. I had the best manager in the game – Pop Foster. He made me, otherwise I might just have got myself into trouble like so many other poor kids. Believe me, you can't know what it can mean to youngsters unless you've been a poor one yourself.'

'The fantasies of "easy money", the lack of accessible vocational opportunities, and the general isolation from the middle-class culture, are similar for those who become professional boxers as for those who become delinquents,' wrote S. Kirson Weinberg and Henry Arond in *The Occupational Culture of the Boxer*. 'The difference resides in the role-model the boy picks, whether criminal or boxer.' Jimmy chose Charles Foster, a tall, grizzled, limping Liverpool-Irishman, who worked on Vancouver's docks one or two days a week as a stevedore. He had fought in the Boer War with the Scots Guards and in the Great War with the Canadian Overseas Railway Construction Corps where he came close to losing both legs after being blown up at Poperinghe in Belgium. His little army pension was the capital that financed Jimmy's first fighting years.

The Fosters of Liverpool were prizefighters. It was the time of the gypsy from Norfolk – Jem Mace, the great bare-knuckle champion – and as a child, Foster watched the magnificent Mace ply his trade. Charlie's uncle, Tom Foster, was a champion before the days of Queensberry Rules and his grandfather ran a boxing booth that toured the fairs. A booth fighter took on men of all weights and sizes, and for every round the challenger stayed, the owner of the booth paid out a pound. Charlie worked on the family booth as a boy, often fighting thirty times a day and he needed to knock out at least a dozen men in a few rounds to eat. 'I took 'em either bareknuckles or gloves,' Foster recalled. 'Wouldn't have done to count 'em. I just took on all as wanted to fight.' Legend has it that Foster boxed the great Bob Fitzsimmons, the first man to be world champion at three different weights, in England at age sixteen. There wasn't much Charlie Foster didn't know about fighting and when he was only twenty-one he took a tough eighteen-year-old from Leeds, Spike Robson, under his management and taught him the trade. Foster was in Robson's corner as his man fought such greats as George Dixon, Joe Bowker, Abe Attell, Joe Gans and Terry McGovern. 'Never won a championship, did Spike,' said Foster, 'but he was the best, easy. The uncrowned featherweight champion of the world.'

'I knew none of those things about Pop Foster then,' Jimmy recalled. 'Nor did I know the bigger things that were later to mean so much to me – his kindness, his quiet, simple wisdom, his tenacity and patience, his loyalty and his unshakable honesty. I wouldn't have suspected he could have all these qualities and still be as shrewd and hard and demanding as it was often necessary to be if you hoped to come out of a business like ours unhurt and solvent.'

Fighting was one of the few ways, at least legally, of making good money back then. The earnings of fighters ranged from $5 paid to palookas in small clubs, to the $200,000, $1,000,000 and $525,000 won by Gene Tunney in his three title fights. A young Jack Dempsey got as little as $2 for a one-punch knock-out in Salt Lake City. Fighters enough above the average to appear in the eight- or ten-round semi-finals on an ordinary bill of the big clubs and arenas got from $1,000 to $1,500 for their evening's work. The preliminary boys drew from $200 to $300 for six-round bouts, from $100 to $150 for four. The amounts paid to top-of-the-bill fighters were determined by their drawing power and that, in turn, was determined by the ability possessed by a fighter to knock opponents cold. It also helped if they were Irish.

The history of prizefighting in America to this time was the history of Irish immigration and in the days when 'No Irish Need Apply' notices were pasted on shop windows, factory gates and workshop doors, boxing was one way to a better life for men who were handy with their fists. Up to the early decades of the twentieth century the majority of those who participated in and attended prizefights were Irish. Then as the roaring twenties roared through America the supply of Irish champions was decidedly unequal to the demand and new immigrant groups crowded the celebrated Fighting Irish out of the picture. The Irish customers were still there and many a Lithuanian, Italian and Jewish fighter changed his name to some Irish derivative to attract a following. But the Irish were almost entirely eliminated as headliners in the game over which they once held sway. 'There are not many Irishmen prominent in the boxing world,' wrote Paul Gallico, the leading sportswriter and author of *The Poseidon Adventure*, in 1934. 'Offhand, I would say that this was distinctly to their credit. Prizefighting is not a very admirable sport.' Europe's poorest, the Famine-era Irish had inundated America's cities and they spent a long time climbing out of what William H. Williams described as 'the worst slums in American history'. They were despised for their religion and pinned down with poverty and social dislocation. But climb out they did and other ethnicities came in at the bottom of the pile and now it was their turn to fight their way out. The Irish had turned to more 'respectable' pursuits. Jimmy McLarnin would become the last of the great pugilistic idols of the Irish in America, the end of a lineage that had contributed more than any other race to championship prizefight history. 'When the stock market crashed and the factory smokestacks were capped, the gyms were full of fighters, career sparring partners were better than main-eventers today, but McLarnin was still better than the best of them,' wrote Pulitzer Prize winning scribe Jim Murray.

'When I was fighting I gave the job everything I had and I trained hard and fought hard,' Jimmy recalled. 'After winning my fights I'd turn a handspring in the ring and Pop Foster would wrap me in an emerald dressing gown decorated with a golden harp. Then I'd head up the aisle behind a bunch of Irish cops and if the fight had happened to be a real good one those wonderfully emotional Irish fans who used to come to my fights would break through the cops and carry me to the dressing room on their shoulders.' Jimmy McLarnin, with his fierce blue eyes, bright green robe and a shamrock on his trunks fought like an Irishman was supposed to fight. He was brave and game and knocked opponents cold. Jimmy became, in the words of one *Ring* columnist, 'an absolute godlike idol with the Irish'.

Jimmy's family took the boat when he was barely three years old. They travelled to Canada in steerage – a journey that left one of his older brothers dead. The Canadian Government was subsidising passages for those looking to become farmers and in the early years of the twentieth century the Dominion attracted more Irish emigrants looking to work the land than the United

States. A butcher in County Down, Jimmy's father Sam McLarnin made four ocean crossings before he took the family to make a go of it planting wheat in Mortlach, Saskatchewan, a village about twenty-five miles west of Moose Jaw. The Canadian federal government had supported an overseas immigration campaign since the 1870s to try and promote settlement of the prairie West. The Dominion Lands Act required only a ten-dollar registration fee, the construction of a habitable dwelling, three years' residence and evidence of cultivation or stock raising and the title to a homestead was granted. But life was hard and when Jimmy was nine the family moved to Vancouver, British Columbia, where Sam ran a second-hand furniture store and raised his twelve children.

Rural Ireland was barely a memory for Jimmy and for most of his life his home was the city. He learned his trade in Vancouver, but the place where he made his money and his name was New York. When the Irish first arrived there was no previous immigrant group to tell them how to act or what to do. So they created a new way of life that allowed them to thrive in the big city, a different world from what they had left behind in Ireland. And much of Jimmy's success and his standing as one of the great sports heroes of America during the Depression was his chameleon-like ability to rework himself into any environment.

For about thirty years controversy had surrounded his birthplace. The wish perhaps being father to the thought, it was claimed by many, his admirers, and some newspapers, that he was born in Dublin. Jimmy caused most of the confusion because for much of the time he would never disclose where he was born. His inevitable reply was 'I'm Irish,' or 'I'm Irish Jimmy McLarnin'. On a trip back to Ireland in 1934 he claimed to have been born in Inchicore when he was in Dublin and when in Belfast, he was from the Lisburn Road. 'Jimmy McLarnin's inability or discrimination to decide whether he was born in Dublin or Belfast today threatened another civil war between embattled residents of the two Irish cities,' commented the *Los Angeles Times*. 'Jimmy himself is a bit vague about the matter. In Dublin he thought, perhaps, he was born in Dublin. Today in Belfast he decided he probably was born here.' Jimmy said he was looking for the relatives who could straighten him out on the matter.

According to the *Belfast Sunday News* back in the 1960s, Jimmy was born in the Lisburn Road area of the city on 17 December 1905. 'His aunt, Mrs McLarnin who resides at Balmoral, says Jimmy's people belonged to the Derriaghy and Lisburn districts. He has a cousin, Mrs Ferris, of Cussick Street, Lisburn Road, who corresponds with him. He also has relations now living in Bangor.' Boxing writer Patrick Myler eventually solved the mystery and found Jimmy's birth certificate. It shows that James McLarnin was born in Hillsborough, County Down on 19 December 1907. The McLarnins soon joined the huge in-migration from the countryside to Belfast, before crossing the ocean to Canada.

Boxing became Jimmy McLarnin's business from the age of twelve. Charles Foster became Pop; he was the boy's manager, friend, father and mother. They became two stand-outs of their times. Pop and Jimmy kept themselves unspotted and held themselves aloof, while at the same time, exacting and receiving every penny that the traffic would bear and retaining it for their own particular and special purposes. Foster was the only manager of his type in the racket. Certainly he was the only one who openly and candidly resented the advances of the racketeers. 'Leave us be,' he would invariably wind up; 'the boy is mine.'

'It must have seemed a little funny to Jim's mother and father – an old guy like me spending all that time with their kid, teaching him the boxing racket,' recalled Foster. 'It never occurred to them, I guess, that he would ever turn into a fighter. Nobody who looked at his baby face thought so either. But I did. I not only thought so. I knew!' The McLarnins were none too keen to see their boy go off with the ex-Canadian soldier. Fighting seemed no kind of business to them and Jimmy was too frail for it anyway. What chance did the child have with the hard-faced, battered men who made a living in the ring? Well, let him go. The experience would do him good, and he'd be back soon enough. Besides, Foster was a kindly soul. The boy quit his job running an elevator, the old man quit his job as a stevedore on the docks and they set off for San Francisco, which was known at the time as 'The Cradle of Fistic Stars' because of the number of great fighters emerging from the city. Jimmy's mother gave him her last $20 and from that day on Jimmy McLarnin and Pop Foster trod the path of life together. 'It's not fair to expect anyone who hasn't been through it himself to understand what you have to do to be a professional boxer. For some the formula has come easier than it came to me. But I am sure it never came really easy to any body. Boxing was my business from the time I was twelve. I had nothing to start with except a quick wiry pair of legs and Pop's promise that he would make me a champion of the world if I did what he told me to.'

A BABY IN THE CRADLE
OF FISTIC STARS

I n the old days San Francisco was a fighting town and all the great prizefighters had been through there. Jack Dempsey showed up broke and beaten a few weeks after Fireman Jim Flynn had knocked him out in less than a round. He stayed a year and by the time he left he was on the way to becoming the most famous man in America. Heavyweight champ and San Francisco native 'Gentleman' James J. Corbett introduced science, refinement, and the white-collar man to the boxing game. He was largely responsible for getting prizefighting legalised in California, and San Francisco became the golden city of pugilism. It wore a veneer of civilisation and culture, but it was still a frontier town at heart. Gold poured in from the mountains and the city was cosmopolitan, brilliant, predatory, adventurous and sporty. Men bet on anything; and they bet everything on a fighter they liked. They flocked to the prizefights with guns on their hips and bags of gold dust inside their coats.

San Francisco had grown out of the lust for gold in the 1840s and prizefighting found a home there. The fighters clustered

around the Tenderloin district, a swarming downtown neighbourhood packed with gambling dens, brothels, billiard halls,
boxing gyms, speakeasies, theatres and restaurants. Legend had
it that it got its name because the cops got extra money for working its streets thereby affording them better cuts of meat. And on
a cold winter's morning in early 1924 a grizzled old man and his
108-pound, 4 feet 10½ inch prizefighter stepped off the *SS
Dorothy Alexander* in San Francisco bay. The kid had been sea-
sick all the way down and when he looked out the porthole
through the morning fog and saw the city hanging up there on
the hills he was homesick too. Jimmy said nothing to Pop, but he
knew that Pop knew anyway. He had never spent a night
away from home and there had never been a night when he
hadn't knelt beside his mother and said his prayers. And for
the previous year or so his mother's prayers had been that
Jimmy would give up on the idea of being a boxer.

Pop and Jimmy had worked together for four years and they'd
both put too much into it to think of turning back now.
Anyhow, they didn't have the money to go back. The boat fares
of $24 apiece had taken out most of Pop's savings and they were
within a few bucks of being broke. With only the old man's
small monthly cheque as a part pensioner of the Great War to
look forward to, Jimmy needed to start fighting. They got off the
boat and headed to the Observatory Club at Franklin and Grove
Streets, a notorious hangout for fighters and promoters. The
usual crowd of muffin-eared sparring partners, punchy ex-pugs
and cigarette-sucking loafers jammed the place. They met Frank
Schuler who was running weekly fight shows at the Dreamland
Rink. Pop told Schuler that his boy had won a dozen or more

amateur fights in Vancouver and was ready to turn pro. Jimmy, with a pair of ring shoes under one arm and trunks wrapped in a newspaper under the other, took off his cloth cap and smiled hopefully. This was a mistake. Schuler looked at Jimmy's round, pink face and said:

'That boy don't need a fight, he needs a nurse.'

'This boy's a lion,' Pop barked at sufficient volume to ensure that everyone in the gym could hear.

'In spite of the way I felt inside, I felt my shoulders squaring too,' Jimmy recalled. Pop marched the boy out of the Observatory Club, but Schuler came after them and explained that boxing was under local police control and that he'd lose his license if he tried to use anybody who looked as young and seemingly defenceless as Jimmy. He suggested they go across the bay to Oakland where the cops were a bit more accommodating. Pop had a long memory. Jimmy couldn't fight for Schuler when Jimmy was a nobody and afterward when he became a somebody, they never went back. But they did take Schuler's advice and took an attic room near West Seventh Street, deep in the black quarter of West Oakland. The $15 for the first month's rent left them less than $4 to eat on until they got a fight or until the next pension cheque arrived. Pop would buy a veal chop or a piece of round steak and a bushel of Brussels sprouts, which he got for a quarter by waiting until the markets were ready to close for the day. The room had one bed, a gas burner and a few dishes. Pop would boil up a mess of Brussels sprouts and he'd fry the chop or the steak, carefully cutting away all the fat for himself giving Jimmy the lean.

When there was no more money they went fishing for crabs.

Late in the afternoon, when the day's work was done, they'd tramp down the Southern Pacific tracks to the edge of the Oakland mole. Pop was an old seaman and dockhand and had made friends among the commercial fishermen who worked off the mole. Pop would borrow a dory and a net and he taught Jimmy how to snare sand crabs. They would put out around dusk and stay out until they had enough for dinner. It was a one-course menu. They'd walk back to West Oakland, Jimmy carrying crabs in a pail and Pop shambling slowly along beside him; they were known locally as the old man and the kid. They walked mile after mile without speaking; Jimmy in a frayed old suit and cap, Pop always in blue denim. 'It wasn't a bad life. Plenty of people have had worse,' Jimmy reflected. 'I wasn't feeling sorry for myself any more. I was just mad – mad because every day I went to the gym I saw a dozen or more fighters I was sure I could lick, and they were working regularly and I couldn't get enough work to pay for a haircut.'

They spent five weeks trying to crash the San Francisco fight game, and failed. 'No wonder you can't get him fights,' said Moose Taussig, a fight promoter, 'he has a baby face.' The name stuck. The hard-faced boxing men laughed at the gruff old man with the wide-eyed boy at his heels. The promoters grew angry at Pop's persistence. Others pitied them. One or two offered them money to go away but Pop wouldn't take it, he wanted to fight and earn the money. All they needed was a chance to show. The boy was a real card. Just give him a fight. They'd be bidding for him after that.

Jimmy trained every day at the Imperial gymnasium as if he was preparing for a title fight. You were either going to be a boxer or you weren't was Pop's belief. If you weren't going to be a boxer you were better off knowing nothing about it. If you were going to be a boxer then you might as well make up your mind that there weren't enough hours in the day, enough days in the year or enough years in a lifetime to learn so much about it that you didn't need to learn still more. Jimmy had sense enough to grasp this point almost from the start. He saw the old fighters – good fighters some of them – hanging around the gymnasiums with no place to go and nothing to do but wait for the next handout. Boxing was one business in which too much experience could be a very bad thing. Getting hit didn't teach you how not to get hit. Getting hit too often slowed your reflexes. The more often you got hit, the easier you became to hit, and the easier you became to hit the more often you got hit.

Nothing was left to chance. The difference between an easy winning fight and a disastrous losing fight, which in itself could mean the difference to a whole career, could be as slim as the difference between one punch that lands and the same punch that misses. And that difference in turn could be as small as the difference between five miles of roadwork and six miles of roadwork, between fifty minutes a day on the bag and an hour, between carrying a shoulder this way and carrying it that way. There were fighters who might have been world champions, but who ended up punch-drunk simply because they made some mistake as small as holding their left elbow half an inch too high.

The Imperial was just a few blocks from where they lived and it was also close to a saloon operated by Tommy Simpson. He was an ex-railway brakeman and Oakland's leading fight promoter who had given Dempsey his shot in the San Francisco area. Simpson started promoting as an assistant to his brother George back in 1905 and was responsible for the debuts of many ringmen who went on to become champions. He promoted in the days of unlimited rounds; saw boxing outlawed in 1914, but carried on under the guise of so-called four-round amateur bouts. When the sport became legal again a decade later he was still in the saddle. Pop pleaded with Simpson to come and see his boy and eventually, one day in February 1924, he got lucky and the promoter came to the Imperial. It was the first time Pop and Jimmy had seen Simpson in the gym. Jimmy had a bundle under his arm that contained a worn out pair of shoes and the faded tights his mother had made. He borrowed a pair of gloves, but there was nobody his size to fight him.

'I'm sorry,' Simpson said. 'If that kid's more than thirteen, I'm Methuselah.'

Pop looked around and the next smallest fighter in the gym was 'Oakland' Jimmy Duffy, the welterweight champion of California. They went three rounds and even though he didn't get a dime for them, in many ways they were the most important rounds Jimmy ever fought. He had to show Simpson that Duffy couldn't hurt him so all through the three rounds Jimmy kept running faster and faster and Duffy kept getting madder and madder. Occasionally Jimmy darted in and hit him a couple of light lefts on the jaw and then he'd scurry away like a jack rabbit in reverse while Duffy came after him, swinging from the heels. By the end of the second round everybody else in the gym had stopped working and crowded around the ring taunting Duffy.

'He didn't see anything funny in it and neither did I, because his pride and my bread and butter were at stake,' recalled Jimmy.

When the third round was over, Duffy wanted to go on but Pop hustled Jimmy out of the ring and over to Tommy Simpson. Still Simpson was afraid to use him. He was afraid he'd get hurt. But the boys told Simpson the old man and the kid were broke so he told them to show up for the curtain raiser on his next card at the Auditorium.

Boxing in California was limited to four rounds and the shortness of the route sped up the pace. You couldn't stall for a second and get away with it in a four-rounder. But there again Jimmy had no intention of stalling. He was a very bashful, self-conscious little chap who rarely talked and blushed as easily as a schoolgirl, but when he stepped into a ring he became feral. Jimmy's opponent was Frankie Sands, a flyweight who'd had eight or nine professional fights. Jimmy knocked him down in the first round and went on to win an easy decision. The purse was $25, which paid the back rent and the gas bill. Simpson had bought a lot of action for very little cash and Pop convinced him that Jimmy was worth at least fifty bucks next time up. Jimmy worked for Simpson again the following week and he knocked out Eddie Collins in the third. From then on Jimmy appeared in seven straight curtain-raisers in seven weeks. In the spring of 1924 it warmed up, the summer fogs from San Francisco Bay started to roll over Oakland and Jimmy McLarnin made his name. He was promoted to the ranks of a 'semi-final wind-up' fighter and the baby face was an asset now; he just looked so different from the usual run of pugs. Jimmy fought most weeks and his purse grew from $25 for the Sands fight to $200 for a match with Frankie Grandetta. They quit eating crabs and Brussels sprouts, started riding on streetcars and bought some new clothes. One reporter described Jimmy's new garb as 'cheap and somewhat gaudy', while Pop acquired a suit of hand-me-downs and a new cap.

'What good is a medal?' a thirteen-year old Jimmy had asked after an amateur bout back in Vancouver. Pop bit the medal, spat and agreed they were not edible. Jimmy's mother disapproved of boxing, so to spare her feelings and to keep himself out of trouble he boxed at the smokers under the name of Jimmy Lane. He fought 'amateur' bouts in Vancouver for a couple of years and his biggest purse was $2.50 credit at the local grocery store. But he saw a chance to get rich and finally his folks had agreed to let him go a-wandering with a grey, cross-grained old Limey who thought the world of him. Pop cooked his meals and treated Jimmy as though he was his own kid instead of just another fighter worth so much on the fistic market. They set off along the long road without even a piece of paper for a contract. Now they had made $1,300 from five months fighting and Pop decided that the pair deserved a holiday, so they returned to Vancouver. There was still $300 left after settling the rent and the boat fare was paid. Pop insisted that Jimmy take every cent of it home to his mother.

Jimmy was courted by local promoters through the summer, but there wasn't a purse to interest Pop Foster. 'I fought in Nanaimo,' Jimmy said years later, 'as hard a bout as I ever had and received $2.50 for my end. What did Vancouver, or Canada for that matter, ever do for us? We had to go to the United States to make any money. Why should we feel grateful? We owe Vancouver nothing.' The old adventurer knew there was nothing more for them in Jimmy's hometown so they struck out on the trail once more. They were as flat broke as ever when they returned to California in the late summer of 1924, but this time they knew there was money to be made. Pop was thrifty by nature, and according to one scribe he was recognised in all languages, including the Scandinavian, as being the final authority on how to make a nickel do half a dollar's work. What Pop Foster didn't know about economy could be written on the head of a pin with a railroad tie. So with every dollar earned from their first campaign deposited on Mary McLarnin's lap, Pop and Jimmy worked their passage to San Francisco aboard a coastal tramp; Pop as a deck hand and Jimmy peeling potatoes and onions down in the mess.

Their first port of call was Tommy Simpson, the only promoter to give them a shot in the long, lean days. But Simpson had run out of opponents for Jimmy so he sent them on to Los Angeles where there were several really good fighters around the boy's weight. He wrote them a letter of introduction to Jack Doyle, the biggest promoter in Southern California. Doyle was based in Vernon and he turned the place into the focal point of boxing in the Los Angeles area. The movie people used to go to the fights and Mae West was a regular. Vernon was famous for prizefighting and meat-packing and the fighters could smell the slaughterhouses from the ring. It was also a little out-of-town, so they could sell liquor there.

Jimmy's first opponent in Vernon was Benny Diaz, a better man than he'd met up until then. According to the *Los Angeles Times*, 'McLarnin, who looks like a kid of twelve, but who fights like a veteran, threw so many gloves at Diaz that the Mexican must have thought everybody around the ring was taking a poke at him. McLarnin won all the way. He is a classy kid.' Next up was Frankie Dolan who fared little better than Diaz. Dolan was given 'as artistic a trimming as local fans have seen for a long time.' The 'cleverest kid to show here in years' was an instant hit at the Vernon box-office. In those days Jimmy really was a 'Baby Face'. When he climbed through the ropes women gave vent to sighs of distress and thought it was just too terrible that the little fellow should be sacrificed. After the fight was over they were still sorry ... but for Jimmy's opponent. Most of the boxing clubs in the Los Angeles area were complaining that little fellows didn't draw at the gate, but Jimmy was selling-out the Vernon Coliseum. 'I suppose I had passed a turning point, but looking back on it, I can't honestly say that I felt much different,' Jimmy recalled. 'My routine between fights was still work and rest – work and rest – work and rest.'

Jimmy's debut as a headline fighter came when he was still shy of his seventeenth birthday. He was matched with Fidel La Barba who had won a gold medal at the Olympics in Paris a few months previously and was just starting out as a professional fighter. They fought two close four-rounders; Jimmy winning the first, the second was scored a draw. A sparring partner's head opened the soft flesh over his left eyeball before the second fight. It didn't show when he was looking straight ahead so Jimmy put a piece of adhesive tape over the other eye to draw attention away from the cut. He lost the tape during the fight, but the injured eye was untouched. 'Fidel La Barba and Jimmy McLarnin are the little cusses who have all Southern California by the ears,' reported the *Los Angeles Times*. 'It has been many years since little fellows have been able to attract the fans as have Fidel and Jimmy.'

Los Angeles was a good place to be a prizefighter in the winter of 1924. Boxing was re-legalised in the State and fights of ten rounds were permitted once more and suddenly there was good money to be made in fighting on the Coast. But the new rules required fighters to get a licence and you had to be eighteen to get one of those. Jimmy, who was sixteen years old and looked still younger, got creative. He wrote away to Mortlach, Saskatchewan, his first home in Canada claiming that he had been born there eighteen years previously, but that his father had forgotten to register his birth and could he please have a birth certificate. It took quite a bit more correspondence, but eventually Jimmy got a birth certificate from Regina and then a boxer's licence in California.

Now that he was 'legal', Jimmy was booked as the main event in Jack Doyle's first ten-rounder in Vernon. His opponent, once again, was Fidel La Barba. Doyle put two thousand new seats in his arena, bringing his capacity to ten thousand – and he needed them all when Jimmy and La Barba got together. Jack Britton, a former world welterweight champion, was at ringside and said: 'I never saw such a bout in all my ring experience. These two boys are marvellous. The boxing game today has not their equal.' Jimmy won another hairline decision and his end of the gate was $3,000, almost as much as he'd earned in all the rest of his life put together, including four years of selling newspapers, a year running an elevator and nearly a year's professional boxing. Pop and Jimmy may have been making real money now, but it certainly wasn't changing their spending habits. 'The roughnecks of the sport world won't know how to take Jimmy as champion,' wrote Paul Lowry in the *Los Angeles Times*. 'He's a shy, retiring kid, and he cares for none of their ways. Nor does Pop Foster. The old man is all wrapped up in the kid. What they do with their money nobody knows. It's cached somewhere and if the truth is ever told the pair are likely to retire from the ring with the biggest pile that anybody except heavyweight kings and their managers have accumulated.' Pop Foster became Jimmy's manager, trainer, mother and father. Every morning he donned the apron and poached the eggs and browned the toast for his boy. In the afternoon he donned the gloves and taught Jimmy how to be a prizefighter. This was a hard game, but Foster was a student of boxing, he was raised in it, and Jimmy had more care – more ideas for his development being applied to him – than any other fighter. Blows stung, they hurt, so the boy learned how to protect himself and he came out of most of his fights without a mark on him.

There had been a lot of hard work and heartbreak and the big purses hadn't come easily. It was a lonely life with thousands of miles of roadwork, countless hours in the gym, a rigid diet and no late hours. Jimmy and Pop moved into two rooms over a grocery store in Echo Park, not far from the radio evangelist Aimee Semple McPherson's temple. There was a playground across the street and now and then Jimmy wandered over after supper and threw a ball around with some other kids. After a while, when it got too dark to play ball, the others would wander off, maybe to go to a show or to buy their girls a soda and Jimmy would go back across the street and go to bed to be fresh for roadwork in the morning. 'I don't think I envied those other kids,' Jimmy recalled, 'but I'd have been surprised if they'd told me they envied me.'

After La Barba came Teddy Silva, one of the best bantam-weights on the Coast. Jimmy floored Silva twice and almost had him out in the eighth round. Silva's nose was broken in the fifth. When the fight was over, Silva put his arms around his opponent and mumbled:

'Thanks for letting me stay, Jimmy.'

'That's all right, Teddy,' said Jimmy, but he felt a hypocrite. Jimmy figured fighting was far too dangerous a business and what you got out of it came too hard to start giving things away – he never carried anybody in his life. Young Farrell and Eddie 'Spec' Ramies were both beaten in six rounds and Pop decided that Jimmy needed to rest. They set off for Gillman Springs where Jimmy lived the life of a boy, not a fighter. He played tennis and golf and returned, sun-tanned and rugged, to Los Angeles where Charles 'Bud' Taylor lay in wait. And Taylor was a killer.

THE HURT BUSINESS

Bud Taylor's shoulder popped out of its socket in a fight with George Rivers in 1924. Taylor stuck out a left jab to keep Rivers away, grabbed his right wrist between his knees, hobbled back, standing Rivers off with his left and tugged at his right with his knees until the dislocated shoulder dropped back into place. It went out again in the next round and Taylor did the same thing. He won the fight on points. Taylor had taken over a hundred fights and his record showed that he fought and usually beat the best men around. He'd killed one man and would go on to kill another. Frankie Jerome and Young Nationalista both died after fighting Taylor and though he was sorry, he never felt at fault, and the raw brutality of his fighting remained undimmed. He was a born fighter with a killer instinct, and now he was going to box a seventeen-year-old boy.

For the first four rounds the Babyface gave the Killer more than he could handle. Little Jimmy was winning all by himself until Taylor switched his attack and beat the kid with countless left hooks over the last six rounds. Jimmy's streak of nearly forty fights without a loss was over. But Taylor was already hailed as the uncrowned bantamweight champion and the decision didn't really hurt Jimmy. Indeed, the following month he was matched with Pancho Villa, the world flyweight champion. It was an overweight match, so Villa's title wasn't at stake, and Jimmy went into the fight a big underdog. He was such an outsider in the betting that even Pop, of whom it was rumoured still had the first buffalo nickel he ever collected, put up $100 and made a bet.

'It just wouldn't be sensible to pass up a price like that, would it?' the old man asked gravely.

Pancho Villa had been complaining of an infected wisdom tooth, but Jimmy and Pop put it down to the usual training camp chatter from somebody trying to build an advance alibi or make what looked like a one-sided fight look closer. But Villa really was suffering and the night before the fight a dentist was called to the champion's room at the Whitcomb Hotel. Dr H.E.R. Pascoe found Villa in bed with the right side of his jaw badly swollen. The swelling extended almost to his neck and, according to the doctor, was 'as hard as my desk'. Villa could barely open his jaw so Pascoe gave him gas and pried his mouth open to cut away the gum and pull the tooth. The dentist warned that the infection had spread throughout the side of Villa's face and down his throat. He told Villa's handlers not to take the fight, but eventually Pascoe was persuaded to go to the Oakland ballpark, where he treated the champion just before he stepped between the ropes with a perceptible swelling on his jaw. According to *Time* magazine, 'a doctor had shot his face with cocaine to dull the pain'.

The rains of the morning had threatened to cancel the fight

but the skies cleared and some twenty thousand people packed into the ballpark. Wild rumours fizzled around ringside. Was Villa going to show? Was the fight fixed? Had the 'sure-thing' boys got to the champion? The betting fluctuated. Villa was 4 to 1 on, but then came the stories and he was no better than a 10 to 7 shot. The champion's manager, Frank Churchill, asked the State Commission, the promoter and the referee to demand that all bets be called off. The Commission didn't 'recognise' betting and could not take such action. Referee Johnson said he would refuse to officiate before calling off bets. Promoter Simpson wouldn't intervene. So Churchill issued a statement: 'I am making this statement for the press just before the contest,' wrote Churchill. 'I am making it in justice to the gamest little man I ever knew. Villa is not himself. But he insists on going through with the fight because he says people came from all over the country to see him and he will not disappoint them. He further realises that Tommy Simpson would be put to a loss of thousands as the contest could not be postponed. Therefore, under the greatest handicap I have ever seen a fighter knowingly enter the ring, Villa will go in and do his best under the circumstances.'

Dr Judson Litchfield of Oakland, the boxing commission's doctor, passed Villa fit. Litchfield found the champion's temperature one degree higher than the norm, his blood pressure perfect and he didn't notice any swelling on the side of Villa's face – in fact, he admitted that he didn't pay any particular attention to the fighter's face. So on a baking hot 4 July afternoon, before thousands of fevered fans, Jimmy McLarnin and Pancho Villa slugged it out for ten rounds and there was no dissention when the referee gave the verdict to Jimmy. Villa's dentist, Pascoe, noted that his patient was hit with several stiff punches on the side of his face and 'unquestionably these blows shook him up and scattered the poison'.

Jimmy awoke the following morning to find himself famous. He'd beaten the world flyweight champion and Pop was deluged with telegrams from promoters in all parts of the country. Jimmy McLarnin was suddenly one of the outstanding attractions in American prize rings and little did anybody know that he was still only seventeen years old. Pop and Jimmy took their takings of $5,919.45 and hid away at the home of friends in Berkeley, and if there was any celebration it was confined to a very few. Within a few days the old man and the kid set off for Vancouver to visit the folks and then a long rest in the hills. There would be no talk of any boxing match while Jimmy was taking to the tall timbers and the wide-open spaces. Before departing the pair called at the editorial rooms of the *San Francisco Chronicle* where someone remarked to Foster:

'Well, you got a nice little chunk of money for yourself.'

'Jimmy has a nice little bit of change,' corrected Pop. 'For me, I don't care much about money. I'm a pensioner of the Canadian Government, you know, and that takes care of my wants. And as for Jimmy, he frankly admits he is glad to have this windfall, because it helps him take better care of his mother and father and brothers and sisters. There's a family of twelve in Vancouver, and they can do nicely, thank you, with a little change on the side.'

Pancho Villa spent the day after the fight with the dentist who extracted three more teeth. His recovery was helped along with news from Manila that he'd just become the father of a ten-pound son; mother and boy were reported doing well. But three days later Pancho Villa was dead. The early reports were confused. It was given out that he died from infected teeth, but many believed it was the unmerciful beating handed out to him by Jimmy McLarnin. Villa died on the operating table at St Mary's Hospital on the morning of 14 July 1925 at 11.10 just as Dr Charles E. Hoffman was preparing to operate upon the Filipino's infected throat. Three or four whiffs of the ether and Villa was dead. All efforts to resuscitate him proved in vain. He never regained consciousness from the moment he fell over on his side. Dr Pascoe, the dentist who had treated the fighter was in the operating room when Villa died. 'I want it definitely understood that I had objections to permitting Villa entering the ring, but was overruled,' Pascoe reiterated.

A coroner's jury decided that Villa died because he had neglected his own health; anxious as he was to please the paying public 'he danced away from strict care of his surely infected jaw'. The jury also decided – at least by inference – that Villa's fight with Jimmy was not the cause of his death. Many witnesses testified at the inquest, many words were spoken and there was a lot of ill-feeling, but the verdict placed the blame on no one, and according to the *San Francisco Chronicle* 'those who knew Pancho Villa, the game fighter, believe he would be as charitable'.

Pancho Villa was not the only fighter to die in such circumstances around this time. Boxing writer Peter Benson believes that the mob had found a way of getting rid of fighters who refused to go along with fixes, and that it was to get a doctor to kill them. 'Harry Greb, Tiger Flowers, and Pancho Villa all died on operating tables of overdoses of ether. Anesthesia was an imperfect science then. But three world champions, two known to have been involved in fixes, all dead within two years from the same "accident"?'

'A lot of people blamed poor Pancho's manager, afterward, for not calling off the fight,' Jimmy recalled. 'I think those who said the manager was responsible for the fighter's death were being too harsh. But I can't help thinking, and couldn't help thinking then, that if his manager had been Pop Foster, Pancho wouldn't have died. With Pop the fighter always came first and so many things could happen to hurt a fighter in the ring that the manager had to be sure that nothing was going to hurt him outside.'

That summer, in Jimmy's words, 'the things that happen in books started happening to me'. He bought a new house for his mother and father and the eight brothers and sisters who were still living at home. The house was in a better district and the seventeen-year-old spent $8,000 on the property and furnished it throughout. Hard up as his family had always been, Jimmy's mother wasn't the sort of woman who'd have let any amount of money change her convictions. But she looked at her boy very carefully and after twenty-three professional fights she couldn't find a mark on him. She seemed to be satisfied that whether what Jimmy was doing was a good thing or a bad thing for a boy to be doing, he at least had a chance to come out of it with his health. The fights had taken their toll on Jimmy's hands however. He'd hit a lot of heads with pretty thin gloves since he was a twelve-year-old fighting smokers in Vancouver. In one of those early fights the promoters had promised everybody on the card a steak dinner after the show. 'We didn't have steak at our house very often and I was looking forward to it,' Jimmy recalled. He broke his right thumb in the first round and the steak turned out to be pretty tough. He was too proud to let anybody help so he sawed away at the meat holding the knife between the first and second fingers of his left. He kept dropping the knife and fork and the steak kept skidding off his plate.

A hard campaign in California had left both hands damaged so they went north to the Gulf of Georgia where Jimmy rowed a boat while Pop fished and at night the precious hands were pickled in a brine-based recipe specially prepared by the old man. With both paws back to their bone-crunching best Jimmy worked on a punching bag in the back yard of the new family home and ran five or six miles to Buffalo Park and back. His route took him past a public tennis court and it was there, in the summer of 1925, that Jimmy McLarnin first saw Lillian Cupit. Every time he ran past the tennis courts Jimmy slowed down in the hope he'd see somebody who knew him and might know her too. One day he did. Jimmy stopped and hung around until he got introduced. He asked Lillian if she'd play tennis with him sometime. She did, and beat him in two straight sets – a professional athlete going on for eighteen beaten by a junior high-school girl. Jimmy decided that if he was going to impress her, he'd better stick to his own game. So for the rest of the summer he re-routed his runs past her house and sprinted down the block with his knees coming right up under his chin. Lillian was invited over to watch Jimmy punch the bag and he hammered it to within an inch of its life.

'Why that's wonderful, Jimmy!' Lillian said.

'I knew she meant it, but I also had a sinking feeling that she couldn't imagine why anybody in his right senses would be doing such a thing in the first place,' mused Jimmy.

Jimmy's summer in the sun with Lillian was extended thanks to Pop. After the Villa fight he had let slip that his fighter was only seventeen and Jimmy promptly drew a suspension from the boxing commission. There was talk of a fight in Canada against an old amateur adversary, Mickey Gill. Jimmy and Mickey were both products of Vancouver's East End and were deadly rivals. In their first meeting as young boys Jimmy lost a wildly disputed decision to Gill on a wet canvas in a ring pitched in a ballpark on a rainy night. They fought again a week or two later and this time Jimmy was an easy winner. A rubber match was staged at old Beaver Club, across from the historic Woodward's building in the downtown eastside of Vancouver. The place was jammed to the roof and the fighters couldn't hear the bell or the referee or anything else but people shouting themselves hoarse. It was supposed to be a six-round fight and Jimmy didn't find out until later that it went seven because the customers were making such a racket. 'What a fight! They were still talking about it when Pop and I left for California,' Jimmy recalled. But all the talk didn't generate the sort of purse to interest Pop and despite several offers to fight in Canada over the years Jimmy never fought there again.

The money was in California and one of Los Angeles' favourite sons, the Olympic featherweight champion Jackie Fields, lay in wait. As soon as Jimmy's suspension was lifted the promoters got busy. A McLarnin-Fields bout had been talked of as one of the outstanding fights on the calendar for many months but Pop had turned a deaf ear. 'I didn't want that fight,' he later said. 'Fields was a featherweight at that time, Jimmy was only a bantam. I wanted Jimmy instead to fight Vic Foley in Vancouver. But Root [the promoter] kept after us, so I let Jimmy go.' The fight was to be staged at the Olympic Auditorium, Los Angeles' newly-built 'largest and finest boxing stadium in the world'. It dwarfed New York's Madison Square Garden and was regularly packed with the cream of cinema society. The customers flocked to the Olympic as much to see the movie stars at ringside as the boxers in the ring. The building stood as lavish testament to boxing's new-found respectability as prizefights shared a stage with political conventions and grand opera at the Grand Avenue arena.

The talk along the Rialto in the build-up was that Jimmy was developing into a knockout puncher. During his training sessions he was said to have broken the nose of Terry Adams, a middleweight, and had Jack Sparr and Joe Garcia, a tough Mexican, almost out with terrific punches. 'This is something entirely new in the McLarnin category of strokes,' reported the *Los Angeles Times*. Pop's theory was that muscle and speed did not make for harmonious ring relations. Jimmy took particular pains during his training periods to prevent muscular development, particularly around the shoulders. He would romp in from his morning road exercises gripping sponges in place of the usual steel weights. It had long been expounded by veteran trainers that the way to insure against arm weariness in a fight was to force the muscles to full-time labour. But Pop believed that speed was the real secret of hard hitting, the faster the punch, the greater the harm. The velocity of the rifle bullet is what causes the damage and Jimmy learned how to hit fast without pulling back his fists.

'During my years in the ring I was often credited with one-punch knockouts,' said Jimmy. 'But I never knocked a man out with one punch in my life and if I had I'd have been thoroughly ashamed of myself. A fighter who knows his business doesn't try for one-punch knockouts. Unless you're boxing an out-and-out ham the absolute minimum for a scientific knockout is two punches – one to create the situation and one to create the knockout. You take those who are fast and send their blows forward with lightning effect and you'll find that they seldom slug away at the heavy bag. They don't have to. Those are the fellows who do their roadwork consistently, skip the rope, punch the light bag and shadow box to maintain their speed and agility. They throw damaging blows.'

There was a story making the rounds that the fix was in for Fields. There was no evidence that it was true but Pop had been mixed up with the fight game for forty years – plenty long enough to know that fixed fights could be arranged without the knowledge of both or either of the fighters. If the mob had got to the referee then the decision could easily be bought. 'You'd better go after this boy right away,' said Pop.

The second round had scarcely opened when Jimmy backed Fields into the ropes and threw an overhand right that landed flush on the chin. Fields fell through the ropes, face down; his head striking the edge of the ring. He got up without waiting for a count. He fell again, but staggered to his feet and reeled towards Jimmy who met him with another right and Fields went to the floor again. Fields took a five count, got up and went down from another right for a seven count. Then came the last juddering right that finished it. Fields was flattened so hard they picked resin out of his shoulder blades for a week. The boys had said that Jimmy wasn't a hitter. They had rated him as a boxer, but there was Jackie Fields, Olympic champion and a sure-fire bet for a world title, flat on the floor. 'I knew it was a hard punch when I threw it and when it landed I knew it was harder than I'd hoped. I heard his jaw crack and he went backward through the ropes,' Jimmy recalled.

'He could hit something terrible, could Jimmy,' sighed Pop.

Jimmy was proclaimed the new 'future champion of the world' as the previous 'future champion of the world' was having x-rays confirming a jaw broken in two places. But Jackie Fields came out of that crushing defeat to embark on a run of victories over leading fighters and eventually to the world welterweight title. For the victor it was very different and as Jimmy admitted, 'I came out of my smashing victory and headed toward oblivion.'

Pop knew it was coming and he had been beset with a worry that dogged him for years. Jimmy was still very young and was rarely the same weight from one month to another. The boy was growing fast and he'd shot up more than six inches between his seventeenth and eighteenth birthdays. He was constantly drawn between weights and it was hard to match him properly. It was obvious that before long he'd leave the featherweights behind and would be fighting lightweights and welterweights. Pop and Jimmy agreed that he should slow down in the ring and give away a little speed for a little more power. As nature was making over his body, Pop was making over Jimmy's fighting style. But while this process was going on Jimmy developed a slight attack of jaundice and during the next year and a half he had to take two fairly long lay-offs because of a series of illnesses. Not even shrewd old Pop really understood just how his boy was changing, how his increasing weight and the effort it took Jimmy to keep it down if he was to remain a particular class was affecting him.

'The only trouble was Jimmy learned too fast,' said Pop. 'His schooling was practically completed before he was old enough to take advantage of it.' Some of his boyish fire had gone, he looked drawn and pale, but he tried to convince himself that it was just a temporary phase; like spring fever or a cold that he would fight himself out of. But Jimmy's condition wouldn't just pass like that and he was lucky not to get hurt more than he did while trudging through this stage of his career – especially considering that his next two fights were against the Terre Haute Terror, Bud Taylor.

It was a match to delight the more ghoulish fight fan, two killers of the ring fighting one another. To make matters worse, the fearsome Taylor was coming into this fight fully fit for the first time in many moons – or so he thought. A week before the fight Taylor had no broken bones, no bruises, no boils – the first time he had been physically all there for a year and a half. Then a nice boil developed on his left arm. 'Now I feel natural again,' smiled Bud. 'I'm lonesome when there isn't something the matter with me. In the last eighteen months I have fought with broken hands, arms out of sockets, sprained ankles, a lame back and most everything that classifies as a physical ailment. This boil won't hurt me for McLarnin. It's just uncomfortable.'

A packed house of ten thousand jeered when, in the second round, Referee Benny Whiteman awarded Jimmy the bout on a foul. Taylor had won the opening stanza during which he'd hit Jimmy low twice, but Whiteman missed them both. The second round had been underway little more than a minute when Taylor landed a low left and was promptly disqualified. Jimmy offered to fight on, but State Commission Chairman Seth Strellinger refused to let it continue, ruling that the referee's decision was final.

The inevitable rematch came a few weeks later and according to one ringside reporter, 'Baby-face Jimmy McLarnin, the Oakland Infant, was just exactly that and no more, in the hands of Bud Taylor, in their return match at the Vernon arena last night. Ten rounds they milled, with Bud outboxing and outsmarting his Coast opponent. The nifty Midwestern mitt artist was simply too clever for Jimmy, and left-jabbed and hooked his way to the verdict.'

'Bud didn't bite me but he did everything else,' Jimmy recalled in later years. Taylor poked Jimmy in the eye with his thumb. The swelling soon closed it and Taylor battered Jimmy for the rest of the fight. The scribes believed the knockout of Jackie Fields had done 'something to Jimmy McLarnin's complexes'. The consensus of opinion was that the thrill that came from flattening Jack Fields had turned Jimmy right-hand crazy. Now when he stepped through the ropes he felt it necessary to knock somebody else out. The master boxer, Pop's honed diamond, had become a brawler. Damon Runyon, the legendary sportswriter, was at ringside for the Fields fight.

'McLarnin once tried to change his style,' wrote Runyon. 'He was at his best strictly as a boxer; then one night he bowled out Jackie Fields with a right-hand smack to the chin. Thereafter, for a spell, McLarnin was "right hand daffy", as we say at the club. All boxers want to be sluggers and belt the boys out, just as all sluggers usually want to be boxers. McLarnin was imbued with the idea of becoming a knocker out, but the Taylor shellacking changed his views to some extent. He went back to boxing, and in the meantime, as he took on weight, his hitting improved. He does not strike an opponent as fast on his feet because he does not jump around much. He has a curious style of slipping punches with his head and body, and he is always in position to punch.'

The boys were saying that Pop Foster had ruined a clever boxer by changing him into a slugger. Jimmy had lost his dignity and was just another mercenary of the prize ring with a manager who was surly and impossible from a social or any other standpoint. Foster, they said, because of his greed for gold had hurried the boy and burned him out. His hands had gone. He was washed up and not yet eighteen. Jimmy regained some standing by knocking out Joe Sangor and beating Joe Glick but then he lost again to Bud Taylor, and to Johnny Farr, and to Doc Snell, a product of Seattle rings and a lethal puncher when he could land his roundhouse swings. Snell beat Jimmy up as badly as Taylor had done in the rematch. 'McLarnin's burned out,' wrote the wise ones of the ring. 'Didn't I tell you that Foster was taking him along too fast. Only in there a couple of years, that kid, and he's fought them all. It takes something out of a boy. His punch is blooey. I'll bet you real dough he never knocks anybody out

again. And his speed – phooey! He looks like a truck-horse, compared with what he was when he fought La Barba and Fields and
Villa. Washed up, done for. He'll never get anywheres now.'

Pop took Jimmy back to Canada and they spent the entire
summer of 1926 away from the ring to allow the boy to grow into
a fully-fledged lightweight. When they returned to California
they also had another member in the team, Jimmy's brother
Sammy. 'They're two fine boys,' said Pop, 'and both will be
champions some day.' The five-month layoff in the Canadian
woods seemed to have done Jimmy some good. He had grown
tougher and the baby face had been supplanted by that of a man.
The campaign of 1927 was better, but still the scribes were after
Jimmy and Pop. The year started with another unimpressive
showing. Tommy Cello, a San Francisco lightweight, fought
Jimmy to a draw. Jimmy won a return match, but it was another
mediocre performance and his eye was cut badly in the sixth
round. He fought some fairly good fights, but he also fought
some fairly bad ones. Jimmy got the decision over Tenario Pelky
of the Philippines, but the customers weren't happy. Pelky got
the cheers and Jimmy gathered the jeers. It was a poor fight and
in the eighth round referee Freddie Gilmour called the boxers to
the centre of the ring and insisted they put a bit more vim and
vigour in their work. Fighters like Farr, Snell, Cello, Glick and
Pelkey were good professionals but none of them were really
going anywhere. Jimmy was trying as hard as ever, but he was
missing punches he should have landed and was getting hit by
punches he should have slipped. 'Jimmy seems to be in the same
position as the fellow who drove up to the hall of fame and sat
down on the steps,' wrote Paul Lowry in the *Los Angeles Times*.

'The spirit to enter was willing but the flesh was weak ... Whatever it is Jimmy McLarnin, once the wonder of California boxing rings, has degenerated into just an ordinary fighter. He may come back. Everybody hopes so.'

Jimmy was heartbroken over the criticism he was getting. The papers said he was through – washed up at nineteen – and he could hear the booing and see the empty seats. Sadly and occasionally tearfully, the promoters who'd been scrambling to show Jimmy McLarnin just a year before told Pop and the boy they just couldn't afford to use them anymore. They couldn't get a fight in San Francisco, Oakland or Los Angeles. They went to San Diego and Jimmy won four fights there, three by knockout, but you couldn't get anywhere in San Diego. They went back to Los Angeles and still couldn't get anything better than a windup before the main event and Jimmy wanted to quit.

He had retired once before. When he was eleven years old his father gave him two pairs of boxing gloves. The boy tied the laces together, slung the gloves across his back and started down Union Street, not far from the docks in Vancouver. 'Some people would call it a tough street, but to me it was a good street because there was always something doing,' Jimmy recalled. 'It was my idea to keep going down the street, a block at a time, putting on the gloves with a new kid at every corner. I licked the kid at the first corner and started for the second corner wondering if I wasn't being too conservative. Maybe after I was finished on my street I could branch out to the other streets. Maybe in time I could work my way down to the docks and get one of the ship's captains to put on the gloves with me. And then I could order the ship's captain to take me to Seattle or San Francisco and I could tie my gloves around my neck again and go looking for Jess Willard [then heavyweight champion].'

At the second corner he met a kid named Wellington Wallace, who was a little bigger than Jimmy, but he was the only kid around. Jimmy took a beating, carried the gloves home and hung them up for a year. Then he met Pop Foster who told the boy he really would be champion of the world one day. 'I was flattered, although a little sceptical,' Jimmy recalled. 'I couldn't quite see how I could get to be the champion of the world unless Wellington Wallace found some other street to play on.' Eight years on he was contemplating life outside the ring once more and secretly hoping that Pop would make the decision for him. 'I'd been afraid to ask Pop the big question,' Jimmy recalled. 'I'd been afraid he was waiting for me to ask it and that his answer would be "Yes". Now I was afraid his answer wouldn't be "Yes". I had $25,000 in the bank and I wanted to quit. I wanted to go back home and eat ice-cream sodas with Lillian, but I had either too much pride or too little pride to go back home on my own.'

THAT'S WHERE
THE MONEY IS

The old man and the kid entered Capone's castle. It crawled with cops, lawyers and divekeepers; doubtful politicians gathered around, as did the women about whom there was no doubt at all. The Metropole Hotel at 2300 South Michigan Avenue, Chicago, was gangdom central and into its opulent lobby limped Pop Foster with the wide-eyed Jimmy McLarnin at his heels. Pop and Jimmy had asked for a quiet, family hotel. Tall, grizzled and nearly bald, Foster was decked out in a newly-acquired suit of hand-me-downs while Jimmy's clothes were new, cheap and gaudy. Pop's clothes often looked as though they hadn't been pressed for six months – and often they hadn't been. They stayed at the Metropole for a week before discovering that the Capones had as many as fifty rooms on the top two heavily-guarded floors. They had asked for a family hotel after all. Gamblers and hookers took private elevators at all hours of the day and night. Pop couldn't figure out how everybody was so well dressed as if they were really rich. Capone occupied rooms 409 and 410, overlooking the boulevard. 'Not too serious a coincidence for a visiting schoolteacher or clergyman, but the kind of thing that can ruin a boxer who hasn't much left but a reputation for honesty,' thought Jimmy. 'We didn't know Capone owned the Metropole Hotel, but when we found out we got out of there pretty fast.'

Jimmy didn't want to go to Chicago. Before leaving LA, he asked Pop whether it was true that he was through and the old man shook his head. If he'd been getting hurt or losing fight after fight, Pop would have made him quit. That had always been the clear understanding between them. Pop said he was through in Los Angeles and through in San Francisco, but that was only a local disease. 'You gave them so many good fights they can't make allowances for the bad ones. You boxed like a man when you were sixteen. They can't understand why you should be boxing like a boy when you're nineteen.' So Pop bought a second-hand Buick and after breakfast one morning he got Jimmy into the car and they started out to see the country. Pop set off with the intention of driving to Chicago, but the Buick broke down in Juliet, Illinois, so they sold it and went on by train. Foster had wired Jim Mullen, Chicago's leading promoter, to ask if he could use Jimmy. The kid's record still looked all right on paper and Mullen offered them a match against a well-known fighter that Pop was sure his boy could lick. The other fighter's manager told Foster that no matter who won or lost it had to be clearly understood that nobody was going to get hurt. Pop promised that Jimmy would kill the other pug and the fight fell through. A replacement was drafted in. Jimmy was working out in a gymnasium in the Loop and knocked out a sparring partner. The replacement developed a severe cold overnight and that fight fell through too. Another prospective opponent, Spug Myers, broke his left hand training so Mullen called for the Meriden junk man, Louis 'Kid' Kaplan, who used to be the featherweight champion of the world. Kaplan was stepping out of his class because of weight and was now a leading contender for Sammy Mandell's lightweight title. 'Offering me Kid Kaplan at that stage of my career was like throwing a drowning man a crowbar,' Jimmy recalled. 'From the time I started fighting until the time I finished I never ducked fighting anybody at or near my weight, but I was tempted to duck Kaplan. My instinct told me I could beat him but my reason told me I couldn't. Pop decided. He said I could win, and we took the fight.'

Kaplan looked like a fighter. A battered nose and brow divided a pair of beautifully cauliflowered ears. He was a short, stumpy lightweight with bulging forearms. Pop sent Jimmy out of the corner with his usual mantra of 'If he can't hit you he can't hurt you.' Jimmy walked across the ring and with the first punch of the fight Kid Kaplan broke his jaw. He was sent crashing to the canvas for the first time in his life. Jimmy had often wondered how it felt and here he was in a strange town looking along his legs and seeing his feet sticking out in front like tent pegs. An old-hand would have stayed down for nine but the nineteen-year-old was too startled to stay down. He got up right away and Kaplan battered him from ringpost to rope. The crowd bayed for a knockout but all Jimmy could hear was a buzzing in his ear and finally, the bell to finish the first.

Kaplan threw another big left in the second. A little longer this time and Jimmy saw it coming and moved to block it. Too late. There was a creak of soles in the resin and a dull, sodden sound and Jimmy was falling and sinking. He came to after bouncing off the canvas. He felt all right, he blinked, realised that he had somehow managed to scramble to his knees and he could see Kaplan's black fighting shoes in the dust. Jimmy watched the referee toll one and regained his feet. Kaplan went for the finish but Jimmy went into close quarters and weathered another round. He didn't knock Jimmy down in the third but Kaplan hit him just as often as he had in the first two.

Jimmy was tired but far from gone as he sat in the corner. Between the first and second and the second and third rounds, Pop had told him to come up a little with his left, to shorten up with the right, to circle to Kaplan's left. Jimmy waited to hear what he'd say now. He sluiced a spongeful of water down his boy's face.

'Jimmy?' Pop said.

The water ran down Jimmy's chest.

'Yes, Pop?'

'Why don't *you* try hitting *him*?'

'Pop was and is a serious man,' Jimmy recalled. 'He knew there was nothing funny in this situation, either for me or for him. But I think that he sensed that we'd both been living with and eating with and sleeping with our troubles so long that it was time we quit taking them so much to heart. I was nowhere near doubling up with mirth at Pop's unprecedented wisecrack. But I went out for the next round feeling looser and more relaxed, less as though the world was going to stop going round if a guy named Kid Kaplan happened to beat a guy named Jimmy McLarnin.'

It was Kaplan's turn to crash to the canvas in the fourth. The customers were screaming. A right cross and Jimmy thought Kaplan would stay down but he was up at three with a puffed and bruised left eye and a face flushed with rage. Kaplan was in a bad way going to his corner at the end of the round. Now Kaplan was fighting angry. Jimmy hit him with a right in the fifth and he stayed down for nine. All through the sixth and the seventh Jimmy hit Kaplan the way he'd been hit in the first and second, but Kaplan wouldn't go down again. Jimmy got so tired hitting him that he could hardly lift his arms. 'After the seventh I was hoping he'd knock me down again, just so I could feel that beautiful, restful floor.' It was the prizefighter's deepest humiliation, falling out half conscious on the floor and not wanting to get up. 'There is an extortion of will beyond any of our measure in the exhaustion which comes upon a fighter in early rounds when he is already too tired to lift his arms or take advantage of openings there before him,' wrote Norman Mailer, 'there are all those rounds to go, contractions of torture, the lungs screaming into the dungeons of the soul, washing the throat with a hot bile that once belonged to the liver, the legs are going dead, the arms move but their motion is limp, one is straining into another will, breathing into the breath of another will as agonised as one's own.'

In the eighth Jimmy smashed a short right to the chin and Kaplan hit the floor. 'I backed into a neutral corner. I don't really believe that God cares who wins a boxing match, but I leaned against the ropes praying that Kid Kaplan wouldn't get up. He got up at three, with his hands hanging down around his knees and his eyes far away.' Jimmy hit him with another right and Kaplan crumpled in a heap and then turned over on his back. He managed to regain his feet at nine. Kaplan's face and body were now taking their toll on Jimmy's hands. He felt the small bones going like snapping bits of chalk. Jimmy feinted Kaplan into position, braced himself and drove his broken right hand to Kaplan's jaw. The pain shot up Jimmy's arm and if that blow didn't do the trick he was beaten. But Kaplan just lay there, staring up at the arc lights as the referee tolled ten. Jimmy came upright again after his customary hand-spring and back flip gasping from the excruciating pain in his hands.

The knockout of Kaplan was a major upset and it changed Jimmy's life. 'Pop and I don't talk about fights much any more,' Jimmy said long after he'd retired. 'But when we do he tells me this was the best fight I ever fought. Maybe he's biased because he alone knows how low I was when it started and he alone knew how much winning it meant to me.' It made Jimmy, that fight. Many years later he admitted to his friend Ed Frayne at the *New York American*, that up to the time Kid Kaplan hit him on the chin he had never taken the fight game seriously. He didn't believe that he ever really had his heart in his work. 'They say an honest confession is good for the soul. I've done everything else I thought would be good for me, so I may as well finish the job,' said Jimmy. 'Those who have seen me in my California fights will understand what I mean. I remember one writer who gave me an unmerciful panning for one of my Los Angeles fights. He called me a poser, a looking-glass fighter and a pretty boy. I think he was a little harsh, but there was something in what he said. I wasn't really fighting. I was playing. I was having fun. I loved to make the other fellows miss, and then laugh at them. I wasn't doing myself justice, and, I realise now, I wasn't giving the fans everything they deserved. I was amusing myself instead of entertaining them.' Kaplan had woken Jimmy up. He had to fight that night.

When they got back to the hotel there was a message to call Jess McMahon in New York. McMahon worked for Tex Rickard, the promotional wizard who had invested $100,000 in the old Madison Square Garden and the day he signed that lease, prizefighting was born as a respectable business. He had made history's first million-dollar gates aboard the glamorous shoulders of Jack Dempsey and now he saw Jimmy as a miniature version of the Manassa Mauler, the man to bring the big gates back into boxing. It was the McLarnins of the ring, and the Dempseys, who made boxing the big drawing card it was in the roaring twenties, and if a promoter could pick up a McLarnin or a Dempsey, he was assured of netting himself a fortune. Rickard knew he had a mint in Jimmy and Tex wasn't one to spurn an opportunity. New York was calling, but Pop wasn't listening, at least not yet. One more like the Kaplan bout and Tex Rickard would be making the offers – instead of Pop going in, hat in hand, asking for a chance for his boy. The process of recreating Jimmy was pretty nearly completed and the difficult period when he was growing into a lightweight was over. He no longer had to keep down to an unnatural weight and he was punching better than ever, too. Pop was ready to take his creation to New York but only on his terms. Jess McMahon wanted them in New York right away.

'Why?' Pop asked.

'McMahon wasn't quite ready for a question as silly as that one,' Jimmy recalled. 'I suppose he knew as well as anybody else that every boxer wanted to come to New York and that if there were any questions to be asked there was time to ask them when he got there. Pop cupped his hand over the telephone and relayed the answer to me. "They're not sure who they want us to fight. They'll give us a $5,000 advance to come and talk terms.'" Jimmy sat on the edge of the bed. Less than six weeks previously he'd been fighting in San Diego for not much more than room and board. He had been told that if he wanted to fight in Los Angeles or San Francisco he'd virtually have to start from scratch. Just two hours past he'd earned $3,000 for the hardest fight of his life. And now Pop was quibbling about taking $5,000 just to go and say hello to a man.

'Thanks, Mr McMahon,' Pop said and hung up.

The McLarnins had always been very far from rich and seldom very far from poor. The first-born son had died in infancy and, as the oldest boy in the family, Jimmy did his bit. He sold papers from the time he was old enough to stake out a stand on the Vancouver docks and stubborn enough to hold on to it. 'I grew up believing that life was good, but that you had to work for what you got,' he recalled. Jimmy set himself the task of earning a dollar a day selling papers, but by the time he was out of school and got down to the docks there were some days when he wasn't taking more than twenty or thirty cents. So when he was just thirteen, Jimmy quit school. Strathcona School was well aware that its poorest pupils had to go out and hustle when they were young and when Jimmy explained to Mr Brown, the principal, that he wanted to quit to start earning money the man didn't give Jimmy a 'lot of high-minded arguments'. To the contrary, he got the boy a job running an elevator at the

Colombia Paper Company for $8 a week.

Jimmy supplemented his income by fighting for pennies pitched in the ring at lodge hall smokers. It doesn't appear in his record and even Pop only got to hear about it a long time later, but Jimmy fought his first fight in public at a smoker at the Second Division Artillery Club on Vancouver's East Granville Street soon after his twelfth birthday. His opponent was a 'fat kid' named Clarence Robinson and they fought four rounds to a draw in what was billed as an amateur bout. But they weren't really amateur bouts and Jimmy got a dollar as his end of the purse. He walked to the club alone on a dark winter night. It was a long trek and near the end of it Jimmy had to cross the Georgia Street viaduct. It was long and dark and full of shadows. 'In every shadow I was sure there was a Chinaman hiding with a long curved knife,' Jimmy recalled. 'I don't remember much about the fight, but I do remember that I couldn't face that lonely walk back across the viaduct. The streetcar fare was six cents. I thought that it would be undignified to ask for six cents so I asked the promoter Rough-house Charley Burns, for a dime. He gave me a dollar and I was a pro before I held my first amateur card.'

The phone rang off and on all through the night after the Kaplan fight and when Jimmy got up the following day Pop announced that they were heading to Detroit to fight Billy Wallace. There was talk that the winner of the Wallace-McLarnin bout was in line for a shot at Sammy Mandell and the world lightweight title. Wallace had the best right hand in the lightweight division and he was a particularly fine drawing card in Detroit. He had written to Promoter Mullen in Chicago offering to fight Mandell for nothing, because he knew he could beat the champion and all he wanted was the shot. Kid Kaplan had taught Jimmy what it felt like to be knocked down and he certainly didn't want any more of that business. Now they told him that Billy Wallace could hit harder than Kaplan ever thought of. That didn't sound so good, considering that Kaplan had almost turned the lights out. Jimmy didn't want any more lessons, so he went in there with his hands up, and didn't make any fool leads, just as Pop had told him back in the basement of Sam McLarnin's store in Vancouver.

'War ain't so much different than boxing in the way it's run,' Pop would say. 'What happens if they send the shock troops over before the gunners have laid down a barrage an' smashed the wire and the machine-gun nests? I'll tell you. The infantry jolly well gets the daylight shot out of them. If a good barrage is walkin' ahead and wiping out the opposition, the boys with the bayonets get a chance to do their stuff. It's like that in the ring, Jim. Go in there throwing that right and you'll have your block torn off you. Fix the way first with your left and then throw the right, like you did at Fields, and it's a different story. The fellow who can box and punch is going a long way, but the fellow who does nothing but punch usually has a short life in the ring, and it ain't always such a happy one, either.'

Jimmy took the referee's decision over Wallace after a furious ten-round bout. It was a tough fight, slam-bang; Wallace was a great little fighter and he made it tough for Jimmy all the way. They punched each other around the ring, but Jimmy was the more accurate and got the nod. The phone rang quite a bit more that night and the next morning Jimmy asked Pop what he was doing. He told him that if he wanted to they could go to New York and fight Sid Terris for 25 per cent of the gate at Madison Square Garden.

It had been a profitable season and before taking on New York the adventurers went home to Vancouver once more with their bank accounts fattened. Jimmy bought himself a heavy insurance policy, subscribed discreetly to several charities and became a Rotarian. Now he was ready. Now he could go. There wasn't any use waiting any longer. New York, here I am! Bring on all your lightweights from Sammy Mandell down the line. It doesn't matter. James McLarnin was going to show his stuff! Boxing had struggled to gain legitimacy in the United States, but in 1920, state senator Jimmy Walker, the soon-to-be-mayor of New York City, established a state commission to govern the sport. Very quickly boxing ranked alongside baseball, horse racing and college football in the sports pantheon, and New York City emerged as the capital of pugilism. It was in New York that the money was to be found, that's where champions were made. Tex Rickard had drawn a dollar mark across the Eastern skyline and the old man and the kid made up their minds to head there. The sport entered its golden age thanks largely to the popularity of the heavyweight champion Jack Dempsey. After Dempsey lost the title to Gene Tunney, boxing, and New York in particular, waited for a new star to come along. And in January 1928 Jimmy McLarnin arrived.

Jimmy was perfect for New York. Not only was he an exciting fighter, a showman who knocked people out, he had the one ingredient that guaranteed a fighter popularity in New York – he was Irish. The tradition of prizefighting in America was that of the Irish fighter, from John L. Sullivan onwards, and the vast majority of the crowds who flocked to the fights were Irish. But by the time Pop and Jimmy arrived in New York the pre-eminence of the Irish fighter was already over. A decade or so previously nearly every champion was either a pure-blooded Irishman or had a strain of Irish blood coursing through his veins. But as the Jews and then the Italians began to establish themselves in New York the Irish were slowly fading into the background in the sport in which they had reigned supreme. 'What is it then that has caused the Irish gladiators to bow to the Jews, the Italians and the Germans?' asked *The Ring*. 'Where in the past every great warrior of the squared circle was an Irish-man, today the leading figures carry Irish names indicative of ring prowess, but the *nom-de-guerre* belongs either to an Italian or an Israelite.' A profitable myth grew up that 'Baby Face' McLarnin was a wild Irishman who loved to get in there and slug until somebody fell on his face – by preference the other fellow, but if not him, then Jimmy.

The greatest Irish fighter of his generation, arguably the last of the great fighting Irishmen, was about to take his bow in New York at a time when the sport was at the height of his popularity. Everybody now knew what Pop had known for years, Jimmy McLarnin was one of the most valuable commodities in all of sports. He was the new star in a giant industry that had an annual take of $60,000,000. There were between five hundred and six hundred fight clubs in the United States, all operating under boxing commissions modelled after that which Jimmy Walker had created in New York. But wherever there was money to be made rackets grew to feed off the industry and boxing was ripe for the taking. It had emerged out of the underworld, a sport for the depraved and the criminal, and there had always been corruption. But in the roaring twenties the scale of the corruption was taken to a whole new level. Boxing was no longer a sport, it was a business that involved millions of dollars. And where there were millions of dollars there were crooks. It was a time when the mobs owned the fighters and decisions were bought or exacted at the point of a gun. Managers and fighters were intimidated. Referees and judges were hounded. Gamblers and fixers had always been a part of prizefighting but in the years following Prohibition huge bootlegging profits had given the racketeers the cash to invest in their favourite game. As Charles J. McGuirk wrote in the *Washington Post* in 1929:

'The fight game is like a great, rich, ring of gold embedded in a morass of filth and slime; or like a brave gallant ship whose bottom is so cluttered with barnacles that she fails to obey her helm and finds herself on the reef of oblivion.'

It was a time when boxing matches were selling out ballparks and attracting million-dollar gates. A well-engineered betting scam on a fixed fight could net millions – and the racketeers wanted in. One of Jimmy's future opponents, Ruby Goldstein, wrote of how one East Side hood, Waxie Gordon, muscled in on him. According to Goldstein, very few boxers lacked a mob sponsor. 'When you're going big in New York, myths grow up around you and your name,' Jimmy recalled. 'The central myth, from which all the others sprang, is that the entire underworld and half-world of the world's second largest city spent the best part of those nine years trying to separate me and my manager, Pop Foster, from our money or our honour, or both. If you could believe half the stories they used to tell on Forty-Second Street and in the lobby of Madison Square Garden, hardly a day passed but I was urged to sell a fight, buy a gold brick or meet a blonde. As for Pop, he could scarcely turn round without somebody shoving a gun in his ribs and demanding that he go back to the sticks and leave somebody's mob to look after his fighter – or waving a sackful of thousand-dollar bills under his nose and suggesting that he arrange for me to take a quiet dive in the fifth.

'I don't say things like this couldn't have happened. There are burglars in any business and I'm afraid the boxing business has always had its full quota. There are – or were in my day – too many gangsters mixed up in boxing and too many gamblers betting too much money on boxing for anyone in his right mind to believe that boxing could be entirely honest.

'But I was never asked to throw a fight or offered a bribe, a threat or any other kind of inducement to throw a fight. Neither was Pop.

'We were told twice by managers of other fighters that their fighters couldn't fight me unless I'd agree not to try to knock them out. Once, in our early days in Oakland, before Pop and I had a written contract and all we had to eat was the crabs we could net in San Francisco Bay, one of those strangely prosperous little men who hang around gyms told me that if I'd get rid of Pop he'd see that I got all the steaks and all the fights I could handle.

'Another time, after things were going better for us, a "New York manager" wrote and urged me to quit wasting my time in the tall timber and come and get it where the going was good. Of course, he added, I would have to place myself in the hands of somebody who knew the right people and had the necessary ins – meaning him.

'None of these propositions got as far as the discussion stage. To the best of my knowledge they were the only propositions of a dishonest or doubtful nature that were ever put to either Pop or me. This wasn't entirely an accident. It was Pop's theory that nobody ever made a proposition without first finding somebody to listen to it – and Pop was a terrible listener.'

Pop suspected every Broadwayite on sight and he insisted that his mail came to him care of Tex Rickard at the Garden. 'The boys tried to put the lug on Foster,' wrote Andy Lytle, of the *Toronto Star*. 'If he was "regular", they told him, nothing was impossible. Jimmy could have lucrative matches. Money would roll in. Foster sniffed, grabbed his mail and walked swingingly away. "They'll come to me," he would say to his cronies: "'they can't do without the boy. 'E packs them in. They'll get no piece of us!'"

On arriving in New York Foster sought out an old friend from the Coast for advice. Ed Frayne had been a sports writer on the *Los Angeles Record* when Jimmy fought in California, but had moved East to work on the *New York American*. Frayne certainly helped ease Pop and his boy's path into Gotham but the old man had some history that went much further back and that was considerably more important for a fighter and his manager trying to make it in New York. Pop knew that there was one man in New York who could ensure that he and Jimmy would be left alone whenever they were in town. It was time to hark back to the old days; to the bare-knuckle fights and the boxing booths, to Jack 'Kid' Berg and to Liverpool. It was time to call on Owney 'The Killer' Madden.

BEAU JAMES
& THE DUKE

Owney Madden watched as Henshaw dropped off the girl at her home and boarded a trolley car. Owney followed, took out his Smith and Wesson and shot Henshaw in front of a dozen passengers. He calmly walked to the rear step, rang the brass bell, strolled off and disappeared into the night. William Henshaw was a clerk who'd just taken one of Owney Madden's girls on a date. Madden had graduated from mob enforcer to the Duke of the West Side. He was the nighttime mayor of New York employing cops, judges and politicians; he owned The Cotton Club and was the gangster his best friend, George Raft, based many of his roles on. And Madden loved prizefights and prizefighters, some said he loved them even more than actresses and showgirls. Madden's involvement with fighters ranged from gifts and no strings loans to controlling interests, and by the late twenties there were very few fighters making big money in New York without giving a healthy slice of it to Owney.

Making money out of prizefighting in the old days was easy. A racketeer went to a fighter and paid him to 'take it on the chin' and then bet on the opponent. The cost of a prizefighter wasn't prohibitive because they fought for a share of the gate and the gates weren't very high. The price went up according to a fighter's standing and champions came higher than palookas. There was a good living to be made in trimming suckers. But as boxing became big business after the Great War things changed. The gates were much bigger, titles were worth a lot more so the fighters cost more. And then the suckers wised up. 'Don't bet on fights', the newspapers advised.

The alternative strategy was to take a piece of a champion or a young contender and either get him the title or protect him in it. This was done by buying officials, paying for crooked decisions and dangerous opponents to lay down. But in the Golden Age boxers were expensive and it would take more money than the old-school racketeer ever made to buy the likes of a Jimmy McLarnin. It was also a precarious invest-ment and the returns were far from certain. Then along came Prohibition, the racketeers got rich almost overnight and prizefighting was a fun investment, especially if you liked boxers and boxing as much as Owney Madden did.

The old man knew all about Madden, who had walked the same roads and hung around the same dressing rooms and fairgounds as Pop had a generation earlier. Madden, like Foster before him, was a native of Leeds who spent his boyhood in Liverpool. As a boy Owney had spent hours watching an uncle fighting for cash purses in halls and boxing booths, the very same halls and booths in which Foster fought for a living. According to Madden's biog-rapher, Graham Nown, he retained a love for fighters and show people, not for the reasons some gangsters found them attractive, but because he found them to be 'real' people. And they didn't come much more real than Charles Foster. 'Many English fighters, like Jack "Kid" Berg, the British lightweight champion, were his [Madden's] close friends,' wrote Nown. 'Some, in the North of England, kept in touch by sending him clippings from the sports pages of the *Yorkshire Post* which he kept in a cigar box.' Now in New York, Madden met Pop Foster, a character straight off the sports pages of the *Yorkshire Post*. 'Owney Madden was a very important man in New York,' Jimmy recalled. 'Usually foreigners, and I was a foreigner, found it difficult to get a fight. Owney Madden found out that Pop Foster was born in Liverpool, and that's where he was born, so he thought maybe I'll give these guys a chance. So from then on I had an awful lot of fights in New York and made big money. So Owney Madden was very kind to us and I'll always have a soft spot in my heart for Owney Madden.'

Prizefight managers liked to be known as 'Doc' or 'Unk' or 'Pop'. Nobody really bought this of course. Anybody who'd been to a movie knew that these men worked with the mobs, manipulating and selling young fighters. 'Doc' or 'Unk' or 'Pop' would bag a fight with his mother. Young fighters were coerced into selling 110 per cent of themselves to various racketeers until they got more into debt with every fight they took. And then with the money gone 'Doc' or 'Unk' or 'Pop' would explain that 'if it weren't for me, you would have been nothing, kid!' It all seemed particularly true of managers called 'Pop'.

So when Pop Foster and Jimmy showed up on the Great White Way the boys nodded their heads and smiled. This kid was a gold mine. He looked like a choirboy and could sing 'Mother Macree', he could punch a horse to its knees and he was an Irishman. And the kid had a manager named 'Pop'. Soon he'd be in Texas Guinan's till four in the morning, driving purple Stutz Bearcats, dating would-be actresses, sitting ringside with Legs Diamond or Dutch Schultz and Charley Lucky. Then there'd be sour investments, law-suits, and the inevitable night when the washed up fighter would take the beating of his life and would have to find his way back to the dressing room by himself and go home in a cab.

The New York boxing writers panned Pop Foster mercilessly from the outset. "Cos we wouldn't give 'em money,' Pop would snarl. He didn't believe in giving a cent of Jimmy's money to any-body – scribe or racketeer – and he wasn't about to change his ways because there was a homicidal gangster taking an interest in his boy. Consent for newspapermen to see or to talk to Jimmy came grudgingly and Pop was 'cordially blasphemed' by the Broadway boys. 'They couldn't get past the upflung guard of Foster and few of them indeed ever exchanged half a dozen words with McLarnin unless Foster was sitting in, ears cocked and eyes alert to everything,' wrote the *Toronto Star*'s Andy Lytle. 'I think the old man deliberately assumed the role of a curmudgeon and a boor at these times … At any rate it proved fairly effective at shielding Jimmy and it assuredly brought Foster no encomiums, not that the absence of praise would out-wardly worry that rugged old warrior. Quite the reverse.'

New York! Glittering Broadway! Jimmy McLarnin had arrived in Gotham-town. The city was basking in the final strains of the Jazz Age where Runyonesque characters patronised speakeasies called Good Time Charley's and prizefighters mixed with mobsmen, chorus girls, gamblers and racetrack hustlers. Jimmy marvelled at the size of Madison Square Garden and blushed at the signs advertising the coming fight between Sid Terris and Jimmy McLarnin. There were men at the box-office already. It was no small job to crash New York – to make people pay out hard-earned money to see you fight. As Jimmy Breslin wrote, 'Prohibition, then, was a time when hundreds danced wildly while tens of thousands stared at the floor and tried to find a slice of bread.' They said New York was cold and hard to failures, but that if you caught its love and admiration nothing was too good for you. Knock him out and Jimmy was made. Fight fans always string with the winners. Put Sid Terris away and Jimmy, the last of the great Irishmen, would pull them in at the gate like nobody's business. Although Jimmy was born in Hillsborough, County Down, and was brought up a Methodist by his mother, Tex Rickard's press release described him as the 'Dublin Dynamiter' and the 'Murderous Mick'.

Jimmy had his first look at Sid Terris when he weighed in at the Commission's office. Terris was a Jewish boy from the East Side and they called him the Ghost of the Ghetto. He packed 'em in when he fought and the New York boxing writers were convinced that Sammy Mandell, the world champion, was avoiding Terris. 'Sammy is not keen to play with Sidney in a local cauliflower temple because he alleges the "works" would be against him,' reported the New York Post. 'The pacific champion leans to the belief that he would be the victim of the (in)famous "works" were he to venture through the ropes for a fifteen round joust with the Jewish boxer over whom he gained a decision before a local cauliflower assemblage.' Pop wanted to take the match at 137 pounds, two over the lightweight limit that Jimmy was struggling to make. The cry went up that Jimmy couldn't make 135 pounds unless he cut off one of his legs. But Terris was being touted as the next world champion and the New York State Athletic Commission ruled that he had to stay in the 135-pound class to be a contender. Pop eventually relented, largely because he believed Terris had slipped back in the previous six months. In recent fights the Ghost of the Ghetto had been floored by Billy Wallace, Phil McGraw and Hilario Martinez.

Terris had never been a champion largely because he never ducked an opponent. While Sammy Mandell was fighting the likes of Teddy O'Hara, Babe Picao, Jack Sparr and Johnny Adams, names familiar only to the keenest ringworms, Terris was fighting the best lightweights in the country, boxers and hitters alike. He didn't draw the colour line and avoided setups and easy marks. 'Who, then, comported himself as a true champion does, Sidney Terris or Sammy Mandell?' asked Paul Gallico. 'Feed 'em tough ones long enough and they all go, even the champions. The champions know it and they come into the ring with little mocking lines at the corners of their mouths and meet their fate. They have read their end in the lines of the newspapers and in the strange rebellion of muscles of which they once were master. But it comes a little harder when a boy has never been a champion.'

As a result of Terris' frequent tumbles to the canvas in recent fights the theory was evolved on Cauliflower Alley – the babbling strip populated by thugs and pugs, mobsters and their molls, cops and conmen that ran behind boxing arenas – was that he went down purposely to pull in the customers, the idea being that they would cluster about in large numbers if the prospect presented itself that Sid would get bowled over. Pop knew different. Terris was on the decline and a match well made is a match half-won. Wearing a saintly smile and bright green bath-robe with a golden harp embroidered on its back, Jimmy took his bow in New York, top of bill at Madison Square Garden. A crowd of 18,000 gave him the 'greatest reception that ever a vis-iting boxer received in a Garden ring when introduced'. But Terris looked good and ruled an 8 to 5 favourite at ringside. At the opening bell the Ghost of the Ghetto stepped around the Irishman and slapped him with light left jabs. Then he stopped dancing and stood flat-footed and nailed Jimmy with a right on the chin that carried everything Terris had on it. Jimmy took the punch and smiled a wistful smile. William Morris wrote in the *Post* that Terris was wearing 'a "this-is-like-taking-candy-from-a-baby" expression on his face.'

Jimmy weaved under a few blows, but then Terris stuck out his left glove and jabbed him. Sid tried it again with the same result. He became bolder and shot over a right smash that was intended for the chin, but landed on Jimmy's left ear. Jimmy was wide open and offered an inviting target, or so it seemed. Terris, now flat on his feet, continued shooting lightning fast light lefts, but then he shot just one too many. The punch missed and Jimmy lashed out with both hands. His left fell short of Terris' chin, but the right landed solidly and suddenly Terris had his nose buried deep in the resin. Terris just sank at first then crum-pled and pitched forward on his face like 'a steer in a stockyard execution room'. His eyes were shut, gloves open. Referee Jack

O'Sullivan tolled off the fatal ten, he could count a hundred over him and Terris wouldn't move a muscle.

'Nine, ten, out!'

'Whillikers, how James does punch!' commented one scribe. 'And where he gets his power is more than I can figure out. He seems to do no more than reach with his hooked arms and gloves and after he hits he leaves his fist there for a fraction of a second. And his opponents cave as though struck by a bullet.' It was all over in one minute and forty-seven seconds. Jimmy turned a handspring and rushed over to Pop standing in the corner with a smile on his weathered face. 'Ringsiders went into hysterics. The gallery was in uproar. Pandemonium, that's the word,' wrote Jack Farrell in the *New York Daily News*. Jimmy rushed to the centre of the ring and gathered up the stricken figure of the man who less than two minutes earlier was the outstanding contender for the world's lightweight title. Terris was still slumped semi-conscious in his corner long after Jimmy had been carried to his dressing room. The 'Ghost' was surrounded by sympathisers who elbowed their way to the corner to offer condolences to the fallen warrior. 'We got a fleeting glance at the water-soaked Terris as he passed the ringside. Tears, real ones, dripped from his ashen cheek, but not a syllable came from his quivering lips,' wrote Jack Farrell.

'I turned mine [eyes] to Terris, who sat shattered in his corner, the tragic Jew, the Jew of the ages, I thought,' wrote Paul Gallico. 'His eyes were still glassed from the shock of the punch, but the sense of his burden had reached his stricken brain and a steady trickle of tears rolled down his thin cheeks. His dark, oriental face, the face of the true Semite, was set in shadowy lines of sorrow and the body that a year ago was made of tempered steel, a body that he built himself from the scrawny frame of a tenement-reared east sider, was limp and broken. He had come to his reward. There in the ring were the two masks of the theatre – the joyous Irishman, a Punchinello, turning handsprings to the merry screams of the throngs – while opposite him Terris, the mask of sorrow filled with bitterness at the fate that had brought him there. The end of Terris may be traced in the last five or six fights. We all knew about it, knew that it was coming, and joked about being present when someone put him on the floor and kept him there, hoping we wouldn't miss it. But it wasn't funny when it happened. There is no mirth in human frustration. I was sorry I was there.'

The crowd rushed the ring and, for the first time at the new Madison Square Garden, broke past the wall of cops and stormed around a victorious fighter. 'The Irish carried me out of the ring on their shoulders and as they swept me to the dressing room a rain of friendly wallops beat me black and blue,' Jimmy recalled. 'I don't mean this in the figurative sense. The bruises showed for more than a week. Just before Pop rescued me at the door to the dressing room a giant of a man gave me a paralysing smack between the shoulder blades and yelled: "The saints be praised, Jimmy boy!"

"Take it easy," I yelled back. "There's nobody up here but us Orangemen.' Maybe it was just as well that he didn't seem to hear."'

Pop teased reporters that the so-called wise guys had fallen for the stories sent out of the training camp that Jimmy was having a tough time making weight.

'Those 8 to 5 guys certainly ran to cover when weight was announced at the state athletic commission,' he chuckled. Back at McLarnin's secondhand store in Vancouver, Samuel McLarnin was celebrating his boy's sensational Gotham debut. 'They didn't think Jimmy could do it,' he chuckled. 'Those New Yorkers can't see anything good outside of that city of theirs. But Jimmy showed 'em, didn't he? I knew he could do it.'

Jimmy had never seen so many people in his life, and never had so many nice things been said to him and about him as he had after that fight. 'I'm as human as anyone else. I like to have people like me. I made up my mind as I was being carried out of the arena that I would finish this job,' Jimmy recalled. Looking like an embarrassed schoolboy, he spent most of the following day at his hotel, where he was swamped with congratulations and offers for ring work. He was heralded as the best Irish fighter since Terrible Terry McGovern. 'I could quit the ring now and live at ease,' Jimmy divulged. 'I own a home at Boyle's Heights, a quiet section of Los Angeles, own a Hudson car and have no worries. I am not married. Pop told me to wait until I am thirty and I'll know better. I like the girls, love them all in fact, but I am not ready to take the big step.' Jimmy claimed that his greatest diversions were long walks and the movies. 'I don't like the stage,' he said, 'but the soft money appeals to me.'

'McLarnin's successful New York debut aroused the Irish in the big city to such an extent that a two-day celebration followed,' commented *The Ring*. 'For all we know it may still be going on. This was the first time in sixteen years that the Celts had a real, honest-to-goodness chance to root for one of their own.' Jimmy was invited to meet New York's Irish mayor,

Jimmy Walker. 'I sure will be glad to meet the mayor,' said Jimmy. 'From what I've read of him he must be a great guy. I know he's going to kid me to death.' Walker, or Beau James as he was known, was the debonair song-writing politician who came to define New York in the twenties. In *Looking For Jimmy: A Search For Irish America*, writer Peter Quinn argues that Walker, in tandem with Jimmy Cagney had the 'blend of musicality and menace, of nattiness and charm, of verbal agility and ironic sensibility, of what is known today as "street smarts", that the Irish, as New York's first immigrant outsiders, had developed … Jimmy belonged to the concrete, to what won the respect of his peers and made him stand out,' and in February 1928 there was a new Jimmy in town, one who overnight had become the idol with the Irish of New York. When the visitor was departing the Mayor remarked: 'One Jimmy to another – get that championship!' In the space of just a few weeks Jimmy had befriended Jimmy Walker, the daytime mayor of New York and Pop had found favour with Owney Madden, the night-time mayor of Gotham. The city really was theirs.

'Gosh, I've had a wonderful time ever since I beat Terris,' Jimmy told the newspapers. 'Everybody has been lovely to me. Everywhere I go they want to take my picture. At nights they call me out of bed to congratulate me. Theatrical offers are piled high on Pop's desk. New York is a marvellous city and they surely give an outsider more than an even break. I'd make it my home if I could drag my folks and my gang of brothers and sisters east. Please thank them all for me for their courteous treatment. I shall never forget my new friends.'

Jimmy was the new sporting sensation of New York. He fired

the shot that started the forty-second international bike race at Madison Square Garden in front of twelve thousand fans as the teams began the six-day whirl. Then he faced the disk to open the New York Rangers-Toronto Maple Leafs ice hockey match at the Garden. This was the kid who just a few years earlier had managed to charm Harry Holmes, a star of the local ice hockey team, to help him crash the gate at matches. Holmes was pushing his way through the crowd into the arena at Victoria, British Columbia, one night, when he felt a tug on his sleeve.

'Mr Holmes, cantcha take me in with ya?' Jimmy asked.

Holmes said Jimmy's earnestness so appealed to him that he gave his pads and sticks to the boy and followed him inside. This became a regular practice until the management put a stop to it, so Holmes got Jimmy past the doorman by pushing the boy through the door while calling him all manner of names for getting in his way.

In New York Jimmy made the acquaintance of a sharp, finely-mannered young man of the world named Ralph Rogers. He was described as possessing more crust than a slumbering crater and more polish than a king's courtier. Ralph loved the high life, he loved celebrities and it was said that he could smilingly crash any gate and talk himself right into any ringside pew with the promoter apologising to him for the delay by the time he was seated. Ralph took Jimmy to his mother's home in New Jersey and introduced him to everyone of note and everything worth seeing. Jimmy soon acquired a poise and a degree of suavity and Ralph even helped Pop to brush up his appearance. Stains disappeared from his waistcoat, and he wore better clothes, shirts and hats.

A crowd of 17,980 had paid $91,985.25 to see the Terris fight. Jimmy's share was $19,645.50, by far the largest purse the partnership had ever taken in. He was signed for a four-day appearance at Fox's Academy of Music for $1,500, and was swamped with offers to appear in half a dozen cities. Pop let Jimmy accumulate $25,000 before he ever took a cent. He wanted his boy to amass a bankroll before he started taking a percentage. Years later old timers related how Foster was one of the toughest managers in history when it came to business. He drove a hard bargain and wouldn't budge an ounce on a weight agreement if he thought that by doing so Jimmy might suffer. The Californian boxing scribes had Jimmy riding into the tank towns as a fighter; they were convinced he had shot his bolt. But Pop said the boys were all wrong. They couldn't get any breaks on the Coast, so he took Jimmy East and made suckers of the experts who derided him.

The day after he beat Terris, Tex Rickard signed Jimmy for a shot at the world lightweight title. Jess McMahon, Rickard's matchmaker, made Eddie Kane, Mandell's manager 'such a flattering offer over a long distance phone that if he turns it down it will be proof positive that he is either mentally deficient, or afraid to let his cold storage champion take a chance with a worthy foe,' commented one scribe. Mandell wasn't mentally deficient or afraid and signed up, even though he was already contracted to Chicago promoter Jim Mullen to defend his title in an outdoor match in the Windy City in July. Mandell had given Mullen his promise to defend his crown against the best contender out there. Mullen picked Jimmy McLarnin as the fighter best qualified to give the champion a good scrap and draw crowds to one of the major league ballparks. One way or another, Jimmy was going to fight Mandell.

'After the fight it looked to a lot of people, including myself, as though I couldn't miss being the next lightweight champion of the world. Pop and I went down to Rickard's office and I picked up a cheque for $19,645.50 and Rickard said he would make me the next lightweight champion of the world,' Jimmy recalled. For the next three days Rickard and Mullen tried to outbid each other for the privilege of promoting the match. Mullen claimed that Pop had given his word that his fighter would meet Mandell in Chicago if he beat Terris. 'I brought McLarnin from the Coast when other promoters said he was through,' said Mullen. 'I matched him with Kid Kaplan in the Coliseum last October and he won the fight by a knockout in the eighth round. I was instrumental in matching him with Billy Wallace of Cleveland in Detroit last December. He won that fight by the decision route. Now that he has shown the boxing world he is a real fighter, other promoters are clamouring for his services. I brought him to the front and if his manager goes back on his word, I will do everything I can to prevent Mandell from giving him a chance to win the title. I am tired of bringing fighters into the limelight and have other promoters try to steal them, I want this match for Chicago.'

Pop denied signing up his protégé for Mandell in Chicago and was open to the best proposition. He had been too cagey to be coaxed into it before the Terris bout and Jimmy was now worth twice as much at the gate than he was before the knock-out. The row brought a smile to the face of many a promoter on the Coast who had dealt with Pop and knew what a tough guy he was when it came to the percentages. Foster always demanded the extra dime. Jim Mullen in Chicago had the moral high ground and the signature of the champion Mandell, but Rickard had the money. Tex Rickard and Jim Mullen had waged a few promotional wars in their time, and Mullen hadn't won a decision yet. Mullen had Mandell signed in an iron-clad contract and he travelled from Chicago to New York to make sure the champion honoured the agreement. He was going to meet with Pop to 'steer him away from the contaminating influence of Rickard'.

Mullen offered Jimmy a $30,000 guarantee to fight in Chicago. Rickard's offer was 12 ½ per cent of the net receipts, the maximum he was allowed to offer a challenger in a title fight in New York State. Each had half the match tucked away and each was determined to swing the other half to his home city. And in the middle was Pop Foster thoroughly enjoying himself. Pop figured that in the long run it would do Jimmy most good to win the lightweight championship of the world in New York fighting for Tex Rickard. After the Terris knockout he had signed with Rickard for a championship match in May, leaving it entirely up to Tex to get Mandell's name on a contract. But all the time Foster knew Mandell was signed with Mullen to defend his title at Chicago. If Rickard couldn't buy off Mullen the title fight would go to Chicago because Tex couldn't fulfil his contract for a title bout in New York. And if this were the case Mullen would have to come in high for the services of Jimmy McLarnin. He had already bid $30,000, and then he raised the ante on Rickard. Fifty thousand dollars, the largest guarantee ever offered a lightweight challenger was bid for

Jimmy's services. Mullen predicted the fight would draw a $400,000 gate at Soldier's Field, Chicago. Rickard described the offer as 'the laugh of the year'.

'Why, he could offer him $100,000,' chuckled Tex, 'for all the good it would do him.'

Mandell would rather have fought in Chicago, where Mullen could guarantee him all kinds of protection against long counts, dodgy judges and other hazards that champions stumbled into when their titles are put in jeopardy. In New York he could expect nothing more than an even break. But Mullen couldn't give him New York money. Mandell had no idea that Jimmy would come into the Garden and become a sensation overnight by knocking Terris over in a minute or so and he realised that if he didn't sign with Rickard he would not only lose the McLarnin match, but that Jimmy, Pop and Tex Rickard would go out and fight somebody else, so his friendship or loyalty, whatever it may have been, for Mullen, was sacrificed on the altar of business. Rickard signed the Mandell-McLarnin championship fight for the Polo Grounds on 17 May 1928. 'It seemed that his Chicago rival, Jim Mullen, has been effectively flattened in this latest of their promotional wars,' wrote Frank Wallace in the *New York Daily News*. Mullen threatened to sue, but Rickard tilted his cigar and said, 'Let him sue, the Chicago lawyers need the money. We've had plenty of talk about injunctions before, but they never stopped a fight.'

From the Terris fight onwards Pop and Jimmy kept coming to New York for lucrative fights and spent as little time there as possible. They usually trained at Gus Wilson's camp at Orangeburg and only came into the city the day before the fight. They always stayed at the same cheap hotel near Madison Square Garden. Pop didn't approve of taxicabs and liked to be within walking distance of the 'office'. And just a few days after the fight they were gone again.

'We made a practice of staying in the wrong hotels – small, chintzy places populated largely by old ladies and Pomeranians,' Jimmy recalled. The night before a fight they'd take in a late show, partly to get Jimmy's mind off the fight and partly to help him sleep a little later than usual the following day. The morning after the fight they'd go downtown and pick up a cheque from Tex Rickard or Mike Jacobs or whoever the promoter was and they'd get out of town again. Sometimes they drove to Long Island, where both Pop and Jimmy owned some property, but more often they'd fly out to Los Angeles or go on up to Vancouver and stay there until it was time to come back east and start training for the next fight. 'So we weren't too accessible to strangers – especially suspicious strangers – and all strangers were suspicious to Pop,' Jimmy recalled. 'I was far more guileless than he was, but I only got close once to striking up a genuine acquaintance with a real live gangster. The day after one of my fights I went downtown with my brother Bob, who had been helping me with my training. We weren't leaving town until late at night and before I left I wanted a piece of lemon pie. In or out of training, I was very careful about my diet. According to my theories and Pop's on food, pastry of any kind has all the health-giving properties of arsenic. But I've got a hopeless weakness for lemon pie and after an earlier fight I'd discovered a restaurant that made the best lemon pie in the world.

'Bob and I were sitting alone eating our lemon pie when the

owner of the restaurant came up and said he'd like to introduce us to some men sitting at another table. We took our pie over and sat down for a while with Legs Diamond and his bodyguard. Prohibition was still in force and Diamond, who was murdered about a year later, was then the undisputed king of the rackets. Bob and I sat around chatting with Diamond and his boys for half an hour or so, mostly about fights and fighters and then we said good-bye and went home.

'I told Pop where we'd been and what we'd had to eat. He frowned a little when I mentioned the lemon pie but didn't say anything. Then I told him who we'd been talking to.

'I never heard Pop use a swear word until I was past thirty. This time it looked close. He didn't say anything for almost a minute. When he finally spoke his voice was under perfect control.

"Jimmy," he said. "Don't ever eat lemon pie with Legs Diamond again."

"Okay, Pop," I said.

"And Jimmy."

"Yes Pop?"

"Don't even eat a nice healthy salad with Legs Diamond."

"I won't Pop," I said, and I never did.'

A BELFAST LAMB TO THE SLAUGHTER

The East End was where most of Vancouver's new arrivals settled. The Great War was finally over and Charlie Foster and Sam McLarnin were watching a few kids kicking a soccer ball around; after a while one of the boys walked over to where his father and the crusty, nickel-nursing old fighter were standing. Foster said, half to the kid and half to his father: 'I could make a boxer out of that boy.' It was the quickness of the kid – his legs. His arms weren't much, and as a matter of fact there was little to him but legs – but they were enough for Foster. He was struck at once with the idea there was a champion if he was taught correctly. The old man said to himself, 'Who can handle him better than you? Get started. Teach the lad. He can't go wrong – he simply can't.' Foster had watched Jimmy for weeks down by a billiard room where the local boys gathered. But Jimmy never played billiards – not enough action in it. He had to keep moving. 'I'll show you how to box, son,' said Foster. 'If you do just what I tell you, you'll be a champion of the world one day.'

So Foster started to teach the boy some of the things he knew about boxing. This was Jimmy's game and there wasn't anything he liked as well; he'd spar ten hours a day if he could. And Foster never saw anyone who learned as quickly. The kid had a knack, an intuition for it. Foster would tell him something, and before he was half through Jimmy had the idea. Not only did he have the idea, but he was able to carry it out. Pop and Jimmy settled down to serious business, just the two of them, and now, seven years later, they were in New York fighting Sammy Mandell for the title. They confounded the city's boxing writers. Jimmy didn't train by the same routine that other prize-fighters followed, he boxed only three rounds a day, and those three rounds with a 'drowsy middleweight by the name of Joe Something who simulates the style of Samuel Mandell about as well as a two dollar bill can simulate a five dollar bill'. Pop was regarded as being scandalously 'near' regarding finances. Parsimonious old Pop, too mean to employ decent sparring partners. 'Foster, who isn't familiar with Eastern wage scales was besieged by a gang of ambitious young sparring partners who were willing to hire themselves out to McLarnin for $20 per day, but Pop, innocent old soul, figured they were trying to take him over,' wrote Jack Farrell in the *New York Daily News*. 'Pop is quite willing to give each and every sparring partner as high as $2.50 per day plus their bed and board, but he couldn't see the twenty-buck gag nohow.'

The McLarnin camp took on an even more threadbare look when it lost one of its unpaid members. Jimmy's younger brother Sammy had been a permanent fixture at the training camps since the Los Angeles days and he often fought on the undercard when Jimmy was the main eventer. Sammy was scheduled to appear in a four-round curtain raiser before the

Terris fight, but he pulled out after injuring an ear in training. Then as they were running on the roads two weeks before the Mandell fight, Sammy told Jimmy that he was going home.

'What do you mean? You've got a fight coming up in a few weeks and I'm fighting for the title,' said Jimmy.

'No James, I'm going home. I'm going to become a minister.'

Next day, Sammy was gone. He didn't even stay to see the fight. He went home and hit the sawdust trail and became a lay preacher.

'Pop Foster, McLarnin's manager, does everything backwards,' wrote one scribe. 'I don't know whether Jimmy eats his meals in the old conventional way, but from what I observed in the gymnasium it wouldn't surprise me if Baby Face started off with his dessert and finished with hors d'oeuvres.' Pop gruffly mumbled that Jimmy had learned to box years previously and if he didn't know how to box now he couldn't teach him enough in two weeks of training to do him any good against Mandell. He was, however, trying to get the idea of a knockout out of Jimmy's head. Mandell wasn't going to go down as easily as Terris and at that time only one knockout was chalked against the champion's record. But Jimmy was happy with his work. 'If the fight ends the wrong way tonight, at least I will never have to reproach myself with having taken the other fellow too lightly. I've always admired Jack Dempsey's attitude in that respect. He always said the other fellow had two legs and two arms, just like me.'

When Rickard took the Mandell-McLarnin bout from Jim Mullen he expected to clean up and talked of a three or four hundred thousand-dollar gate. He had made great sums of money with lightweights before. There hadn't been a light-weight championship fight in New York since Benny Leonard whipped Lew Tendlar in the Yankee Stadium six years previously. That fight had drawn $472,000 and it wasn't really a lightweight fight at all. The combatants had made a pact to come in overweight as 'Philadelphia lightweights' or 146-pounders. The weighing-in ceremony was held in secret. But despite the suspicion surrounding the fight they stormed the box-office windows and contributed all that money to see a lightweight championship contest in which neither fighter was a lightweight. Leonard won and soon retired because as Westbrook Pegler, one of America's most widely-read columnists of the time wrote, 'it would have killed him to make that weight again and he wished to be good to his mother'.

But the Mandell-McLarnin fight was proving to be a hard sell for Rickard largely because the customers in New York didn't regard Mandell as a real champion. The lightweight title was a very historic one, but most of the history had happened before Benny Leonard retired and the title retired with him. An elimination tournament was staged to find a new champion, but that descended into farce. Sid Terris chose to stay out of it and Mandell was eliminated on a foul early on. Chilean contender Stanislaus Loayza broke his ankle and somehow or other, with the best three lightweights out of it, Jimmy Goodrich was crowned champion and then promptly lost it to Rocky Kansas, 'the Ancient Mariner of the lightweight division'. According to Paul Gallico, 'the title to Kansas when he finally won it was no more than a watch to an amateur – something to hock or sell'. Kansas stepped in with a young challenger,

Sammy Mandell, and lost on a decision, although the boys knew that Kansas was 'protected' in his loss for $50,000. That's how the Rockford Sheik became the lightweight champion of the world, and having gone to so much trouble to get it, he tucked it away for a while. 'Thus, the celebration tonight is for the exhuming of the crown,' wrote Gallico, 'because for a long while everybody thought Sammy had thrown the key away.' In the two years he had held the title Mandell had failed to give a prominent contender a shot. Sid Terris, who had been the most deserving, was ignored by Mandell's management. Terris fought them all and Mandell fought no one. But that's the way the fight business was conducted by smart people; Mandell was the unmarked champion, Terris had been punched to nowhere.

Mandell and Jimmy had shared a dressing room on a few shows in California and were pretty good friends. Jimmy was recovering from a serious illness at the time and Mandell was carrying a rib injury. 'I remember we were both a little downhearted, and we used to console each other,' Jimmy recalled. 'I always liked Sammy personally. I still do, for that matter, but that won't help his chin any if he gets in the way of my right hand Thursday night.' The night Jimmy beat Kid Kaplan in Chicago, Mandell sat just behind his corner and shouted for the Irishman throughout. 'I will never forget the one voice and the one face that cheered me on when things looked blackest. I can still see him standing and shouting encouragement from a ringside seat,' said Jimmy. 'He smiled, waved and shook hands together as if to wish me good luck when I entered the ring. He let me know that he was pulling for me. I appreciated his sympathy, but I know he had a little selfish interest of his own. I had heard before the fight that none of the lightweights wanted to meet Kaplan, and I realised why after we got through our little session. He's the toughest man I ever saw. I can believe that Sammy drew a sigh of relief when he saw me put him out of the running. I don't say that in a boasting way, I'm willing to take my hat off to the Kid. One dose of him is a great sufficiency. The other boys are welcome to Kid Kaplan. I don't crave his society any further. I'm not selfish that way.'

This match may not have been pulling the gate but big money was being laid. 'No matter who wins, half of Broadway will go broke and the other half will double its orders to the bootleggers,' commented one scribe. 'There's so much bet on this fight that the Bulgarian national debt looks like candy money for the children compared with it.' The match had a strange, unfamiliar appearance of complete honesty and honest prizefights were so rare that the customers still regarded them with some suspicion. Mandell ruled a 7 to 5 favourite the day before the fight.

With impossibly good timing, considering how slowly the tickets were shifting, Jimmy was served with a summons in a $20,000 damage suit during the weigh-in. The complainant, Hjalmer Mogren, was a 'placid Viking' retained by Pop who alleged that Jimmy was unnecessarily rough during a sparring session. Hjalmer was willing to do anything but cover up his jaw, however his services didn't cost much, so this defensive flaw was overlooked. Inevitably Jimmy's fist came in contact with Mogren's jaw and broke it. Mogren sued for $50,000, considerably above the market price, and Jimmy's claim to be a killer puncher was reinforced a hundredfold. The boys called him the 'original rigor mortis kid'.

Andy Lytle, the sports editor of the *Toronto Star* was sent to New York to cover the fight. At first he couldn't even find Pop and Jimmy, 'nobody around the fight rialtos seemed to know much about them except that Foster covered up his boy craftily and none of the racketeers and chisellers could fasten a fang on him.' He tracked them down to a walk-up apartment, five floors up and six flats back. Pop was cooking on a gas plate when the reporter walked in. 'The place was ill-ventilated and reeked of hot grease and bad airs,' wrote Lytle. 'Jimmy was briskly doing nip-ups and shadow-boxing while Pop prepared breakfast. I said it was an odd place to find a potential champion. "Sss'ssh," cautioned Jimmy, "it's Pop's idea. He wants to keep away from the mob. Nobody knows where we've ducked to. That's the way I want it, too."'

Pop was an old guy, but he was afraid of no man and the boys liked to tell the story of a night when Jimmy was going to fight in the Garden and a couple of hoodlums walked into his dressing room. Ignoring Jimmy one of them said to Pop:

'Your boy is going out in the second round.'

Pop glared at him, then at his companion.

'Get out of here,' he said. 'Both of you.'

The hoodlum who had talked took out the artillery.

'And take that with you,' Pop said, 'before I take it away from you and stick it down your throat. You and your gun! Who do you think I am, coming around here and making faces at me and showing me a gun?' The hoodlums went. In the circumstances there didn't seem to be anything else for them to do. After all, they weren't going to shoot him in the dressing room or, for that matter, anywhere else. Pop had courage and smartness enough to know it. 'Just for that, we'll knock their boy out, Jimmy!' he stormed, as he chased the thugs from the place – and Jimmy did just that.

Despite all the speculation over Jimmy's ability to make the weight, it was Mandell who was a quarter of a pound over when he jumped on the scales. The champion was given time to knock off the additional poundage, and after a light workout he came back and moved the beam at the 135 pound notch; Jimmy was checked at 134 ½ pounds. But across town the forecasters informed Tex Rickard that rain was in the offing, and he immediately called the show off until the following night. Jimmy had struggled to make the weight and the postponement really should have helped him. He wouldn't have to weigh-in again the following day so he could take back everything he'd boiled out of himself and step through the ropes closer to his natural weight. Both fighters rested at their hotels but Jimmy seemed particularly upset at the turn of events.

'I was in a happy mood when I drove into New York from my training camp at Pompton Lakes,' he wrote. 'It was the day I thought would never come – the day I was to fight for the championship. Then I got the shock. It was postponed, and I would have twenty-four more long hours. I don't feel any too cheerful about it. There's no use kidding myself, nor kidding the public. I was right yesterday afternoon, righter than I ever was in my life. I was counting the minutes until ringtime, and I felt the time would never pass. It was a blow, and a heavy one. However, I guess Mandell feels as badly as I do. That's some consolation. I know I would rather have gone through with the fight if there was any possibility that it could be staged. The money didn't matter. The victory was the big thing. I guess I'll feel a lot better about it after a good night's sleep, but it was a bitter disappointment ... This waiting business is hard on the nerves.'

Tex Rickard took fright at the cloudy skies again the following day and he postponed the fight once more early in the afternoon. It would have been a perfect evening for boxing and not a drop of rain fell but Rickard, believing that his luck had fled and the advance sale had not been up to snuff, put it off for another couple of nights. And then it really did rain. 'Apparently his old pal, Mr Pluvius, took this sleight to heart,' commented the *New York Daily News*. 'Jupe had always given Tex better than an even break, and it looked as though the promoter wasn't playing cricket. So yesterday he turned on all the faucets and the rain made the "big flood" look like a misty afternoon.' It was only the third time in twenty-two years of boxing that Rickard had been compelled to postpone an outdoor fight because of weather and the first time for a double postponement. Jimmy was edgy and wanted it over with. Rickard, not satisfied with the advance sale, thought another day's delay would help. But then the continual downpour of rain set the affair back for a third time. Now the commission would insist on them weighing in again, for fear that the lightweight battle would turn out to be a duel between welterweights – just as it did way back in '24 with Leonard and Tendlar. Mandell scurried back to Gus Wilson's place at Orangeburg but Jimmy and Pop stayed in New York working and sweating in Grupp's gymnasium.

Mandell had been kept out of New York for about three years. He had put up some good fights there before he disappeared in about 1925 and was a good card then. But after he won his dubious claim to the lightweight title, his manager, Eddie Kane, felt that it was best policy to steer him around New York. But both Foster and Kane had the outdoor bug that inflicted the managers of apparent drawing cards and they let the match grow cold. A Mandell-McLarnin match would have filled Madison Square Garden just after Jimmy had beaten Sid Terris, but Rickard, the fighters and their managers thought they could fill a ballpark with this one and they waited until the summer. The three postponements had only served to quiet the public interest and a howling sky toward the end of the day kept much of the usual last minute trade in the comforts of the speakeasy. It was cool enough to make overcoats comfortable. The grass at the Polo Grounds was damp underfoot and the stars and a new thin moon shone overhead when announcer Joe Humphreys stepped through the ropes. Jimmy entered the ring at 9.41pm, the champion followed a few seconds later. The fighters sprouted goose pimples as soon as the robes slipped from their shoulders. Neither seemed particularly happy. Jimmy tried a smile without much success while Mandell sat soberly looking at the floor. Foster hovered over Jimmy like a parent over a brand new child.

The referee gave his instructions and the bell rang. The first fifteen seconds of a fight could often be the fight. 'It is equivalent to the first kiss in a love affair,' wrote Norman Mailer. From the opening bell Jimmy looked like an inexperienced boy trying to fight a champion and he fought just as Mandell would have wanted him to. Jimmy charged into the champion and was stabbed to ribbons by Mandell's left hand. The Irishman had lost his temper by the third and he backed Mandell into a corner and unleashed ten or more swings to the head and body and missed every one of them. Whenever Jimmy managed to rush Mandell to the ropes, the champion calmly straight armed him with an open left glove which covered the challenger's face and smothered his nostrils. Mandell arched his body backwards and let Jimmy's gloves go whistling past his ribs. '[Jimmy] boxed with a worried look on his otherwise placid features and the look of concern increased and grew as he discovered the first man he could not hit,' wrote Paul Gallico.

Through all the rounds it was the master working his pupil. Jimmy was game and willing but simply couldn't land, while his own pink cheeks felt the constant stabbing of Mandell's gloves. Then the pink cheeks deepened to a dull red as a crimson smear from his nose spread across his face and his left eye was shut tight in a bloated and discoloured lump.

'[Mandell] stuck his thumb in my eye,' Jimmy said many years later. 'I couldn't see out of this left eye for three weeks. He was a dirty fighter. He was a great guy, but he used to give you that thumb.' Mandell switched his attack and tore away at Jimmy's body with cruel left hooks that left his waistline banded with the impact of all the blows the champion landed. Half blinded, Jimmy kept walking into the barrage and his blood painted a red pattern on Mandell's body.

The 'I told you so' stories were being rattled out on ringside typewriters before the halfway point. Jimmy had trained all wrong. His one sparring partner, a slow-moving welterweight, was no preparation for the lightning fast Mandell. It was Pop Foster's fault. Jimmy didn't miss a single sock; he managed to get his face in the way of the punches every time. Pop looked on from the corner as his boy, sheepish and befuddled, missed enough swings to run a powerhouse for thirty days. 'There was just one thing everybody, including me, overlooked in the calculations. That was Sammy Mandell,' Jimmy said many years later. 'I never took any fight lightly. I knew that Sammy was very fast, very hard to hit, and that he had a very quick and busy left hand. But I was utterly and absolutely sure that I was going to beat him. I trained harder for him than I'd trained for anybody before, but I almost enjoyed the training this time because I kept telling myself that I was finally going to make it all the way to the top.'

Mandell didn't hurt Jimmy – not in the way a fighter means when he says he's been hurt – but by the time it was over Jimmy's left eye was totally closed, his right eye was nearly shut, his nose was puffed up and bloody and his lips were cut as though broken glass had been ground into them. Mandell was generally credited with winning fourteen of the fifteen rounds and sentiment passed quickly enough as it always did. Jimmy was cheered wildly at the start but when he took his battered body and sad heart back to the dressing room he was alone save for his seconds. The fickle mob swarmed around the champion. Jimmy stood with his head in hot water for half an hour to try and reduce the swelling around his eyes. 'The left eye had a ten-storey house on it,' commented Russell Crouse in the *New York Post*. 'Parts of the nose were reported flying over Danbury, Conn., a little after 11 o'clock and should reach Paris at 2pm tomorrow afternoon if they follow Lindbergh's route. The mouth looked like a sunset, with a little ketchup.' Pop said he would take his boy back to the coast for more seasoning. 'We brought him over here about one year too soon.'

Andy Lytle returned to the dimly-lit, badly ventilated quarters near Columbus Circle. 'What shall I say to the folks back home about your battle for the title?' he asked.

'I just couldn't get at him, Mr Lytle,' Jimmy said, with tears in his eyes. 'He was too smart for me, wasn't he?'

Pop shoved the writer away. 'Leave the boy be. The fight's over. The boy fought well. It was close.'

'Close, hell!' Lytle retorted. Pop always managed to come up with a triumphant description of a losing battle, although this one was more reminiscent of Mark Twain's character who said: 'Thrusting my nose firmly between his teeth, I threw him to the ground on top of me.' Jimmy wanted to quit and was inconsolable for days. Ed Frayne stopped by the apartment an hour after the fight and Jimmy was holding an ice pack to a badly swollen eye and sobbing. He was so ashamed he wouldn't look up. 'I'm not going to fight any more, Eddie,' Jimmy said. 'I can't go out and look people in the face ever again. I've sunk every Irishman in America.'

The morning after and the reputations of two prizefighters had been completely transformed. The boys were trying to figure just where Mandell now stood in relation to his predecessors as champion. He had been regarded as an accident rather than a champion, a clever boxer and a businessman who held the title by grace of careful matchmaking. He couldn't 'punch hard enough to break an egg.' But now they were wondering just how Mandell would have fared with the lightweight greats; Gans, Nelson, Wolgast, Ritchie, Welsh or Leonard. Jimmy, who had become a popular idol overnight on the strength of one spectacular knockout over Sid Terris, was dismissed. 'After the

Mandell fight we didn't get right out of town. I didn't even want to get out of that apartment. I couldn't bear the thought of going back to Los Angeles to face my friends. I couldn't bear the thought of going back to Vancouver to face my family and my girl. I couldn't even bear the thought of going down to the corner for a paper.' It was probably just as well that he avoided John Kieran in the *New York Times*:

A fight fan complains that Jimmy McLarnin didn't get enough credit for the courageous way in which he kept tearing into Sammy Mandell in their recent collision at the Polo Grounds. That leads to a general discussion on how much 'aggressiveness' should count in a bout where 'aggressiveness' consists chiefly in walking forward and blocking a number of punches with the chin.

It recalls a recent incident in a quiet suburban community. A small boy came home with a disorganised nose and a big lump over one eye. He told the usual story.

'You ought'a see the other guy.'

'What did you do to him?' queried a fond parent. 'Did you knock him out?'

'No, but I busted his hands.'

Jimmy had taken a very public beating, and so had Tex Rickard. The match was a 'bust', the first Rickard had had in some time. 'Mr Rickard is so unaccustomed to "busts" that his ordinarily placid countenance bore an expression so sad last evening that some of the clients felt disposed to break out into tears on his behalf, until they remembered that Mr Rickard

Above: The McLarnin clan in Vancouver, Jimmy back row second from right
Below: Jimmy 'Babyface' McLarnin

Above: Jimmy and Pop in the early days in Oakland
Below: Jimmy McLarnin and Tommy Cello

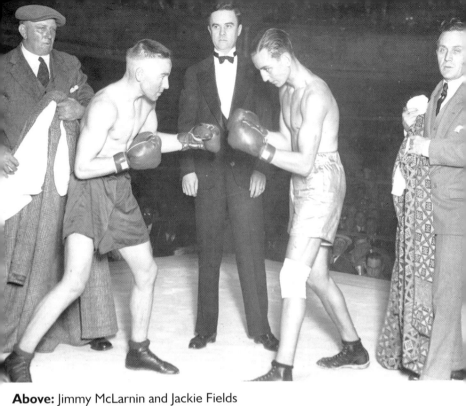

Above: Jimmy McLarnin and Jackie Fields
Below: Sid Terris is counted out in the first round of his fight with Jimmy at Madison Square Garden, 24 February 1928

Above: Tex Rickard (left) and Pop Foster (right) look on as Jimmy demonstrates the punch with which he knocked out Sid Terris
Below: The only photo to capture Jimmy mid-air during one of his famous back handsprings. He has just knocked out Sammy Fuller in the eighth round of their bout at Madison Sqaure Garden in December 1932.

Left: Jimmy McLarnin, World Welterweight Champion 1933-35
Inset: Jimmy 'the Jew Killer' beats Ruby Goldstein in New York on 13 December 1929

Above: Jimmy and Al Singer, 11 September 1930
Below: Jimmy and Benny Leonard, 7 October 1932

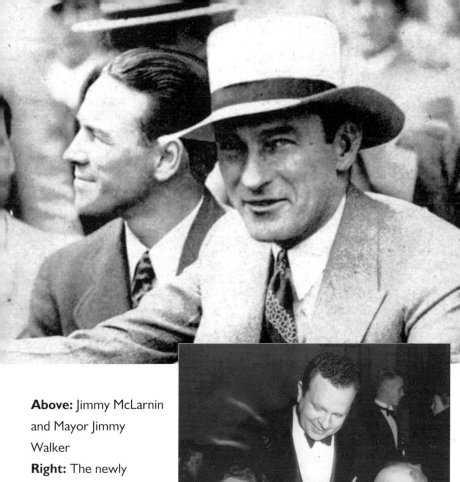

Above: Jimmy McLarnin and Mayor Jimmy Walker

Right: The newly crowned welterweight champion and his manager talk to Joe Mann (centre), in the Blossom Room of the Roosevelt Hotel at a dinner dance in Hollywood, 1933

ACME PHOTO

Above: Jimmy shakes hands with Young Corbett III in Los Angeles, 29 May 1933
Below: Two members of a life boat crew furnish Jimmy with an impromptu piece of gymnasium equipment at Gus Wilson's camp at Orangeburg

Los Angeles, Calif. — By a first round kayo Jimmy McLarnin won the world welterweight title — 2 minutes, 37 seconds.

seldom, if ever, cries for them,' wrote Damon Runyon. Rickard had expected to draw $400,000 with the show, but he took just a quarter of that. He certainly figured to sell most of his chairs, but there were yawning gaps in the grandstand and the bleachers. Back in Chicago Jim Mullen must have smiled as he heard the tidings on the gate. He had offered Jimmy $50,000 for his bit on the match in Chicago and Mandell even more. 'Tex really wanted us to win that 1928 fight with Sammy Mandell for the lightweight title. He had tremendous plans for Jimmy after that one,' Pop recalled many years later. 'Mandell won that fight by slapping and flipping, tactics that are illegal today. He would just slap and back away with Jimmy after him. My boy was brilliant in the last five rounds and really tagged Mandell in the fourteenth, but it was too late.'

Jimmy had carried the cheers of New York into the ring against Mandell, but he took nothing out but a bruised face and a sad heart. Mandell chopped him into raw meat, and the right hand that had cuffed Kaplan and Terris into oblivion got nowhere near Sammy Mandell. 'No delegation of Hibernians escorted McLarnin to the train when he went back West with old Pop Foster,' wrote Jack Kofoed in the *New York Post*. 'He was just another fighter – this Belfast lamb they had been bally-hooing as a tiger.'

Jimmy needed to get back on Rickard's cauliflower patch as soon as possible. After Mandell's master class Pop decided his boy needed someone who was much easier to hit and Phil McGraw, a fighting Greek florist from Detroit, was perfect. McGraw, 'the iron-jawed pansy peddler', was a tireless, persistent plodder who never stopped trying. He wasn't hard to hit but

McGraw could take 'em on the chin and come back for more and fighters usually gave up on the idea of trying to knock him out after a few rounds. The customers loved the fighting florist and a match with Jimmy would sell; McGraw would meet the Irishman at his own game – that of pegging punches. Indeed, 11,570 customers paid $33,154 to see it, the largest indoor crowd of the summer season at the Garden.

McGraw, as usual, came out swinging. Jimmy waited and let Phil dent the air with left and rights as he sized up his opponent. This took half a minute and then Jimmy let fly with a right to get the range, then, five seconds before the hand on the big time clock underneath the gallery registered the two-minute mark, a right to the chin sent McGraw through the lower rope and on his way out of the Ninth Avenue side of the ring. Phil clung on to the canvas and was pushed back into the ring by newspapermen after taking a count of four. Jimmy, scenting a quick finish, slugged McGraw to the mat for the second time with a left to the chin, but the florist got up before the knockdown timekeeper could swing his gavel. Another left crashed through McGraw's guard and sent him through the ropes in another section of the ring. Jimmy moved in and staggered his man with lefts to the chin and a right hook to the jaw. McGraw took a four trip to the canvas and then just stood there like a punchbag waiting helplessly with Jimmy whaling him with both hands. Referee Jack Dorman wouldn't allow any more, much to the displeasure of the tin-horned gamblers who'd wagered on the florist to go the distance. McGraw had been knocked out for the first time and Jimmy had retaken New York in less than a round. 'I've seen great fighters in my day,' remarked Tex Rickard, 'but none to equal that boy as a slugger since the days of McGovern.'

Jimmy's next New York appearance was in a courtroom. On 3 July 1928, the State Supreme Court wanted to know whether Jimmy preferred to knock his opponents senseless or merely outpoint them. The plaintiff was Hjalmer Mogren, the sparring partner with the $50,000 suit and a broken jaw. Mogren said he was unable to work again at catching punches for a year. Did Jimmy wheel out his heftiest wallops, 'without informing or advising those called upon or employed by him to train and exercise with him?' Was he careless in breaking Mogren's jaw? Had he used more force than was necessary? 'Unofficially, McLarnin thinks that the minute Terris lasted under his fists and Phil McGraw's eradication in less than two minutes settles that,' reported the *Associated Press*. The case was dismissed.

'This suit raises a fine point in the manly art of modified murder,' commented Bill McGeehan. 'Obviously, it is necessary that champions and contenders must test their punches before they go into main events. They pay sparring partners upon whose anatomy they experiment. In sparring practice the top-notchers cannot 'pull their punches' to any great extent because that might get them into bad habits. Of course, they wear heavier gloves in practice, but even with the extra padding it would seem that there is considerable shock power left ... For the maintenance of the cauliflower industry and for the advancement of the manly art of modified murder there must be a certain number of mediocre fighters kept around for experimental purposes just as there must be a supply of guinea pigs for experiments in surgery and medicine. The life of a sparring partner is a tough one, almost as tough as that of the guinea pig while it lasts. Generally speaking, there is no more future in the life of a sparring partner than there is in the career of a guinea pig. In both instances it is a short life and not a merry one. I do not recall any instance of a guinea pig that achieved fame or fortune.'

The cauliflower industry didn't care to admit that it was desirable for one fighter to knock the other out, but if it appeared that a fighter was not trying to do this he would more than likely be hauled before the Boxing Commission and charged with not putting forth his best efforts and the promoters just wouldn't hire him. For the purpose of making boxing legal the boys had to maintain that it was a contest of skill. For the purpose of luring the customers they looked for prizefighters that could knock another senseless. Prizefighters like Jimmy McLarnin. 'I gather that the charm of Mr McLarnin is due to the fact that he tries to knock all of his opponents horizontal in as brief a space as possible,' wrote McGeehan. 'He is not always successful, but it is apparent that he is in there trying to attain that consummation with all of the earnestness that is in him.' That earnestness kept the promoters, the scribes and the customers happy and Jimmy left Broadway a hero that summer.

On their way back to California, Foster and McLarnin Inc. stopped off in Detroit for a match with Stanislaus Loayza. 'Promoters are just discovering that the one chance now to lure out anything resembling a crowd is to offer a card replete with flying fists that seem to mean business,' wrote Westbrook Pegler. 'Too many dance acts have sapped a lot of ring enthusiasm. McLarnin and Loayza have not yet become even mildly interested in terpsichorean efficiency.' A sweltering crowd of 18,000 paid $88,000 to see it, a record for a lightweight fight in the Midwest. They got four brutal rounds. The fight was even for the first two but soon after the start of the third a series of right hands weakened Loayza and sent him to his corner in a bad way. An old wound over Loayza's left eye was slashed open in the fourth and a left hook to the head followed by a short right flush on the chin left the Chilean draped over the lower rope. He fell back and attempted to regain his feet but was still on his knees when the referee reached ten.

Pop and Jimmy spent the summer in California and then returned to Detroit for a fight before another season in New York. Jimmy had been signed to fight Tommy Grogan of Omaha but a few weeks out his opponent was changed to the Chicago featherweight, Ray Miller – and Ray Miller was bad news. The match was staged at Detroit's Olympia Arena and as early as the first round it was evident that there was a bad night ahead for Jimmy. Miller tore into the Irishman from the first bell and opened a deep slash under his right eye. A vicious left hook sent Jimmy back on his heels. Few in the crowd thought it was more than a flash in the pan. Miller, a blonde Chicago youth with a devastating punch in either hand, gave away five and a half pounds in weight and was a 1-to-5 shot in the betting. You could get 3-to-1 against Miller hearing the final bell. But he gave Jimmy an unmerciful beating in one of the boxing upsets of the year. Miller came charging out of his corner in the sixth and knocked Jimmy reeling into the ropes with a left to the jaw but somehow the Irishman managed to keep his feet with the Chicagoan standing over him, whipping over vicious left hooks. Jimmy took another beating in the seventh and he seemed on the point of collapse, his face a bloody smear when the bell rang.

A left to the injured eye had opened the cut that Pop had been doctoring between rounds. Bleeding profusely, Jimmy sat down in the wrong corner at the bell. His seconds entered the ring and rushed him to his own stool. Blood was streaming from the cut and it couldn't be stopped. It kept dripping – no, gushing – so horribly that Pop refused to let his boy take any more. Jimmy, bloody and groggy, sat in his corner. It was the first and the only fight Jimmy would ever take that he wasn't still around at the finish. 'Ray Miller hit the hardest,' Jimmy said over half a century later. 'I still think he had lead in his glove. I really do. I never got hit that hard in my life. He was a pretty sneaky guy – he and his managers.'

RIGHT FIGHTER, WRONG TIME

Before boxing the most popular betting sport in New York was rat-baiting. A hundred rats were tossed in an eight-foot pit and a fox terrier killed as many as it could in a set time. It took the best dogs about half an hour to kill all one hundred. Just like boxing there were trainers and handlers, referees and time-keepers, even catchweight matches. In rat-baiting dogs of different sizes were matched in contests of how long it took for the animal to kill its own weight in rats. And to keep things interesting, men in boots jumped in and stomped along with the terriers. The most infamous rat pit in New York was Kit Burns's Sportsman's Hall, an all-round three-story entertainment centre replete with bar and brothel. Kit Burns charged as much as five dollars admission for rat-baiting at a time when admission to human prizefights cost fifty cents. Blood sports of all sorts were central to the street culture of New York and the battles in the rat pit and then the prizering mirrored street warfare. The gangs of New York started out as ethnic enforcers, protecting rival turfs and at a time when Irish, Jewish and Italian gangs held sway it was no coincidence that the majority of prizefighters were Irish,

Jewish or Italian. Each immigrant group that came to America produced great fighters as they struggled to assimilate into American society. The ability to fight was a matter of status among peers so boys learned to fight early. And most fighters were influenced to draw on the gloves by another boxer in the neighbourhood or by a family member.

Prizefighters are recruited from the ranks of poor boys and their changing ethnic composition mirrors the changing ethnic composition of the poor of the big cities. First came the Irish, then the Jewish then the Italian. The traditions of the ethnic group as well as its temporary location at the bottom of the heap determined the number of prizefighters it produced. When the Irish arrived in the big cities of North America, individual and gang fights were encouraged. The most feared and respected member of a gang was the best fighter and successful boxers became heroes to the boys in the slums. Boys like Jimmy had little hope of anything other than unskilled, hard, manual work so fighting for money and prestige was very alluring.

When the old man and his slightly battered kid eventually made their way back to New York, Pop was in quite a different mood than the one he exhibited prior to the Ray Miller fight. He had been holding out for big purses but was now looking for matches to re-establish his protégé. Sensing that Pop might be weakening the boys tried once more to get a piece of Jimmy. Members of the Garden board of directors attempted to subsidise Jimmy's talents with the promise of lucrative fights at Rickard's emporium. 'Charges that Madison Square Garden is attempting to purchase and furnish its own stable of boxers to fight under the corporation seal during the fall and winter threw the private suite of Mr Tex Rickard into something resembling a turmoil today,' reported the *Washington Post*. 'Stories have been heard that Jimmy McLarnin and Johnny Risko were warned that Madison Square Garden's cards might know them no more unless they deeded over a percentage of their management to certain interested parties.' Rickard grudgingly admitted to reporters that, 'certain corporation officials might have lent money to ready managers to advance their fighters'.

Jimmy was down and he had to begin all over again and in starting off with Joe Glick at Madison Square Garden he wasn't handing himself any the best of it. Jimmy had fought Glick on his travels around Los Angeles a few years previously, and although the Irishman was given the decision, the former buttonhole maker from Williamsburg was far from convinced that he had lost. Glick was a smart fighter and a savage body puncher and he had come along considerably since losing to Jimmy. He was coming into this match off a string of wins – barring a dropped decision to Cowboy Eddie Anderson out in the sticks somewhere – and Glick was now a contender for the lightweight championship. Glick's career had been in and out for several years. Just when it seemed he had reached a point where no one could beat him, some one turned around and gave him a smacking. But if he beat Jimmy there was a shot at Ray Miller in the offing, and then Mandell for the title. The fight was sold as the clever Jewish boxer against the fearless Irishman. Jack McAuliffe, the retired undefeated lightweight champion, wrote of how Jewish fighters had come to dominate his old stomping ground:

'Joe Glick comes from the old Fighting Fourteenth Ward of Williamsburg, the home of champions and statesmen. The ward is the home of the Nonpareil, Jack Dempsey.

'There wasn't a Jewish lad in all the Fourteenth Ward in the "old days" and it seems strange that one should now come from that district as an aspirant to the lightweight championship which Nonpareil Jack Dempsey and myself brought to that ward. It is funny that most of the Jewish boys who succeeded in the prize ring came from Irish neighbourhoods. Benny Leonard came from an Irish section of New York's East Side. Joe Choynski and Abe Attell came from Kearny's Sand Hills of Frisco.

'The Fourteenth Ward bred fighters. There wasn't a boy in the neighbourhood that didn't have a "shiner" as we called them in those days. And any young man that didn't boast a broken nose or a couple of loose teeth simply didn't belong in the fourteenth.

'On North Nine Street were the toughest fighters in the ward, and the further down you went the tougher they came. Dempsey and I lived in the last house. Big Ed Garrity, from North Eighteenth Street, would come down every Sunday morning, and in the middle of the road, which we called "Cork Row", he would yell, "I'm a Galway; I'm a Galway man."

'In Ireland when the Galway men and the Corkians met there was always a fight.'

But just a few days before the fight all talk of ethnic rivalry ended. Tex Rickard, the promoter who'd helped take boxing from the spit and sawdust clubs to the million dollar gates, died.

It was a funeral such as New York had never seen before.

'From his palm-banked bier in Madison Square Garden to his grave in Woodlawn cemetery the man of the crowds belonged to the crowds,' reported the *Chicago Tribune*. They piled into the Garden ten thousand strong and fifteen thousand more filed past the great bronze coffin before Tex went on his last journey. Among the last past the bier was a delegation of boxers and managers including Joe Glick and Jimmy McLarnin, who were to trade punches on the very spot where the dead promoter laid before they carted him away amid much pomp and splendour to his final resting place. 'Just what effect this will have on the gladiators is doubtful, but regardless of how good the fight is the fact remains that the old Garden will not feel the same even though the capacity crowd that Rickard always loved to watch trickling in will be there,' wrote Jack Farrell in the *New York Daily News*.

Rickard had been laid to rest but on the night of the Glick-McLarnin fight the Eighth Avenue palace he built was crowded with fight fans baying for blood. Jimmy had gone from the next lightweight champion to the 'cherubic seven-day wonder from the Coast' and several New York boxing writers picked Glick to beat him. The Irishman had become just another pug with a sock and a heart, trying to rebuild a bloated reputation. More than nineteen thousand customers showed up and they stood bareheaded, banked from the floor to the topmost gallery of the Garden. Jack Dempsey stood with announcer Joe Humphreys in a darkened ring. Through the stillness came the haunting notes of 'Taps', and then Humphreys' '…and may his soul rest in peace. Amen.' To add to the strange atmosphere in the

Garden, Jack F. Apdale, a lion tamer and vaudeville actor, died while awaiting the preliminary bouts.

> Jimmy was nimble,
> Jimmy was quick,
> Oi yoi, Oi yoi,
> He murdered Joe Gleeck
> – A noisery rhyme alreddy
> Jimmy Powers,
> *New York Daily News*

Jimmy was slow in getting started and dropped the first round to Glick, but from then on he ripped and hammered his way through nine rounds of slugging. He barely wasted a punch. This was another incarnation of Jimmy McLarnin, a 'beautiful fighting machine'. Glick complained after the fight that he had been worried by the 'sardonic grins' of Dai Dollings, Jimmy's trainer, during the rest periods and by Jimmy himself. They used this means of strategy to worry him and succeeded, claimed Glick. It created sufficient column inches to stoke up a rematch a month or so later with the Jewish fighter promising not to pay attention to opposition grins.

Glick was knocked out inside two rounds. He'd started well. He came out to the sound of the bell flourishing a wide left hook. But Jimmy was faster and landed four left-handers to the head in a row. A right collapsed the hinges of Glick's knees. He began to go. Glick took his chair with a bloody nose. Jimmy dropped his defence and ran forward, whipping left hooks. They ripped Glick's eye and his mouth. One of them dropped him in a corner. He was down on his side and the customers screamed. The timekeeper yelled 'ten' but Arthur Donovan, the referee, was a good second behind as Glick got to his feet. He ran but Jimmy chased him easily and wiped his chin with a left and Glick sank again. He looked sick and his eyes rolled. Then a frenzy sent him riding across the ring, both arms swinging. The crowd cheered Glick on, but Jimmy reached with a long right and laid the end of it on his opponent's chin. Glick sank to the floor, his right knee gave way first and he went on his back. This time the referee concluded the count. The crowd stood up and yelled as Glick grovelled on the floor. He had gone the way of all fighters who lead with their chins. The ring floor thumped as Jimmy threw a handspring. Glick motioned as though he wanted to continue. The referee told him to sit down.

Jimmy was still a sell-out attraction and he put a capacity crowd into New York's Madison Square Garden despite being stopped by Ray Miller not that long ago. New Yorkers liked big punchers – that's why Jack Dempsey was such a gate attraction for a long time. The relative fortunes of Jimmy and Sammy Mandell, the lightweight champion, served to illustrate the point. The previous year Mandell had laid his title on the line for Jimmy to shoot at. Jimmy was soundly beaten, but the reverse didn't hurt him and where Mandell had been making dimes since that match, Jimmy had made thousands.

Such was the demand for his next fight, a rematch with Ray Miller, that the sidewalk hawkers had bought up thousands of tickets and were selling them at inflated prices along Broadway. The Garden box office had to be closed down and advance sales sent by mail, no more than two per customer. Fight fans loved nothing so much as a puncher and here were two, each as aggressive as a wolf that had gone without its rations for a week.

'The scientific side of the art of self-defence always slips into the background when a pair of punchers drift along,' wrote Grantland Rice. 'There may be a world of science in boxing and the artistic appeal may be heavy, but they both get crowded back when a McLarnin and Miller begin starting a few from the floor … This age, whatever its other faults, is in motion. There is a lusty demand for action, and you can get more action from two offensive machines than you can from two defensive parties. Maybe this is not as it should be but that happens to be the way it is,' wrote Rice. 'McLarnin and Miller proved in Detroit that the main idea of the evening was decapitation, if possible, and this idea is as popular in New York as it was in the Mid-West.'

But after all the ballyhoo the fight was a bust. Nearly twenty-one thousand customers had packed the Garden arena to the gunwales and paid a record gate of $111,855 to see it, but far from being the predicted war, the fighters seemed to have too much respect for the punching power of the other. Ray Miller's father had died only a few days before the fight and Jimmy seemed haunted by memories of Detroit. Jimmy was the 2-to-1 favourite largely because he carried a ten-pound weight advantage and the result was of little importance to Miller. The dough was already in the house and his share of it was 25 per cent, win, lose or draw. It was usually good to win the decision for the sake of future engagements, but on this occasion it wasn't necessary. Miller had been promised a shot at Sammy Mandell in Detroit for the title if he was still on his feet at the end of the tenth round and in reasonably good condition.

The decision went to Jimmy, but his margin was slight. It was another highly-touted affair for which too much had been forecast. When Jimmy was given the nod he turned a couple of handsprings while some of the customers felt that he might have used a little of this energy in the course of the fight. The judges were unanimous in their decision, so was the crowd. It wasn't good. Jimmy had entered the ring with a bad cut under his right eye and Miller showed up wearing a white patch over his left lamp. Neither was disturbed at the end. Both fighters were armed with knockout punches, but they played a safe game. A referee of the old school would probably have chased the pair from the ring. Not once during the ten rounds did the highly-vaunted left hand of Miller, which tore Jimmy's face apart in Detroit, land on target and not once did Jimmy's knockout right reach Miller's jaw. There wasn't a mark on either boxer at the end. Jimmy won because he carried whatever fighting there was – a case of a guy who could fight trying to fight a guy who wouldn't. The paying customers, some who had paid $75 for a $10 seat, spent most of the fight booing and jeering.

'It was evident from the start that these two tired young businessmen cherished no animosity whatever against each other,' commented Bill McGeehan. 'For the first two minutes of the opening round neither gladiator made a hostile gesture at the other. After having watched these things for more than a quarter of a century I do not recall having seen before one bout where not even a slap was exchanged for that length of time.'

Another New York campaign was over and Pop and his boy returned to California for the summer, and even though two disappointing matches with Miller had damaged Jimmy's reputation they were big bankrolls richer. Whenever he'd get back to the Coast there'd be several offers to fight in local arenas. But old Pop just shook his head.

'Why should my Jimmy fight here when he is the sensation of New York?' he would ask.

In the summer of 1929 matchmaker Hayden Wadhams of the Olympic offered $20,000 for a fight with Jackie Fields. Pop turned it down. He wanted $30,000. Ancil Hoffman dangled $15,000 before his eyes for a match with Young Corbett III, a San Francisco southpaw, in the Bay City. Pop just laughed.

'That's not New York money,' he said.

Pop and Jimmy had made tens of thousands of dollars in the East, but the pair still lived the same way as they did in the old 'pork-and-bean days'. Even when the money started to roll in they kept on riding in upper berths. Pop was still a crusty, nickel-nursing Englishman. Whenever they went back to Vancouver the pair stayed in a $5-a-week hotel and Pop was stunned at a suggestion that they should move to more comfortable accommodation at $5 a day. It was good enough in the old days and there was no reason for changing now. The summers were spent on the Pacific Coast, partly in Los Angeles and partly in Vancouver. Jimmy had a gymnasium fixed up in the woodshed of the home he'd bought for his family where he trained with the boys of the old Methodist mission days, now grown men.

Jimmy continued to grow and by the winter season of 1929 he was ready to move into the welterweight division. He made his New York debut at the new weight against veteran local fighter 'Sergeant' Sammy Baker on 9 October 1929. It was viewed as an eliminator for the welterweight title now held by Jackie Fields – the same Jackie Fields that Jimmy had knocked out in two rounds when they were both lightweights. It lasted a second over two minutes. With the crack of the bell Jimmy moved out and crossed Baker with a right hand that floored the soldier for a count of nine. Baker tried to clinch but Jimmy landed four rights to the jaw. Baker stood up straight, closed his eyes and fell to the canvas. Referee 'Kid' McPartland went through the motions of counting him out, but Baker couldn't hear a thing. He was stone cold. They picked him up and 'his body folded in the middle like a hinge' then they dragged him to his corner, sat him down in his chair, and it was fully three minutes before he was able to leave the ring. Baker sat unconscious in his corner; 'his head wobbling wildly on his shoulders' while Jimmy danced around the ring and put on his still warm bathrobe. It wasn't a one-punch affair such as the New York debut against Sid Terris and it gave the customers a good opportunity to see the spectacular new welterweight version of Jimmy McLarnin. Jimmy was mobbed and it took the combined efforts of a dozen special policemen to get him to his dressing room.

Now the talk was of a world's welterweight titular brawl between Jimmy McLarnin, Irish contender, and Jackie Fields, Jewish champion, and right in the world's biggest boxing town to boot. But before chasing titles Jimmy wanted to settle an old score. The memory of his first world title fight at lightweight against Sammy Mandell still hurt. 'Going over the Mandell fight in my mind, and talking it over with Pop, I couldn't find any excuse for telling myself that Sammy had me licked,' Jimmy recalled. 'Maybe on some other night it would be different. No matter how I looked at it, no matter how many excuses I tried to make for myself, the same answer still kept coming up. Sammy Mandell had me licked, period. But I wanted to fight Mandell again. In the next year and a half it got to be an obsession with me.'

Since beating Jimmy at the Polo Grounds in New York back in May 1928 Mandell had fought out in Janesville and Flint, Indianapolis and Peoria, Grand Rapids and Muskegon, while Jimmy had established himself as the biggest draw, outside the heavyweights, in New York. Some pugilists held titles, but it was Jimmy McLarnin who made the dough. Even world champions like Mandell struggled to make money unless they fought an opponent of the McLarnin type. Mandell was also struggling to make the lightweight limit and so had set his sights on the welterweight championship and the quickest and most lucrative way to a bout with Jackie Fields was to remove Jimmy McLarnin. Mandell had given Jimmy a lacing as a lightweight, but he found that at 143 ¾ pounds the Irishman was too tough even for his marvellous boxing ability. Mandell entered the ring the favourite but Jimmy was too strong and too aggressive for him. The Irishman concentrated his attack on Mandell's body, delivering a terrific hammering to the lightweight champion's mid-section. Jimmy then switched to throwing left hooks at Mandell's head. He came close to scoring a knockout in the sixth with a clipped right to the chin and then again in the tenth when he rocked the champion with both hands to the head.

'Jimmy was too eager,' said Pop. 'If he had let Mandell come to him instead of always forcing the fight I doubt if Sammy would have gone the distance. He's only twenty-one and he is learning fast.' Jimmy was credited with six rounds, Mandell two with two even. It was the first decision Mandell had ever lost, and his first defeat since being knocked out by Joey Sangor in 1923, when he was just getting started as a major fighter. 'I showed 'em, didn't I Pop?' Jimmy shouted through a cut lip after they had crowded through the lanes of admirers. 'Pop felt as good as I did about the fight,' Jimmy recalled many years later. 'But he wasn't letting either of us forget that I still didn't have a championship. 'You licked the right fighter at the wrong time, Jimmy,' Pop reminded me sorrowfully.'

It seemed like America would collapse to its very foundation. The first tremor was felt on Black Thursday, 24 October 1929, but the experts tried to spread calm insisting that the markets would recover. Everyone ignored them. In a frenzy of self-preservation thirteen million shares were traded to the point where the ticker machines couldn't cope with the weight of business. Worse was to come of course. Five days later the Stock Exchange collapsed with losses totalling $3,000 million, then the banks folded and the factories closed and the unemployed wandered through the streets. There was a joke in New York that hotel receptionists were asking, 'Do you want the room for sleeping or jumping?' The roaring twenties were over; a decade of abandon, well-heeled gangsters, flappers and jazz music. The great party had ended.

In the first important prizefight after the stock market crash of '29, and despite the fact that bankrupt ex-millionaires were falling like ticker tape from skyscraper windows, a crowd of 18,608 paid $106,992.36 to watch an Irishman fight a Jew at Madison

Square Garden. Over on the East Side, Ruby Goldstein was an idol, the Jewel of the Ghetto. When he started out Goldstein was going to be a great champion, a clever boxer who could hit very hard. But then the opponents got a bit tougher and there were doubts about his temperament, even his courage. As the boys used to say, you can't look into a man's soul and tell what he will do under fire. He had been going well until he bumped into Ace Hudkins who came off the canvas to knock Ruby out. Goldstein put Sid Terris down only to have Terris come up to fan him over. Ruby had looked like a world champion against dubs and a dub against the stars. The Jewel of the Ghetto was a little tarnished but he was still the idol of the Jews of the lower East Side.

'The little Ruby with the large eyes that glitter like mica is a strange character,' wrote Jimmy Powers in the *New York Daily News*. 'He looks and talks and acts like a thousand and one of his countrymen that swarm the curbs of the lower east side. He wears the same Tyrolese burgundy hat. His vest is as extremely cut and double-breasted. He has the same flamboyant purple handkerchief peeping out of his breast pocket. The same dagger-pointed highly polished shoes decorate his feet. Little Mr Goldstein is just like a thousand other Mr Goldsteins.'

The sportswriters of the time used ethnic stereotyping as a form of shorthand to write about fighters. The Italians were tough, always willing to take a few shots to land one of their own. The Irish were brave, Jimmy's performances, whether good or bad were usually described as 'game' and 'full of heart'. The Jewish fighters were clever, but when they came up against Jimmy McLarnin the scribes began to question their courage in the face of this Irish warrior. There was a rumour along Cauliflower Alley that Goldstein wasn't even going to show. 'I learned from some of Ruby's closest friends that the young man is feeling just as cheerful as a guy about to walk through the little green door at Sing Sing and that he amused himself all Wednesday night tearing up the bed sheets,' reported Jack Farrell. 'I also understand that Manager Hymie Cantor became so fidgety over his fighter's playful antics that he doubled the watch and that he has applied to Albany for one or two national Guard units to convoy the badly frightened young man to the arena, but such canard is not to be taken seriously.' One newspaper felt compelled to inform its readers that Ruby 'isn't carrying around any railroad time tables around in his pocket and that is sufficient proof that he isn't contemplating any out of town trips within the next few days'.

Pop and Jimmy, as usual, stayed out of New York for as long as possible and continued to confound the critics by not employing any sparring partners during training. 'As usual, he has no high priced human shock absorbers to work on as it is getting too near Christmas for Manager Pop Foster to take the zipper off his moss covered pocketbook,' wrote Farrell.

There may not have been so many dinner jackets and evening gowns as usual, but the seats were filled. Joe Humphreys prophetically announced the bout as 'ten rounds or less'. Jimmy was given a good hand but the East Siders nearly tore the roof off when Goldstein was introduced. 'The Ghetto sent a pale, frightened-looking Jewish boy into Madison Square Garden last night to fight Jimmy McLarnin, the Irish welterweight they call Baby Face,' wrote Paul Gallico. 'That is a misnomer.

McLarnin's face is a fighting skull out of which gleam vicious, piggy eyes and the mouth is a thin, cruel line.'

Goldstein made the packed house shake when he twice lashed at Jimmy's chin in the first round. He let fly but two punches, right hands at Jimmy's wide-open chin. 'Then with panic and terror in his eyes and that sad, sick look in his face, he looked disaster in the face,' wrote Gallico. Jimmy was pecking away with short, spiteful hooks, one of which landed on the side of Goldstein's face and he sank to the floor. He got up, but he looked hurt and was wearing a 'most unearthly pallor'. But he lasted the round. Meanwhile, backstage at the Apollo Theatre, clustered around the horn of Willie Howard's radio were Willie, his brother Eugene, Jack White, the comedian, and the acrobatic sensations, Mitchell and Durant. Sam Taub had just concluded his broadcast of the first round.

'It won't be long now,' gasps White. 'Some fight,' breathes Willie.

'*That is the bell for the second round*,' intones the radio. '*McLarnin*—'

A callboy pounded at the door. 'You're on, you're on,' he screamed. Cursing and moaning, the Howards, White and Mitchell and Durant trouped on stage for the 'Nations' number of the show. When they returned ten minutes later the radio was quiet. Not until they reached the street and got the early editions did they learn what had happened next.

The Jewel looked pretty good as the second round started. He stepped around and flicked his left jab into Jimmy's eyes. But then Goldstein was trapped with his back against the ropes. Jimmy caught him with two hooks, first left and then right and

Ruby went over the middle strand, folded in half. He fell on the narrow ledge outside the ropes and into the hands of the *Evening Post*. Doc Morris and Jack Kofoed, the newspaper's boxing writers, put up their arms to stop Ruby's fall. Referee Lou Magnolia rushed over and leaned through the ropes. 'Don't any man lay a hand on him!' he shouted down. The count had reached five. Ruby clawed his way through the ropes, untangled his buckled legs and at nine he was on his feet. But his eyes were unseeing and his arms were raised no higher than his waist. He was standing there waiting for the left, right, left, right with which Jimmy hit him into complete insensibility. Ruby pitched limply to the floor and was counted out. Jimmy hurtled through the air in a double handspring while the referee picked Ruby up in his arms and carried him to his stool. Jimmy turned another handspring and then followed the sorrowful caravan to Goldstein's corner. 'The Jewel of the Ghetto is a gem of paste,' concluded the *New York Post*. A victory-drunk rooter brushed Pop aside and grabbing Jimmy's hand he exclaimed: 'I knew you'd do it kid! Who ever said Goldstein could fight?'

'Whoever said he couldn't is crazy,' Jimmy replied. 'He took some terrible punches. He is a great little fighter, only he can't take it and it's a pity he can't.'

One of Goldstein's seconds however, was visibly disgusted. The fact that Ruby picked himself off the floor twice after being dropped with huge punches didn't seem to matter. 'Why, he was licked going into the ring,' said the cornerman. 'But he took more than I ever thought he would. He ought to hang up those mitts. Fighting is not his racket.'

'He was licked before going into the ring' became the lasting legacy of the McLarnin-Goldstein fight. The press began to infer that Jewish fighters didn't have the heart to fight an Irish warrior like Jimmy McLarnin. 'Jimmy has made a speciality of beating Hebrew fighters,' wrote Jack Kofoed. 'He dotes on it just as Battling Nelson did in trimming Negroes.'

The promoters looked around for young Jewish fighters to match with Jimmy. There was a plentiful supply, most of the leading fighters at or around Jimmy's weight were Jewish. It was a simpler time and nobody rioted no matter how the fights came out, they just paid up. Just like in the days of rat-baiting at Kit Burns's Sportsman's Hall blood sports were an intrinsic part of everyday life in the poor neighbourhoods of New York.

'It was just a business,' said Jimmy. 'This was the Depression.'

THE DARLING OF THE
DEPRESSION

Abie's Irish Rose, an unlikely romance between a Jewish man and an Irish woman, was the longest running production on Broadway in the twenties. Its author, Anne Nichols, attributed the play's popularity to the 'spirit of tolerance' that ran throughout America. Half the population of the United States lived in cities by 1920 and these places were so multicultural that tolerance was a practical necessity and Americans of different ethnicities had to find a way to get along.

The Irish and the Jews were regarded as strong, unmeltable ethnic groups, but *Abie's Irish Rose* preached a message of tolerance as a fundamentally American value. In one scene a priest and a rabbi discuss their time in the war. 'I gave the last rites to many Jewish boys,' said the priest. 'And I to many of your Catholic lads,' the rabbi replied. 'We're all on the same road, I guess, even though we do travel by different trains.' The reality on the streets was that this tolerance was very much a work in progress.

Jimmy was the greatest attraction the prize ring had known since Jack Dempsey and Benny Leonard retired. Jimmy could knock a man out with either hand – not all fighters could, not even very good fighters. Promoters all over the country practically grovelled at Pop Foster's feet, and the old man rarely considered a bout unless he was assured at least $20,000 for his end. 'Jimmy McLarnin,' wrote Wilbur Wood in *The Ring*, 'is the nearest approach to the famous gladiators of the old school developed in many years.' Titles were passed around with abandon and were often won by proxy instead of punches. They didn't mean as much as they used to. The fact that a second-rater held a championship wasn't going to make him draw the crowds and the fact that Jimmy held none wasn't going to keep the cash customers from coming to see him. Jimmy had more than a championship; he could box and he could knock people out. He also had colour. Jimmy McLarnin was going to fight and that was enough for the paying patrons. The New York Commission apportioned to champion and challenger 37 ½ per cent and 12 ½ per cent respectively, and in the summer of 1930, at the height of his popularity, Foster wasn't about to let Jimmy fight for 12 ½ per cent of any gate. It was a choice between the title and money for Jimmy and for him and Pop it was an easy decision. Jimmy had six sisters and five brothers and he managed to send them all through school; even during the depression they never wanted. 'Foster,' wrote Andy Lytle, 'starved and beaten by the wings of a cruel earlier fate, was equally determined to wring the last pound of his juicy flesh in all of their fight contracts.' Champions demanded such a huge fee to risk their title against the Irishman that promoters were left with nothing for themselves or for Jimmy. There was more in it for him when he tackled contenders so Jimmy passed up the crown wearers.

Furthermore, Pop felt, and justly so, that Jimmy was the bigger drawing card, hence he expected as much as the title-holder for his boy's services. Then there was the problem of cashing in on the title once you won it. Champions got all wrapped around with commission red tape and lost money in the long run.

'It doesn't matter apparently what the balance of the bill is so long as Jimmy McLarnin is on it,' wrote Jack Kofoed in the *New York Post*. 'The fans raid the children's banks to get enough for admission money.' Jimmy's popularity showed just how little a world title mattered at that time. He had already knocked over half a dozen champions, had made plenty of money and was looked upon as the best fighter in the world. In the old days champions were revered and a title was a valuable commodity, but the cauliflower industry was in decline, champions had cheapened their titles and very few were regarded as real drawing cards. Many dodged the best contenders and took on set-ups over the weight. Time and again champions had been soundly walloped without losing their titles and Jimmy was often the one doing the walloping. Pop and Jimmy worked their way back East in early 1930 and stopped off in Chicago where they picked up $18,541.89 for a rubber match with Sammy Mandell. Jimmy won every round. After the fight Mandell said: 'He has a perfect left hook now, something he didn't have when I first beat him. That left is so good that he hurt me far more than he did with that dynamite right of his. It's no great trick to get away from a right hand, but if a fellow possesses a corking left hook, he's bound to nick you.' Mandell was still the lightweight champion but he couldn't draw flies. Jimmy could and Sammy was prepared to give a few pounds and take a punch or two because of the Irishman's pull at the box-office. Jimmy, on the other hand, didn't need to spot weight to anybody. 'There is no reason why I should get down to some ridiculous weight to meet a lot of these fellows who think they would like to meet me,' said Jimmy. 'If they want the chance, they will have to come in at my weight. I'll not go to theirs. I wouldn't think of asking Mickey Walker or any one of those other 160-pounders to come down to 150 pounds to meet me. So why should these little fellows, the light-weights, the Bergs and the likes, ask me to do something like that.'

The welterweight division was enjoying a new lease of life around this time. Joe Dundee, a lantern-jawed fighter from Baltimore had guarded the title carefully for a few years, but when Jackie Fields finally beat him there seemed to be a big welterweight match on a monthly basis, and the man who featured in most of them was leading black fighter Young Jack Thompson. He flashed into the limelight following a two-round knockout of Joe Dundee in Chicago. Dundee was still champion at the time and the only thing that saved his title was a pre-fight stipulation that it was to be a non-championship affair.

By the time he was matched to meet Jimmy, Thompson had an astonishing career of 259 fights and only one knockdown against him. His life had been filled with the flurry of grimy adventure, with hasty contests in Rocky Mountain mine towns and fights along the Mexican border where the ring retained some of the careless, rowdy glamour in which it originated. Young Jack was the last obstacle in the way of a fight between Jimmy and Jackie Fields for the welterweight title. Jack had trained with Jimmy in Los Angeles and wasn't afraid. 'There is nothing about Jimmy McLarnin that will scare a real fighter,' declared Thompson. 'I'll tell you. Most of the fellows who have fought McLarnin were licked before the bell rang. The weird tales of the things he did to people with that hard wallop he packs had them frightened stiff. But I sampled his wallop during a mixup in a gymnasium several years ago and man, I'm gonna tell you that I honestly believe he can't hit one bit harder than Mrs Thompson's boy Jack.'

In March 1930, when the soup kitchens were the only establishments that didn't report a dramatic decline in business, Pop and Jimmy staged another raid on New York. Jimmy, as *The Ring* described him was the 'darling of the depression'. The magnetic power of the McLarnin name attracted $77,868.21 into the box office and the Garden was packed to see Jimmy scrap out a ten-round decision in a fight he came very close to losing. Jimmy caught Thompson with a big right in the opening round but the punch was accompanied by a sickening, cracking sound. Jimmy's fist connected with Thompson's forehead instead of his jaw and his right hand broke with the best part of ten rounds to go and a championship match with Jackie Fields on the line. With his right out of commission Jimmy was forced to do much of his fighting with his left.

All those years ago when Pop arrived at Sam McLarnin's second hand store in Vancouver to give Jimmy his first lesson he found the boy repainting some old chairs.

'Do it with your left hand, Jimmy,' Pop said.

'Gosh, Mr Foster,' said Jimmy, 'I can't paint with my left hand.'

'I know,' Foster said. 'That's why I want you to do it.'

For the next sixteen years Pop bullied Jimmy into using his left hand whenever possible. Aside from the countless lefts thrown at the bag or in sparring Jimmy was told to chop wood with his left hand, row a boat with it, haul in fish nets with it, throw darts with it. 'When Pop started on it my left hand was as left-handed as it's possible for a hand to be. When he finished with it, it was the best hand I had.' Which was just as well on the night he fought Jack Thompson. Behind on points and faced with defeat, Jimmy came out for the later rounds and launched an attack consisting almost entirely of left hooks. He chased Thompson all over the ring and as the final bell neared he smashed his broken right onto Thompson's head. If the right hand had to go – well, let it go. His rally in the last two rounds was enough to get the unanimous decision of referee Jimmy Crowley and judges Harold Barnes and George Le Cron. The customers booed the decision and Young Jack Thompson shrugged his shoulders. 'He realised that fighters of colour always climb into the ring with two strikes already called on them,' wrote one scribe.

'If you could have taken the green bathrobe and the harp of Erin on it, the smiling Irish eyes and the unmistakable Hibernian name of McLarnin over into the opposite corner in Madison Square garden, who do you think would have won the fight?' asked Bill Corum. 'I think Young Jack Thompson. McLarnin, the current idol of the cauliflower customers and what the boys glibly call the best draw in the business got two breaks in this rousing encounter – a broken hand in the first round and a lucky decision at the end of the tenth. It was just an ordinary, everyday

Garden variety of bad decisions. A draw would have been fairer and a verdict for Thompson would have been fairer still.'

Jimmy was laid off for six months so he and Pop went to Alaska and fished for salmon while his hand finished healing. Thompson, the loser on the night, was given the title shot against Jackie Fields in Detroit. It was reported that Fields had signed for the fight over his manager's head. A guarantee of $75,000 awaited Fields for a title fight with Jimmy in New York later that summer but the champion was prepared to risk his crown because he'd already beaten Thompson twice and there was the no small matter of a $37,500 guarantee. Thompson was the sole support of his mother and three sisters in Los Angeles in addition to maintaining himself and his wife and he wasn't about to let this chance pass. He beat Fields in fifteen gruelling rounds but had exactly $14.85 jingling in his pockets as his financial reward for winning the welterweight championship of the world. Thompson had been guaranteed $10,000, but agreed to accept only $2,500 as training expenses if he succeeded in winning the championship, with the full $10,000 if he lost. It was a deal that had a little insurance for everyone. Thompson was going to walk out of the ring with the title or ten grand while Fields had the blow of losing his crown softened by a bigger bank roll. After paying his bills Thompson was left with less than fifteen bucks but now he was the champion and the offers poured in from promoters across the country. Ray Alvis, Thompson's manager, turned down $75,000 for a title defence against Jimmy in New York insisting that he would take $200,000 worth of overweight matches unless he got $100,000 for a championship match. But this was 1930 and there were no $100,000 guarantees out there, not even if Jimmy McLarnin was involved.

Pop proclaimed Jimmy the uncrowned welterweight champion of the world and signed for a lucrative, overweight match against the new lightweight champion Al Singer. It didn't hurt that Singer was also Jewish. It was Singer's first ring appearance after taking the lightweight crown by knocking out Sammy Mandell in just one round and it was the first time that Jimmy had swung into action for five months. A bunch of boxing scribes were whooping it up in one of the better and more civilised downtown restaurants and someone suggested a little pool on the outcome of the Singer-McLarnin prizefight that evening. Three wallets made their appearance before one of the boys said, 'Wait a minute. Maybe this isn't such a good fight to make a pool on. Maybe it's a good fight to do nothing at all.' And so the wallets went back again, and somebody started a discussion as to just what kind of fight might be a good one to bet on and the speeches were quite conclusive, a sort of unanimous chorus of 'None!' One might trust a match where both parties hoped to advance their fortunes and ambitions, but certainly not one where one of the participants was meeting a man in a lower weight class. The history of overweight matches was not a brilliant testimony to their purity. The actual difference in weight was not as much as implied by the match. If Singer had come in as a lightweight and Jimmy as a welterweight it would mean a twelve pound pull. But Jimmy had signed to do 142 on the scales and Singer came in at around 138, which reduced the handicap to four pounds, or at the most six, depending on how much Jimmy put on between weighing and fight time. But no matter what they weighed, in the minds of the public, the Irishman was a welter and Singer a lightweight, and in these glum, lawless racketeering days overweight matches just could not acquire that above suspicion look.

Jimmy's right hand still bore evidence of how hard he hit Young Jack Thompson on the head. It was gnarled and scarred, bulging where there ought to be have been dimples and sinking in where knuckles ought to have been. Jimmy said it was as strong as ever but he wore sixteen-ounce gloves for safety's sake as he boxed his sparring partners in the build up. A rumour started that Jimmy still had a bum hand. That switched the odds from 8-to-5 McLarnin to 13-to-5 Singer. The boys who spread the report overlooked just one detail; they forgot to take a sounding of Singer's chin. The crowd of 30,000 that poured through the gates of the stadium, paid $200,000 to see the battle, lured with the prospect of seeing a fast and furious bout which would end in a knockout for one man or the other.

Singer started as if he would win just about as quickly as he had over Sammy Mandell. He leathered Jimmy with a series of right and left jolts to the jaw that forced the tips of the Irishman's knees to the canvas. Jimmy regained his balance and straightened up before a count could be started. Singer also furnished the big moments of the second round, as he boxed and punched better than he ever had in his career. Then Jimmy shook Singer up with a left hook and he seemed to relax. He had acquired the proper feel of Al's chin and it was clear that there was bad news ahead for the world lightweight champion. Jimmy walked in reckless of consequences and threw punches with the high assurance that one of them would finish the lightweight champion of the world. One did.

Shortly after the third round got under way Jimmy dug a few lefts deep into Singer's stomach and backed him to a neutral corner. Jimmy nailed him with a left hook to the chin that made Singer's knees sag and he fell forward and lay prostrate with gloves clasped over the back of his head, bobbing and kicking up puffs of resin as he pounded the canvas with the toes of his ring shoes. Singer was hit so hard he thought his neck was broken. The referee barked the count close to Singer's ear and at nine he had laid his red gloves on the soiled and threadbare plush of the ropes and pulled himself up. Jimmy had backed off to the opposite corner, his lips rolled back in a grin as he watched his opponent writhe. He lost track of the count and when Singer got up he thought the referee had said, 'He's out.' So according to custom, he took off in a handspring amid the gnats swarming under the ring lights and landed, standing face to face to face with a wobbling but still upright, Singer. The referee had actually called, 'He's up.' Singer had the presence of mind to throw a weary right hand punch at Jimmy's head. Jimmy recovered from the shock in time to duck under it.

'He's hitting you: hit him back,' yelled Pop, and Jimmy, thus advised, exploded a right in the lightweight champion's face. Singer spun and fell face down with his gloves on the back of his neck. Jimmy kept an eye on Singer until they'd carried him to his stool. The referee got to ten this time and Jimmy took to the air again, turning two cartwheels and landing perilously close to Singer's seconds, who were trying to salvage their boy. Singer was more carried than escorted to his dressing room by police and it took the defeated, but not deposed, lightweight champion just four minutes to take a shower, dress and leave the stadium.

'He's the greatest puncher I ever met. I'm broken hearted, that's all,' said Singer.

It was the most exciting nine minutes of pure fighting seen in New York for many a year. Celebrities cluttered the doorway of Jimmy's room. He was just about to leave for his hotel when Jimmy Walker came through the door. 'It was the treat of my life. Come down and see me before you go. Don't forget,' said one Jimmy to the other.

After the fight a number of boxing writers mocked the so-called 'In-the-bag' boys, saying in effect: 'Yah, you old cynics. See, the fight was honest after all.' One of the leading 'in-the--bag' boys around town was Paul Gallico who made his name by writing a column on how it felt to be hit by heavyweight champion Jack Dempsey. Gallico operated on the premise that all fights were potentially fakes until they proved themselves otherwise. 'I feel called upon to take a good deal of personal credit for the up-and-upness of the proceedings last Thursday,' wrote Gallico. 'What would happen to the boxing racket if old Gallico and a couple of kindred colleagues were not around screaming "Fake" at every turn, I shudder to conjecture. Thursday morning, for instance, Brother Parker and I both screamed: "If McLarnin doesn't stop Singer within three rounds, it's a phoney." McLarnin stopped Singer within three rounds. Ergo, it wasn't a phoney. Three cheers for us!'

It was easy to see why Singer's handlers had signed for the match. Their man was risking nothing more than his reputation, but some of the scribes believed he was taking a terrible chance mixing with Jimmy just a few weeks before a scheduled championship bout with Tony Canzoneri. He never really recovered from the beating he took against Jimmy and very soon Canzoneri had knocked him out in a round and his title had gone. Although he was only twenty-one years old, Singer's big-league fighting career was over. He had gone from a soda jerker in a little store to world champion in three years but a questionable bit of judgement sent him into battle with Jimmy McLarnin and the effects of the beating he took that night seemed to have lingered with Singer. 'Jimmy McLarnin was perfect for a kid's fantasies,' wrote Pulitzer-prize winning columnist Jim Murray. 'The uncrowned champ. The word on the street was, he couldn't get a title shot because he wouldn't play ball with the mob. So he beat up all the mob fighters in over-the-weight contests. It didn't have to be true. We believed it. And that was enough.'

Not far from the press row sat the legendary Benny Leonard, the former lightweight champion, who had been tutoring Singer in his recent matches. From his seat Leonard was seen ducking the long left hook that Jimmy let fly but that Singer did not. He was then spotted letting a few punches go. When Singer lay flopping on the canvas Leonard shouted, 'Take nine!' Singer did, and one more for good measure.

According to a long catalogue of vaudeville jokes and burlesque skits, there should have been a riot at the Yankee Stadium. Certain racial boasts had preceded the encounter, and there was sporadic fighting between groups of Jewish and Irish boys in the stands. But the match was notable for a lack of bitterness, very few derogatory racial taunts were hurled and the ringside crackled with sharp humour. 'One test of the literature of an age is the accuracy with which it reflects the contemporary mood and time, commented the *New York Times* after the fight. 'On that basis many public events in New York City have proved that *Abie's Irish Rose* was a faithful picture of a certain phase of mid-town life here. What did not happen at the Yankee Stadium when Jimmy McLarnin knocked out Al Singer bore out much of the message of Miss Nichols' drama.

'There really seems to be a good deal in the solemn conclusion of anthropologists, based on New York City observation, that the Irish and the Jews, when their numbers are fairly matched, dwell together in an amity which suggests fundamental respect and great enjoyment by the one race of the humorous powers of the other.'

Jimmy was on a two-year winning streak and, though he hadn't yet won the title, he had beaten most of the good fighters at or near his weight and the victory over Singer was proof positive in the minds of the boxing writers that Jimmy McLarnin was now the best fighter in the world at any weight. 'The only one who might give McLarnin an argument on this point is Mickey Walker,' wrote Grantland Rice. 'McLarnin and Walker come closer to expressing in action just what the fight game should mean than any other two men. And this is largely because they work along the lines of attack and not defence. The mental attitudes of both are all along offensive lines. This is the factor that made Jack Dempsey the most popular of the fighting machines. It is doubtful if Dempsey ever thought in terms of self-protection or defence. It has been the manly art of self-defence with Dempsey, McLarnin and Walker, and there are not many who walk along the same road.' Much of Jimmy's popularity with the fans could be traced to his early habit of knocking his opponents into a cocked hat.

But he had also built a reputation for giving the best he had, and in these dark times that counted for a lot. Jimmy knew only too well what it was to be poor, as poor as the boys in the unemployment queues who read about his exploits in yester-days newspapers. Jimmy believed that since the public paid him a fat living for boxing he should do his best every time he stepped through the ropes. It certainly wasn't the modern idea, which was one of the reasons why the ring racket wasn't in a healthy condition. Jimmy was affable, well-mannered and candid. It sounded much better for a fighter to say that he fought for glory, rather than for gold, but Jimmy said he was fighting for a bankroll and in these bleak times people understood that. He never learned the delicate act of ballyhoo, yet the people paid to see him fight because he was as sincere in the ring as he was on the street. 'McLarnin is one of those queer fighting men who believe they can whip anyone within reasonable distance of their weight. The species is virtually extinct these days, which is one reason Baby Face is so popular,' wrote Jack Kofoed. 'Jimmy has added a gay note to the gloomy symphony of the ring. His hand-some face, complete good nature and absolute honesty have been fine additions to his great ability. Even hard-boiled fight fans find it easy to recognise the spark that burns within him.'

'In the old neighbourhood, you had to have favourites,' wrote Jim Murray. 'Mine was easy. He was Irish. His name was Jimmy. And he knocked everybody out in one round. Sid Terris, Ruby Goldstein, Phil McGraw, Sergeant Sammy Baker, Joe Glick and finally the lightweight champ himself, Al Singer. It was important that your favourite be a puncher. My ballplayer was Jimmy Foxx, the home-run hitter. You never picked a bunter, a jabber, a blocker. Even the guy who threw passes was considered kind of a sissy.'

Jimmy was supposed to be invincible right about now and New York loved him. Only once had he disappointed the city, and that was with Ray Miller. Since then every customer had been given his dollar's worth. As one scribe wrote, 'attractions like Baby Face pack 'em in even when there isn't enough money to pay the butcher.'

CAN SUCH THINGS BE?

The fight was the like of which the Garden patrons often heard of, but seldom saw. The sheer violence of it all was too much for some. Al Goldie of Newark, a guest of New York Americans owner William Dwyer, was overcome during a frenzy in the sixth round and dropped dead in his seat.

'Sometimes a guest accompanies me to a fight, someone who has never seen a fight before,' wrote Paul Gallico. 'And so luck would have it they witness the spectacle of a fighter who has his opponent on the verge of a knockout beat a helpless opponent to the ground and the sight leaves them sick and disgusted. And one of them once said: "How can you sit there, completely cold and calloused? Have you no feelings left? Doesn't it turn your stomach? Or do you just get so hardened that you don't care?" … When I see the coup de grace administered to some poor, fogged, taffy-kneed, glassy-eyed, quivering fool and he falls at my feet a-tremble and blowing little bubbles of red froth from his mouth, I say to myself: "Yes, that was cruel." And then I look at the strong, proud champion who has done this, and his retainers are hugging and kissing him and a hundred hands are reaching through the ropes to seize him. And I say to myself at that time: "My boy, eventually you will get yours in somewhat the same manner, and in all probability I shall be sitting exactly where I am now, watching you get it." Jimmy was about to get his and Gallico was there to see it.

Justo Suarez, an Argentine fighter, was signed to be Jimmy's next opponent in a ten-round bout at the Garden on 21 November 1930. But Suarez was given a sixty-day suspension for transgressing a New York State Athletic Commission ruling and the Garden matchmakers signed up Billy Petrolle as a replacement. Petrolle was a brawler from the high plains dubbed the 'Fargo Express', the best fighter never to win a championship, said the boys. He climbed into the ring in a dirty old Navajo blanket, had incredibly long arms and was a murderous puncher. Even so, the scribes didn't expect the Fargo Express to provide too much opposition. 'The general idea along Orange Juice Gulch is that Petrolle will finish on the floor in about the same state as a Bismark herring after having been packed in a barrel for several weeks,' commented Jack Kofoed. Petrolle had been stopped twice by technical knockouts, but had never been flattened. He was no boxer, but a rugged tearing battler with a big punch in both gloves. According to one scribe he lacked 'just enough fighting brains to try to match right hands with McLarnin. And that will probably mean his undoing … I don't see where he can escape being annihilated.' The seers and soothsayers of Broadway also thought Petrolle to be a soft touch and Jimmy went into the ring a 7-to-1 choice to win the decision and an 8-to-5 shot to score a knockout.

Jimmy had spent two months training for Petrolle with a clear idea about the kind of fight that would take care of the Fargo Express. Pop had built his boy into both a fighter and a boxer, so no matter what type of opponent he was in against he had, in theory at least, the ability to take his opponent into the kind of bout in which his natural style and talents would be of least use to him. Billy Petrolle was a fighter, so the plan was to stay away from him at first, to wear him down gradually and then, if possible, to knock him out. But Jimmy came into the Petrolle fight having knocked out four of his last eight opponents in three rounds or less. 'Somewhere between the time I got up from my stool and the moment when Petrolle and I met in the middle of the ring I got the idea that there couldn't be any harm in making just one quick, tentative try for the fast knockout against him,' Jimmy recalled. 'If it didn't work, okay, I could forget about it. I still wouldn't be committed to making Petrolle's kind of fight.'

'Keep boxing him,' Pop shouted through the first.

'Sure,' replied Jimmy.

That was what he meant to do, but Jimmy still had this other idea in his mind. After all, he was a 7-to-1 favourite and Petrolle hadn't shown anything in the first to suggest that, even at that price, Jimmy was an overlay. Early in the second Jimmy spun Petrolle a little with a left to the body and saw what he thought was an opening to the jaw. 'You don't get time to reason these things out, of course, but after you've had fifty or eighty or a hundred fights your decisions, quick as they have to be, do have reasons behind them,' Jimmy recalled. Petrolle was still carrying his left nice and high, but Jimmy thought he could come over it with a right. It was as hard a punch as he ever threw. Petrolle's left was still well up so the punch had to start a little high. The Fargo Express started to duck as it landed. It caught him on the top of the head and it broke Jimmy's hand. 'I don't know how the top of Petrolle's head felt but I thought the top of *my* head was coming off,' Jimmy wrote. 'Pain shot up my right arm from the broken hand and exploded right above my eyes and for a moment I couldn't see anything but a white-hot blur. Then I pulled Billy into a clinch and by the time Patsy Haley, the referee, had pulled us apart I was all right again.'

Jimmy had broken the same hand in two previous fights and he knew what had happened from the way it felt. He'd managed to win both of those other fights and he still thought he could win this one. The x-rays showed later that he had broken the thumb in addition to rebreaking the old fractures on the back of the hand, but once the first stab of pain was over it didn't feel too bad. Petrolle hit him two or three hard lefts and a solid right before the round ended, but Jimmy was in pretty good shape when he went back to the corner. He knew he was in trouble, but he didn't think it was serious trouble.

Trouble aplenty arrived in the fourth, however. Petrolle threw a long left that nailed Jimmy on the jaw. 'If you get a good punch on the button you see a pool of white light and then a dark curtain drops across the pool. I didn't feel myself hitting the floor. But I picked up the count at four. I started to get up and then remembered I shouldn't get up until nine. I watched Haley's hand and pushed myself to my feet just as it was coming up for the last time.' Jimmy scrambled to his feet just as Referee Patsy Haley had his arm poised for the final count. Disregarding the frantic calls from Doc Bagley, his chief second, to 'grab 'im' Jimmy stepped right in and swapped punch for punch.

'Usually a fighter doesn't want to keep his knees straight, but there are times when he wants to get himself straight just to prove to himself that he can do it. I couldn't. I felt my knees sinking.' said Jimmy. Petrolle sent a right swishing through the Garden air that landed high on Jimmy's left cheekbone, slitting an ugly wound under his eye and sending him sprawling to the canvas. It wasn't quite as good a punch as the first one and it didn't black Jimmy out, but it knocked him down through its force. Jimmy went back on his shoulders and felt the canvas hitting him. 'If anything was hurting me I was not aware of it. I just felt hopelessly weak and the question in my mind was not whether I should stay down till nine but whether I would be able to get up at nine.' Jimmy got up. Jimmy always got up. He dropped across Petrolle's shoulders and stuck to him, half falling and half clinging, until Haley drew them apart. Jimmy saw another left coming and swayed under it and grabbed Petrolle. Haley yanked him away and Jimmy tried to get his hands up. 'In my nightmares I had dreamed about a time when I wouldn't be able to get my hands up, in the same way that other people dream of the time they'll be walking down a busy street with nothing on. Now my hands weighed 8,000 pounds each and I couldn't get them up. I went into a low crouch, trying to get my head down to the level of my hands, and I bobbed and weaved the best I could.'

Petrolle came out to finish Jimmy in the fifth, but the Irishman forced the Express back time and again with short left hooks that bounced off his chin like a rubber ball. Jimmy won the round. He threw both hands at Petrolle and when the right landed he hardly felt the broken bones. The tight bandage and the tight glove held the broken bones in places and kept the swelling down. His hands were too heavy to hold up and block Petrolle's punches but by using his shoulders and upper arms, they weren't too heavy to throw. Jimmy and Billy kept throwing punches at each other. They seldom missed or tried to make each other miss. When the bell went to end the fifth both stumbled toward the same corner. Jimmy felt a desperate tug of triumph as he saw Petrolle trying to beat him to *his* stool. He looked for Pop, but Pop wasn't there. Then Jimmy realised it was he, not Petrolle, who was headed for the wrong corner.

They fought toe-to-toe in the remaining rounds, but just when Jimmy was in the throes of a rally Petrolle would lash out with that murderous left hook and stop him dead. Jimmy simply couldn't find any defence for Petrolle's mitts; he walked right into the carnage, hoping to land a punch that would turn the fight in his favour. 'Many an Irish fighter will win on his gameness and his refusal to admit that he is licked more than on his ability. I don't think I ever saw a gamer exhibition than that put up by Jimmy McLarnin when Billy Petrolle was bouncing him off the deck, three bounces to a round,' wrote Paul Gallico. 'A knockdown is merely a knockdown whereas to more temperamental races it instils terror and discouragement.' At the end of the seventh, Mayor Jimmy Walker left the Garden; he couldn't stand it anymore. Walker's timing was impeccable as usual as his old friend was hopelessly licked in the eighth and Petrolle brought the gore from his badly bruised mouth in a torrent. The Express hit him so hard on the liver with that left hook that Jimmy was bilious for a month. His eyes were closing and there was a lot of blood around his nose and the crowd was yelling at Haley to end the slaughter. While Pop was sponging off his face the referee came over to the corner and leaned across his back.

'I'm going to stop it,' he said.

'Please don't stop it, Mr Haley,' begged Jimmy.

'Stop it,' Pop demanded.

'Please don't,' pleaded Jimmy. 'I can still beat this boy.'

'No,' Pop said. 'You'd better stop it, Mr Haley.'

Haley let it go on.

'In all my years with Pop that was the only major argument I won from him and the only major argument I wanted to win from him,' Jimmy recalled. It was nearly two years to the day since Pop had tossed in the towel in the eighth round against Ray Miller in Detroit. Jimmy's eye was oozing blood and Pop decided enough was enough. Jimmy was furious and didn't speak to Pop for three weeks. Finally Jimmy spoke. 'Please, Pop, don't ever stop a fight to save me. The fans pay money to see me fight. They don't want to see me quit. If I am to be stopped, let my opponent stop me.' Pop wanted to call this one off, but Jimmy would have none of it. He reminded the old man of the Miller fight and Pop left the ring while Jimmy finished the bout.

'For more than half my life Pop Foster had been more than a manager to me. He had been a mother and a father, a brother and a Dutch uncle, a teacher and a friend. Our relationship being what it was his capacity to watch me take punishment could not possibly have equalled my capacity to take it. For once I honestly thought my judgement was better than his. I honestly thought I could stay on my feet for two more rounds. I honestly thought I had some kind of chance of winning. Anyway I wasn't quitting. I was fighting for money, but I always tried to earn the money. Once the bell went I felt that mercy was a luxury no fighter could afford to give or expect to receive. These were hard standards but they were of my own choosing. They were not the kind of standards that you could change when the going got tough – not and hope to live with yourself.'

Haley let him go out for the ninth and somehow Jimmy won the round. He just about navigated the tenth as well though he dropped his hands to his sides once and Petrolle nailed him with a left hook that nearly floored him. 'I recalled the smashed, bloody figure of Jimmy, reeling under the terrific impact of Petrolle's merciless wallops; yet as he stood in the ring, bathed in his own gore, hardly strong enough to keep his hands up in defence, he wouldn't give in,' Nat Fleischer wrote in *The Ring*. Jimmy heard the final bell but he didn't have to wait for the decision to know it was unanimous and for Petrolle. He took it standing up, like a fighting man, and the final gong found him still on his feet, battered and bleeding, thoroughly whipped, his right hand fractured, but still smiling. Jimmy's face offended the finer sensibilities of certain patrons and the following day editorials appeared in the press asking if such brutality should be allowed to continue. His face knocked him from the sports page over into the editorial page, where there were ringing denunciations of such brutality, under the heading, 'Can Such Things Be?' A crowd of 12,512 brought gate receipts of $47,992 to see what one New York paper called 'the greatest fight in the memory of man'. Broken hands? Sure, but alibis didn't help. It didn't matter why you failed, it was the result that counted. Somewhere along the road every prizefighter caught it as Jimmy caught it against Petrolle. Jimmy paid in full. For the first time in his life he even looked like a prizefighter. They had nicknamed him 'Baby Face' and he performed his own executions wearing the bland countenance of a choirboy. After

Petrolle had done with him he suddenly wore all of the badges of his trade – the split nose, the swollen cheekbone reaching up to meet the upper eyelid and shut off the light, the puffed line framing what was no longer a mouth, but just a wound.

'I did not feel sorry for Jimmy McLarnin last Friday night at the Garden,' wrote Paul Gallico. 'I admired his bravery; I loved him for it. What man didn't? But I didn't begrudge him his licking. The inexorable workings of the law of compensation call forth little emotional response. In his best days he gave it. Eventually he was due to take it. No one escapes. Fate has been owing him a beating a long while. I have rarely seen a little man so mangled in a fight. O, just and dependable laws! Is there really, then, justice of sorts in this world?'

When the law was invoked one of two things happened in the prize ring. The loser either cried against the greatest and only justice in the world, or he was a thoroughbred, looking his end squarely in the face, fighting with a smile slightly tinctured with bitterness on what was left of his face. Jimmy went as the thoroughbred. 'It was one of the worst nights in the old neighbourhood since the time Notre Dame got beat by a last-second field goal,' wrote Jim Murray.

'Pop was crying when we got back to the dressing room,' Jimmy recalled. 'I didn't feel like crying until we got back to our room in the Bretton Hall Hotel at eighty-sixth and Broadway and looked in the mirror and saw for the first time what a mess Billy had made of me. Staring back at me out of what I could see of my eyes was the question every fighter has to ask himself some day. 'How many more like this can you take before the damage moves inside? Or is your brain the only one that can never be hurt by punches?"

'Well, I guess that's that,' said Jimmy.

'We'll see,' Pop replied.

Jimmy fasted for a week as he often did after a hard fight, whether he won or lost. He'd drink nothing but fruit juice and nibble a little lettuce and celery. An animal that was sick or hurt or weary stopped eating to give its system a chance to rest up and Jimmy thought the treatment made sense for a fighter who felt the same way. His kidneys bled on and off for three weeks, but the doctors said there was nothing permanently wrong with them. After the swelling went down his hand set cleanly and Jimmy changed his mind about giving up.

In Columbus, Ohio, Mr William C. Willard, Vice President of the Huntington National Bank and Vice president and Treasurer of the Columbus Savings Bank shot himself dead. Back in New York, bankers were trying to figure out a scheme to save the Bank of the United States, one of the newer and smaller banks on which there was a run following the breakdown of a thousand million dollar merger. Long lines of depositors gathered on hearing the news, but by the following day very few had kept up their futile vigil and those who did show were persuaded by the police to leave. One of the Bank's largest depositors initiated legal proceedings for the recovery of $1,500,000 that he needed to 'meet current expenses'. Only forty-eight hours before the announcement that the Bank had suspended payments, Jimmy McLarnin walked into a branch and took out all $65,000 from his account there. He and Pop were on their way to Vancouver when the news broke.

The old man and his battle-worn kid spent the winter on the

coast of British Columbia. They did a little hunting and chopped some wood and in the early spring they moved into a little cabin at Smith's Inlet and went salmon fishing. Pop had a commercial license and he and Jimmy would go out together in a rowboat with a gill net. Hauling the long net in and out of the water helped his shoulders and the constant exposure to salt water was good for his hands and a lot less monotonous than sitting around holding them in a pail of brine. Pop, naturally, had his own method of dealing with injuries of that kind. 'I just rub skunk oil on it. That fixes it all right, but it has to be a powerful skunk.'

They read in the newspapers that Petrolle had been knocked out in the first by King Tut in St Paul, Minnesota. That was Petrolle out of the picture. Pop started talking about challenging Young Jack Thompson for the welterweight title. Jimmy said nothing. The rowing and the fishing went on as the days got longer and the mornings warmer. The New York papers now told how the Fargo Express had avenged King Tut and knocked him over in five. Pop still wanted Thompson, but there's only one fight out there for Jimmy; beating Petrolle was more important than any world's championship.

Return fights were notoriously difficult to sell because they never figured to be as good as the original. It wasn't like a movie – the characters didn't do the same thing over again. Ray Miller and Jimmy had fought a terrific fight in Detroit, but when they re-matched them in the Garden they had to shoot guns off in their ears to wake them up. Billy Petrolle had little to gain by beating Jimmy again unless he could knock him out. And Jimmy was always going to be pretty careful of how he sailed into

Petrolle this time. 'How does it feel to fight a fellow who had taken a "duke" over you?' Jimmy was asked. 'I never think of those things – it never seems to affect me. I am happy to be getting another chance.'

'They say the memory of the average fight fan is shorter than a midget's stride,' wrote Jack Farrell. 'The fact that the layers are out betting 2½-to-1 that Jimmy McLarnin wrecks Billy Petrolle sort of proves it.' Up to the time he bumped into Petrolle, Jimmy's New York career had largely been a long series of knockouts against the greatest lightweights and junior welterweights of the day. Even in defeat, his superlative courage overshadowed the sensational punching of his conqueror. Both boys were punchers. The customers liked them and they were lined up at the box office a few days before the fight, and when that happened most of the seats were going to be filled. Or so the cauliflower industry hoped. Times were hard and the old boxing business was stumbling into a fight that would leave nothing more to its imagination. The return match with Petrolle would be a defining moment for Jimmy and for the future of boxing in New York. There was no more attractive match, nor two more popular figures in all of America. If this fight couldn't pack Madison Square Garden, nothing would. 'From the attendance of this match boxing will learn whether its present low estate is a slump or a permanent depression,' wrote Ed Frayne in the *New York American*. 'There will be no further room for guesswork.'

Petrolle stoked up the hype. 'I knew I could lick him before I ever met him, either on the street or in the ring,' said the Express. 'He shouldn't fight little fellows that carry the fight to him, he should box the big slow ones who are so hard to hit. Just by his style, I know I can lick him.'

'He's a hard-boiled egg, without any pose, that Italian from Fargo, with a natural dislike for Jimmy, just as an Airedale hates all cats,' wrote William Morris in the *New York Post*.

The maximum price of $10.40 a seat, which included a couple of bucks for the Government, reminded the customers of more prosperous nights in the same house and got them storming into the lobby early in the evening. The dress suit trade, which used to occupy the first rows of the ringside section, had been absent since the Depression had really started to bite, but according to Westbrook Pegler, 'peering into the glare of lights with an alcoholic blink, the attendance was happily reminiscent of the late Rickard's time and the gory operatics of Berlenbach, Delaney and Michael McTigue ... In fact, some brazen optimist, identity unknown, did come down to the ring wearing a boiled shirt, and it shone there amid the last year's Worsteads and shiny serges, a lily blooming in a soup lunch.' What they were using for money nobody thought to explain, but the *bon vivants* over on Broadway were reported to have booked a lot of business on Jimmy to win. 'Possibly the entire traffic didn't exceed $25, however, for a party can run up a reputation as a big oil man from Oklahoma with a flash roll of not more than five singles nowadays,' commented one scribe.

Mr Charlie Hayden of Hayden-Stone, the financial house that had staked Tex Rickard the price of building the new Garden half a dozen years previously, sat with a certain look in his eyes 'as of a landlord looking over the property to see how the tenant is getting along'. He must have been pleasantly impressed, the bout drew a gross return of $82,377, the best haul of the year. Jimmy entered the ring in his green bathrobe and with his features gleaming with slip oil to skid the blows away. Petrolle, 'the ugliest mortal in the ring since Johnny Wilson was touring around as middleweight champion behind a nose like a bare foot', sat quietly in his corner, wrapped in a robe cut from an old horse blanket. How would Jimmy react to the shellacking Petrolle gave him? When he stepped back into the ring and saw the Fargo Express in the opposite corner would he see himself on the floor with toes turned up for nine and wondering if he'd get up? When a guy has had a damn good licking it was a handicap to be a thinker. And Jimmy was a thinker. And what about the hands? Had they set properly and healed? Petrolle was always in there with his head down and a straight right was as liable to catch him on top of the head as on the chin. Would the first crack on Petrolle's skull jam the bones in front of his wrist right up again?

The scars of battle had rubbed the ethereality from Jimmy's angelic countenance. Billy fixed him with a glare and Jimmy smiled. He was still smiling as he crept out of his corner, moving slowly and cautiously far to his left and far from Petrolle's left hooks. Jimmy looked quite something; a lightning left, a bone-crushing right, when the bell rang the punches came from every-where. He grouped his punches in a series, a number of small, sharp left hooks to the face, then a hard left hook, as his right flicked across and banged the Fargo Express on the face. Petrolle was always coming forward but he ran up no score and as often as he went looking for trouble he found it with his face. Jimmy had been caught in a careless moment early in the previous fight and Petrolle proceeded thereafter to chop him apart. He wasn't going to get a chance to repeat the trick. Petrolle landed only a few glancing lefts to Jimmy's face in the entire ten rounds and his only reward, aside from the money, was a constant slugging of left hooks and right crosses to the chin. Petrolle's courage earned him the plaudits of the fans. No matter how much he was beaten – and he was given an unmerciful beating – the Fargo Express kept tearing in, punching the air with tireless fists. Jimmy had taken spectacular vengeance in return for one of the worst beatings that any fighter had absorbed under the Garden lights. Petrolle's already badly beaten countenance was minced up and swollen out of shape while Jimmy walked away unblemished and apparently not much fatigued. *The Ring* described his victory as a 'masterpiece'.

The same night of the return fight with Petrolle in the Garden, Young Jack Thompson, the current incumbent of the welterweight title, was fighting a main event across the river in Newark. The next day Foster tossed Jimmy a newspaper clipping on the comparative gates. Jimmy had drawn $86,000; Thompson had drawn $2,400. 'Sooner or later one of them champions will get hungry,' Pop predicted. 'We can afford to wait.'

Barring the Petrolle-McLarnin rematch it had been a sorrowful summer on Cauliflower Alley and there were no signs of any bull movement in the market as the season waned. The sorrowful summer promised to be followed by an even more woeful winter. Madison Square Garden had a lease on the Yankee Stadium, and they had to do something to keep the franchise, so a Petrolle-McLarnin rubber match was made, a big outdoor show in August 1931. 'Messrs McLarnin and Petrolle have continually violated the rules of the prizefighters' union,' wrote Jack Kofoed. 'When they are inside the ropes they insist on fighting. Stalling and fouling have no part in their programs. What can you do with fellows like that? Nothing, except pay for ringside seats when they are booked.' As well as settling their year-long squabble both fighters had their eyes glued on a real fistic plum dangling a little further along the trail – a promised 'big shot' against Benny Leonard, the season's prized comeback. Leonard, one of the greatest of them all, had put his name on the list of old fellows who needed the dough. If they hadn't gone broke through bad investments they would have left the rough business to younger men. The old champion was fighting virtual set-ups to get him ready for big game and some lucky fighter was going to fall heir to one of the juiciest purses of the year. The top price for the bout was $9.10, which was now regarded as serious money by customers who were digging up $25 exclusive of war tax; state tax, head tax and all of the other taxes a few years previously. 'Many of the boys have the dime but not the nine dollars,' wrote Bill McGeehan. 'There are a few who have been able to dig up the nine, but find it hard to raise the last dime. It might be good judgment to knock off the nine dollars or the dime.'

'From the interest displayed so far in the contest, such customers as are lured into the place will have a lonesome night unless they are allowed to sit close together,' predicted McGeehan. 'It should be a good spot for anybody who wants to woo the solitudes. The fight, according to some reports of the advance sale, might be held in a couple of telephone booths without anybody's feeling overcrowded.' To whip up some enthusiasm, Petrolle's manager, Jack Hurley, claimed that

Jimmy had a·yellow streak and the Fargo Express expressed that Jimmy was a coward. It was built up as a grudge fight. 'So far as I was concerned it never was,' said Jimmy. 'A boxer who takes his work seriously has no more time for grudges than he has for pity. I assumed that Hurley and Petrolle said what they were saying either to help the gate or to needle me into doing something I knew better than to do. I didn't think they really meant it.'

It was a muggy night and as the first preliminary went on the half moon was a blur behind a veil of clouds. Only a few of the crowd felt the heat enough to shed their coats. The 145th and 155th Street bridges from Manhattan to the Bronx and the avenues leading to Yankee Stadium, leased by Madison Square Garden for outdoor summer events, were filled with squads of police although there was no danger of a sell-out or even half a one. There was no money for ringside seats in the summer of 1931, not even if Jimmy McLarnin and Billy Petrolle were fighting. The ballpark was a large place, and the customers were down to a mere 15,000, which as owner Col Jake Ruppert would say, was nobody in his spacious orchard. It would have been a cosy fit in the Garden, with its capacity of 20,000, but in the vastness of Yankee Stadium, the customers looked no more than a small huddle. The tiers of the triple-deck stands were patterned with groups of a few hundred scattered through the vast arena with yawning gaps between. Only a comparatively small area of the field was covered with ringside seats, and behind these, back of the infield, quickly assembled clusters of the 'regulars', who didn't get many chances in those days to foregather in friendly conversation to discuss the vital topics of the day. The Garden went into the red, but not very deep; Jimmy and Billy were in there on a percentage and when fighters worked that way the loss was mutual. Everybody took a swim. 'Holding this out of doors in the largest ball yard there is was something like turning out the militia to stop a quarrel 'twixt man and wife, and a great flattery to the boys,' commented Westbrook Pegler.

And so the boxing game absorbed the ominous tidings of Madison Square Garden's first outdoor promotion of 1931 and the day of $10 ballpark shows were dead and cremated. 'John J. Fan not only will not pay ten bucks, but he also refuses to pay one buck if the ringsides are priced at that figure,' commented Ed Frayne in the *New York American*. 'He figures the cheaper seats are too many counties away if the top is too high. Rather than Hoboken, he stays home.'

But those who had found the dollar bills were treated to another ten-round thriller, a third blood-curdling episode. Jimmy sledged his way to a decision and even though Petrolle took a terrible beating he was game and aggressive right to the very end. Petrolle went down twice without being hit but from the force of his own missed right swings. He was sprawled in the centre of the ring in the fifth but got up before the knockdown timekeeper could grab his gavel. Again in the eighth, he missed and went down on one knee. Petrolle's determination to get within range made him an easy target and Jimmy barely missed with carefully timed left hooks and right crosses. The Fargo Express finished with a badly busted mouth, a ripped right eye and cauliflowered nose. Toe to toe, punch for punch, Jimmy slugged away with Petrolle to prove that he could hit the harder and possessed as much courage as his opponent. Jimmy tried to escort Petrolle to his corner at the final bell, but Billy was having none of it and he shook off the Irishman, swinging him clear across to the ropes. That was the nearest Jimmy came to getting hurt.

'I beat Petrolle very badly, much worse than I ever beat anybody before or since – worse, most of the boxing writers said, than he had beaten me the first time around,' Jimmy recalled. It was a unanimous decision but the scribes were worried about Jimmy's inability to knock Petrolle out. Some attributed it to chivalry, others to revenge. One of them, remembering what Hurley and Billy had said about Jimmy before the fight, wrote: 'McLarnin made his answer last night and made it with a studied cruelty and viciousness that came straight from the heart. Toe to toe, punch for punch, he slugged Petrolle into submission and then deliberately set to work to slash his detractor to ribbons.'

'Neither theory was correct,' said Jimmy. 'I didn't feel sorry for Billy and I didn't feel mad at him either. My failure to knock him out was of his doing, not mine. If I had wanted to forget about defence and take the chance of catching another of his long lefts on the button, I guess I might have put him away. But it would have been a mistake to try.'

Billy went into Jimmy's dressing room afterward and asked him if he remembered a hard right hand he'd hit to the stomach in the eighth round. Jimmy said he did.

'You nearly killed me with that punch, Jimmy,' Petrolle said. 'My nose was bleeding. The blood was trickling down from my nose and I was swallowing it. When you hit me that one in the stomach I nearly died.'

They shook hands. 'I know how it feels, Billy,' Jimmy said. And so Jimmy and Billy dissolved their profitable partnership, which had drawn gross receipts of around $175,000 in three fights. Jimmy invested much of his share in a house at Massapequa Park, Long Island. He already owned an entire block bounded by New York Avenue, Glengariff Road and Avoca Avenue, near the Sunrise Highway. Pop also owned twenty lots on New York Avenue. 'Every time I read about the glamour attached to the prize ring in general and the career of Jimmy McLarnin in particular I think about my fights with Billy Petrolle,' Jimmy wrote. 'We all know how it feels, even those of us who were lucky and handed out two or three for every one we took. That's why, whenever somebody asks: "Was it fun, Jimmy?" I try specially hard to give the right answer if the person wants to know happens to be a kid with stars in his eyes and a promising left hand. For one in ten thousand the money can be fast. But even for that one it never can be easy.'

THE INWARD
APPARATUS OF A
SECOND-HAND JOB

In 1932 the Dow-Jones Industrial Average, which had reached an all-time high of 381 in September 1929, bottomed out at 41. The economic slump no longer felt like a fleeting phase, the bottom had dropped out of everything, including prizefighting. After the third Petrolle fight Jimmy took a year off. He spent most of the time letting his hands heal, playing golf and enjoying the rewards of his hard-earned gains. And, of course, there was always Lillian waiting for him back in Vancouver.

'Jimmy McLarnin strikes the writer as a veritable miracle, in that there has been so little change in him, outwardly and inwardly, in over ten years,' wrote Damon Runyon. 'He does not drink. He does not smoke. He does not swear. And yet Jimmy manages to find life interesting and entertaining. He has his own modest diversions when he is laying off from ring activity, and while they might not strike the average reader as particularly exciting, they suffice this young Irishman from Vancouver. He plays golf, goes to the movies, hunts, fishes, and – rumour from the West

Coast tells us – does a bit of sparking. This alone can keep a man well occupied. His savings bring him a nice income, and by fighting once a year McLarnin keeps his nest egg nice and warm.'

Times had changed since Jimmy whipped Billy Petrolle at the Yankee stadium the previous summer and his drawing power as one of the town's favourite fistic idols was going to be tested. In the old days Jimmy's appearance in the ring guaranteed a gate of over $100,000, but in 1932 any show that drew forty grand was doing very well. Pop wasn't a man for dropping his prices however, so he became 'a newly joined-up member of the anti-Garden society'. The Garden thought Pop's fees a bit steep and the idea was to ignore Jimmy until Pop relented. But the McLarnin tag was still 35 per cent and all Pop dropped was Madison Square Garden. He took his business to Timothy J. Mara, who had been a bookmaker, coal baron, stock broker, professional football promoter and was the best friend of former heavyweight champ, Gene Tunney. Jimmy's return to the ring marked Mara's first appearance as boxing promoter and leader of the anti-Madison Square Garden forces in New York City. The opponent chosen was Lou Brouillard, who'd briefly held the world's welterweight title the previous year. Brouillard was a strange fighter in that he was neither an orthodox boxer nor a southpaw. He started out boxing with his left hand extended in the usual manner, had a rib broken and then turned slightly southpaw to protect the injury. Southpaws usually hit hardest with their left hands, Brouillard was better with his right. If Jimmy could come back to take the measure of the French-Canadian, after so long a layoff, it would rank with the best of his ring achievements, especially as he was also spotting the southpaw three pounds. He sparred with the best-conditioned left-handers available, and was reported ready, but Jimmy was rusty with inaction and no one could afford to be rusty in the same ring with Lou Brouillard. Foster never would have considered a heavier southpaw for Jimmy, especially after such a long lay-off, until his dispute with the Garden, but then he was willing to fight anybody for an opportunity to show up his old pals. That was prizefighting, a promoter was never made by his friends; his best assets were the other promoter's enemies.

It was apparent from the opening bell that Jimmy's layoff had done him no good. He was slow, his judgement of distance was poor and he found it extremely difficult to solve the mystery of Brouillard. It was a rugged, tough fight full of mauling and clinching. Brouillard was so much bigger and stronger and Jimmy took a real manhandling in the clinches. He found his range as the fight wore on but, handicapped by a swollen right eye that puffed up quickly at the end, he was punched out by the final round. Brouillard was a hard and willing opponent and he got the popular vote of the crowd as well as that of Referee Patsy Haley and Judge Charlie Lynch. Judge Charles Mathison thought Jimmy had won. Jimmy finished the imbroglio with his body scarlet from the punishment administered and a deep cut over his left eye, suffered in the sixth round when the two bumped heads in a clinch. The crowd was estimated at 23,000 and the gate at $35,000. Tim Mara lost $4,800 on the match, but went back to Saratoga Springs laughing about it – 'his good humour apparently incurable'.

There was talk of Jimmy being through; that he intended to

get married and didn't want to fight any more. Before the fight Lou Brouillard was just one of a numerous band of ex-welter champions, but suddenly he become a very troublesome guy to a lot of people along the rowdy Rialto. Not only had he damaged one of the very few cards left in the boxing business he was also the mud in the coffee of those who had been carefully preparing a Benny Leonard-Jimmy McLarnin match for public consumption in the Fall. This match was a natural and it had been in the making for over a year. Leonard retired as lightweight champion back in 1925 and nailed the boxing gloves to the wall with heavy spikes. He said he'd never take them down. The experts figured that Benny had accumulated close to half a million dollars in the days of the fistic gold rush. He drew the largest lightweight gate in history – $452,648 – with Lew Tendler in New York and he drew another $367,862 with Tendler in Jersey City. Now like a lot of other citizens in those years he was back out of retirement. There was only one reason why a fighter who was once rich and who quit the ring as emphatically as Leonard did would wish to come back. He was a cautious man with a dollar and he had financial advice that seemed infallible, but so did a great many other people. He thought he had enough money to last him the rest of his life, then came the crash and Leonard suddenly discovered himself quite a bit short of enough.

Seven years on and Leonard was still New York City's favourite gladiator and there would be no lack of customers, especially for a fight with Jimmy McLarnin. Benny had lost his hard-earned money and the quickest way of getting at least some of it back was to fight the biggest draw in town. Even though one was regarded as an ancient of thirty-six years and the other as a fighter who seemed to have seen his best days, there was more interest in this fight than in any the Garden had shown in a long, long time.

'The indoor cauliflower season will open at Madison Square Garden Friday night with the venerable Benny Leonard and Baby Face Jimmy McLarnin in the Battle of Nothing In Particular,' wrote Bill McGeehan. 'Apparently there is no reason at all for staging the fight excepting that Benny can use the money. So can young McLarnin. After all, perhaps that is just as good a reason as any for holding any fight.'

Much of the press attention was given to the patriarch, as it were, of the Judean traders out to avenge the previous insults to his race by the flailing fists of a gentile and an 'Irisher' at that. Jimmy was written of as the Jew Killer; the record books showed that when the Irishman had beaten the leading Jewish boxers of the day in the ring, they stayed that way. What became of Terris, Sangor, Singer and Goldstein after they met Jimmy? According to one scribe, 'they went into the record books along with the semi forgotten men of Cauliflorida.' From the day Benny Leonard announced to the world that he was coming back to the prize ring he talked about fighting Jimmy McLarnin. The scrap took up an angle frequently emphasised by the fight promoters who ran clubs in neighbourhoods thickly populated by fans of each race, that a match between a Jew and an Irishman possessed powerful box office appeal. 'I'm going into the ring with McLarnin as an undefeated champion of the world. I emphasise that,' said Leonard. 'I wanted this one – set it as the goal of my comeback – because I thought McLarnin was the best in the class. There's nothing to that stuff about my coming back to fight him because he beat all the second Benny Leonards.'

Meanwhile Pop Foster was going around town spiking stories that the McLarnin family was turning to evangelism as a pursuit. A rumour had been bruited about since the Brouillard loss that Jimmy was due to follow in the footsteps of his brother Sammy who was already exhorting along the sawdust trail. 'Tain't so,' said Pop. 'Jimmy isn't as interested in fighting as he was at one time, he has plenty of money, and perhaps he will retire in time. But not right now.' Pop was also blushingly taking some credit for Benny's comeback. 'I had a hand in that,' he said. 'Benny wasn't getting rid of the weight at all until I suggested the way to do it. He couldn't perspire properly. I told him to diet, prescribed orange juice in the morning, no lunch, just one meal a day. That broke up the fat layers, and now Benny's in splendid shape for one after a seven-year lay-off.'

Leonard had prepped on the usual number of chumps, wet and dry tankers and fall-down men, which meant that nobody had a real line on him. In his thirty-odd fights against second-raters since starting his comeback the old champion had not shown evidence of a real wallop. He claimed that he had to be careful, to find out what he possessed by the way of stamina and not to risk getting a finishing punch. But there was never a fighter who was improved any by getting old. 'Old Uncle Benny comes to Madison Square Garden next Friday night to fight a young Jimmy McLarnin a ten round bout,' wrote Paul Gallico. 'There will, I suspect, be a large gathering of addicts present for this event because it presents many interesting and charming features. Chief of these is the undeniable handicap of Uncle Benny's wheel chair. There have been fighters who have fought ten rounds on a bicycle but I never heard of anyone going that distance in a wheel chair. And what with his ear trumpet, false teeth, hot water bottle and Rejuvenator Tonic, your Uncle Ben Leonard is going to have a busy time in there keeping the Irishman from punching him on the chin, head or body. The Irishman has a great record for punching Hebrews – he has whipped every Hebrew he has met and smart as Uncle Benny is, it is a question whether he can overcome the handicap of his wheel chair. At that it is a more mobile vehicle than crutches.'

Leonard's apparent faith in his ability to beat Jimmy was based on a few sparring tilts they staged when both were boarders at Gus Wilson's Orangeburg camp. 'I can never think of my fight with Benny Leonard without also thinking of my fight with Al Singer,' Jimmy recalled. 'Benny, who came out of the East Side, too, was the model for and in some cases the adviser to all those East Side boys I'd been fighting. While I was training for Singer, Benny spent several days in my camp at Orangeburg. I knew Benny was scouting me on Singer's behalf and Benny knew I knew it and we got along fine. I didn't think he was going to see anything that he hadn't seen before.'

Leonard got into the ring with 'the outward form of an athlete but the inward apparatus of a second-hand job'. He had nothing but his old knowing and intuition against a fellow ten years younger, stronger and more resilient. 'The once thick, slick black hair of Benny Leonard's, rarely ruffled from its careful parting by an opponent in the ring, had thinned out until even the most crafty combing failed to conceal the white skull underneath,' wrote Westbrook Pegler. Of course Jimmy stopped Benny Leonard. The end came with but five seconds of the sixth of a scheduled ten rounds. Jimmy stood off staring at the wretched figure before him. He could do anything he liked. A right uppercut to shock the old guy out of his crouch? An overhand right to the back of his skull to knock him altogether loose? A left hook to the ear to set him staggering? Referee Arthur Donovan didn't give him the opportunity and he waved Jimmy away as Benny's head sagged and his rounded body bowed forward. But at least Leonard was still on his feet at the moment of his final, official demise. 'That must be said for him,' wrote Westbrook Pegler. 'He probably did not know whether his feet were beneath him or waving over his head. He was very weary. He wanted to lie down and pant and rest and breathe. Anybody of the age of thirty-six – and there must be quite a few of us at any given time – will understand how Benny must have felt.'

Leonard knew that his only chance was to finish Jimmy in the first round or the second, at the latest. Leonard began boxing like the old Benny Leonard. He was pretty fast, stayed on the defensive, kept away from Jimmy's hooks. Then he shot out that famous right hand and Jimmy's knees wobbled. A left ripped the bridge of the Irishman's nose. But just before the bell, Jimmy blasted back with a left hook to the chin and Leonard's chance had gone. Beyond that it was just a matter of ducking and trying to stay alive. 'Every time McLarnin hit Benny a good solid punch Ben started to come undone all over at once,' wrote Paul Gallico. 'He was just like a second-hand car that knocks up against the curbstone – all the parts start falling out at once. His legs would get wobbly, his wind would go, his eyes would glaze and he could do nothing but stand pitifully and take it. And when he tried to do some of his old-time footwork and feinting he looked as silly as a grandmother attending a fancy ball in kiddie rompers.'

Leonard had been sopping up Jimmy's punches with elbows and gloves and using a lot of acreage to keep out of range. But a right on the head early in the sixth stunned him. His legs went dead. He couldn't get away. Jimmy moved in, belting him heartlessly on the head. Leonard's mouth was wide agape, gulping air. That's one thing about old fighters, no matter how good they were, they came apart quickly when tapped. Leonard had no resistance to the punches, no elasticity or recovery. There was a gasp from the crowd as the old champion's chin dropped down to his chest and he covered his head with both hands and elbows. There was a stir of sympathy and pleading shouts from the old-timers who had memories. A right then a left then another left to Leonard's half covered head. Jimmy looked pleadingly to the referee as Leonard reeled about the ring. He backed away and covered up, the referee looked away from Jimmy's gaze so on Jimmy went. 'The crowd was with him, but Nature was against him,' commented *The Ring*.

'Every now and then Benny would pull me into a clinch and whisper: "Listen, kid, let's not have anybody getting hurt around here." I didn't say anything,' Jimmy recalled. 'But I was glad when Arthur Donovan threw his arms around Benny just before the end of the sixth.' Donovan knew that Leonard couldn't fetch another punch. There was some booing among those who had bet heavily on Leonard going the distance, but Leonard, as the late John L. Sullivan put it, 'took the old pitcher to the well just once too often'.

The attendance of 21,733 was the first standing room only

turnout at the Garden since the depression hit boxing. With $65,315.15 in the box office and one in every four of the dollar bills coming to him, Benny had got what he needed. 'Is it tragedy that a nonagenarian of thirty-six years is tapped lightly on the rib and ears by a fighter ten years younger for 25 per cent of $67,000 eight years after his prime when any one of 20,000 men that you might accost within a five-minute walk of the place would gladly give up a gallon of his blood in the transfusion room of Polyclinic Hospital, across the street, for a five-dollar bill?' asked Westbrook Pegler. Prizefighting was Leonard's business, the only business in which he was ever successful, and the bout with Jimmy was the last closing-out sale. 'Was it a hard fight?' Jimmy was asked some weeks after the bout. 'Leonard was old,' he replied in a 'tone of reverence one employs for the dear departed'.

'You are old, Benny Leonard,' James Archibald said,
And I always heard tell you were bright;
But my punches you blocked with your ribs and your head,
Do you think at your age it is right?'

'In my youth,' Benny said, 'I was clever and fast,
A champion courageous and strong.
I refused to believe the parade had gone past,
But now I'm convinced I was wrong.'
John Kieran, *New York Times*, 11 October 1933

Next up old Pop Foster got one of those matches that he dearly loved for his boy. Firstly, it was a good money fight, which was always a strong consideration for Pop, and secondly, it was a match that gave Jimmy a decided advantage in the weights. He had no compunctions of conscience in this respect. A match in which Jimmy had the edge in size was evidence of shrewd managing, and Jimmy nearly always had the edge. From the very beginning Foster always drove a hard bargain on weight. Pop worked on his old-time theory that a match well made was a match half won, and certainly a manager was doing alright for his boy when he got the best of poundage. He nearly always got his way because Jimmy drew big money at the gate. That's why other fighters wanted to fight him. Or more accurately, that's why the managers of other fighters wanted their fighters to fight him.

'He'll be picking on Little Billy, the Lilliputian, next,' wrote Damon Runyon. 'Well, why not if Little Billy will take the match, and it figures to draw any money? (And, say, don't think McLarnin is any cinch over Little Billy if Billy happens to get good and sore!) The purpose of matchmaking is to draw money. If McLarnin can draw money with opponents at a physical disadvantage with himself, he'd be a sap not to take them.'

'I believe I hear someone mumbling about "sporting spirit",' added Runyon. 'In my altruistic moments I occasionally think that of myself. Then I remember that when a fighter is finally around with marbles in his mouth, and flat tires, no one is willing to lend him anything on any "sporting spirit" he might have displayed in the days of his puissance.'

The Sammy Fuller-Jimmy McLarnin fight at the Garden was not an example of the most brilliant matchmaking and Pop had probably pushed this one too far. The fighters were mismatched to the extent of a ten-pound pull in the weights and a laughable discrepancy in height and reach. 'Sammy Fuller looks like something hauled down from one of the cornices or buttresses of Notre Dame de Paris,' wrote Paul Gallico. 'He is a gnome, a dwarf with tiny legs and a massive head and torso and a curious, gargoyle-like face with extruded lips and big round eyes like aqua-marine marbles. He has a most amazing muscular development. His short arms are masses of bulging biceps and sinews. His shoulders are lumps and knots of muscle. His black hair pours over his face like the hair on a golliwog. He is a brisk and aggressive specimen, brave and game.' Fuller's manager, Dan Carroll, seemed more concerned with bandages than weight. Like many big punchers Jimmy had ruined his hands by hitting too many of his opponents too hard on the head, and as Bill McGeehan once wrote, 'you might as well try to dent boiler plate as to even annoy an opponent in the manly art of modified murder by hitting him on the head'. Fighters were not allowed more than six feet of soft bandages and two feet of tape but rival managers had long suspected that Pop made up his own rules. Pop was going to have his gauze measured out for him this time. 'We're not going to spot horseshoes and blackjacks in addition to ten pounds in weight,' said Carroll.

Fuller only managed to reach Jimmy about five times in eight rounds before getting himself very thoroughly knocked out. It seemed to please Jimmy's rooters, but most of those at ringside found it neither edifying, nor in any way beneficial to the Irishman. He got a good booing from time to time and he looked like a corner bully picking on one of the smaller boys. Fuller was knocked down for a nine count in the first round by a stinging left hook to his bearded chin. A similar blow sent him to the canvas in the second, but he sprang up instantly with the 'stupid little smile pugs affect to show they are unharmed'. Jimmy bullied Fuller in the third, mauling him, shoving him backwards, twisting him off balance and ripping up cruel rights that brought blood trickling from puffed lips and mashed nostrils. By the seventh Fuller was doing nothing but giving Jimmy free tries at goal. In the eighth Fuller was dropped by a left hook then Jimmy chased him to the ropes and lashed out with a vicious right hand that crashed against his face and drove him backwards. Fuller's head missed the top rope entirely and he was bent backwards over the middle strand, swinging out over the press row. The spring of the rope bounced him back into the ring and he pitched forward, half on his side, and there he lay. He tried two or three times to roll over as the referee, Pete Hartley, took up the count. His head and shoulders were in the ring under the bottom rope, with the rest of his body outside. At the count of six he was on his hands and knees. He tried to get up, but the bottom rope was in his way. It held him down. He crawled a few inches. As the referee said 'ten', Fuller lifted his hands from the floor, but he was still on his knees and out – knocked out for the first time in his career. Lusty boos and jeers had greeted each of Jimmy's rallies and when Fuller wearily toddled out after the knockout to congratulate his rival he was roundly cheered. The Garden matchmakers had gambled on Fuller's ability to put on a good show against Jimmy as a way of advertising a forthcoming lightweight championship bout between Fuller and fellow Italian, Tony Canzoneri. But Fuller was outclassed and Jimmy lost stature and respect because he knocked off only a small lightweight and took eight rounds to do it after he had Sammy on the deck in the first for a count of nine. 'Not one hero, but two, had some of the shine rubbed off,' wrote Paul Gallico. But the fight, at $5 tops, drew a net of $22,000 – exceptionally good for those times.

'I was keenly interested in many ringside comments on the battle, especially so because of the change of opinion of former ardent McLarnin supporters who hissed and booed Jimmy for no other reason than he was protecting his own interests by using Fuller as a target at every opportunity. Why those hoots and catcalls?' asked Nat Fleischer in *The Ring*. 'Come, fans, let's be fair. Give McLarnin the credit due him. Keep him in the sport that needs such fighters as he. Don't disgust him with his vocation so that he will hang up his gloves at a time when there are so few real battlers left in the ring.'

Every fighter at or anywhere near Jimmy's weight wanted to fight him. They could make as much money taking a beating from the Irishman as they could from half a dozen fights against other boxers. For Sammy Fuller and his manager such a payday was worth the risk; for Jimmy McLarnin it was just business.

IT COULDN'T HAPPEN
ANY OTHER WAY

The welterweight division had been a mess since Joe Dundee took the title away from Pete Latzo back in 1927. The title bounced around between Tommy Freeman, Young Jack Thompson, Jackie Fields and Lou Brouillard until no one knew or cared who the champion was. Jimmy kept out of the melee, largely because Pop thought the title was more bother than it was worth, and, since he and Jimmy were in the game for money and in only a lesser degree for the glory, there was no point to winning one. If Jimmy was champion the ring 'politicians' would take charge of his career because title-holders were restricted by commissions and often were not free to fight whom and when they pleased. Jimmy felt he could make just as much money and have a better time doing it if he didn't have a crown tilted over his brow. Although never a champion, he got the bigger slices because he was the attraction.

'Perhaps so, but every fighter is dazzled by a championship,' argued Jack Kofoed. 'To some it means more than money ever could. I have an idea McLarnin, in these fading days of his career, inclines towards the welterweight crown.'

It may have been the booing after the Fuller fight – Jimmy was certainly growing tired of the critics who accused him of ducking men his own size. It may have been that the Brouillard and Leonard fights had dented his prestige. It might have been the Depression and the reality that there just wasn't the money around any more. By now Jimmy had $250,000 cached in eight different banks throughout the country as well as the real estate on Long Island and a soap factory in Oakland. Foster had $75,000 put away in a Vancouver bank as well as fishing leases in Alaska. He wanted to go back to the fishing game when Jimmy's fighting days were over. There was no further inducement for Jimmy to continue unless the championship was at stake and in the spring of 1933 Pop Foster decided it was time for Jimmy to have a crack at the title. 'It was pretty exasperating to sit and watch the merry-go-round whirling past without getting a chance at the brass ring,' Jimmy recalled. 'After all, the word "champion" has a ring to it.'

Jack Kearns and Ray Alvis, the managers of Jackie Fields and Young Jack Thompson respectively, had been trading the welter crown between each other for a few years and they tried to get Pop Foster to enter the fold and keep the title in the family if Jimmy won it. If he was willing to sign away part of Jimmy or to enter into an agreement to have Jimmy fight none but boys belonging to the stable of the syndicate that now controlled the welterweight championship, Pop could get his boy a title fight. 'But that's not my way of doing business,' said Pop. 'Jimmy and I have never been involved in a crooked deal since we started and we won't begin now, not for all the money in the world.'

'And that is why McLarnin was kept on the sidelines so far as a championship affair as concerned,' commented *The Ring*. 'He wouldn't play ball with the mentors of the titleholder. He would agree, only as he always has, to play ball with the fight fans. Honesty was the policy of the Foster-McLarnin combine.'

Jimmy wasn't the only leading fighter to be squeezed out of the welterweight championship picture. For several years he had shared the title of 'uncrowned king' with an Italian fighting out of Fresno, Raffaele Capabianca Giordano, who fought under the name Young Corbett III. Corbett on the Coast and Jimmy in the East had polished off all the contenders, and Corbett, in particular, kept beating the champions – but always in non-title bouts. When Corbett was working his way up to the title he took the toughest he could find, whenever they could be induced to meet him. He often accepted a very small end of the purse just to get the fight. He whipped Jack Thompson when he was welter champion. Thompson made Corbett fatten up and come in officially overweight so that it could not be a title fight, which turned out a very wise decision when Corbett flattened him for a nine count in the ninth round and nearly finished him in the tenth. Jackie Fields also made Corbett come in overweight to keep the title safe, and had reason to congratulate himself when Corbett hammered him all over the ring and took the decision. The Italian had taken the small end of the purse in those battles and he agreed to take a smaller end still when champion Jackie Fields consented to give him a title fight. The champion's manager Jack Kearns also insisted that Corbett and his manager, Larry White, come into the fold. In the event that Corbett should win, Fields was to get the first tilt at the new champ. The match was made for 25 February 1933 at the Seals'

Stadium in San Francisco; and Jimmy and Pop were ringside to see Corbett relieve Fields of the title in ten rounds. The Italian had rescued the welterweight championship from the clique that was handing it around from fighter to fighter like a pair of dice in a crap game and he had no intention of waiting around too long to capitalise on his title. One defence, perhaps two, and he was ready to retire. He had been close to hanging up the gloves once before, but the stock market collapse wiped out the $50,000 he'd saved and invested and he had to go back to fighting again. Corbett lived with his family in Fresno and spent his time running a gas station when not in a training camp or away fighting.

'My mother wanted me to stop after I had won the championship. She pleaded with me that I had won the title, and said I could get a nice job at $5 a day, and that was plenty for me.'

'She has never seen me fight, and I never went home after a fight if I had been hurt. She never knew I could get banged up until she caught me unawares after the Fields bout in San Francisco three years ago … I was butted early in the scrap, and got quite a cut over the eye. I went out to my aunt's after the fight, and my mother was there. She's been after me ever since to quit. But my dad, he's different … He never misses seeing a single one of my fights.'

After taking the small end of so many purses, and having other champions make him come in overweight to keep their titles safe, Corbett might have been excused for responding in kind and going out for easy money. But the quickest way to grant his mother's wishes was to turn down the overweight, non-title fights with no danger attached and take on the most dangerous puncher among the welterweights as his opponent in his first fight as champion. He offered to take Jimmy McLarnin on at weight in Los Angeles, with the title at stake. Both champion and challenger were popular on the Coast and with the cry growing for a bout between the pair, Pop, by granting Corbett's demand of a $35,000 guarantee, finally succeeded in getting a title shot for his boy.

Young Corbett III had seen Jimmy fight just once, almost ten years previously when Jimmy first broke into the fight game around San Francisco. 'Little did I think at that time that the day would come when Jimmy and I would be battling for the world's welterweight championship,' said Corbett. 'I know he's a great little fighter. His record proves it. I doubt that he is as tough as Jackie Fields. By that I mean that Fields is awfully hard to hurt – he's rugged and sheds punches that would stop most boxers. Perhaps McLarnin is just as tough this way, but I doubt it. I know Jimmy is a great hitter and I'm not underestimating his ability in the least.'

Everything was set for Wrigley Field in Los Angeles in late spring of 1933. The champion would get his guarantee and Jimmy agreed to 22 ½ per cent of the gate. But there was one snag. Before agreeing to let his fighter, Jackie Fields, defend the title against the Italian, Jack Kearns had thoughtfully tied up Corbett in an ironclad contract. If Fields lost he would be entitled to a return match and Young Corbett III couldn't fight Jimmy McLarnin or anybody else unless Jack Kearns tore up his contract and Jack didn't tear up anything for nothing. Jack Kearns was a very different creature to Pop. It was said that Pop still had the first buck he ever earned. Kearns had made a million and had spent a million and now in the teeth of the Depression he met more cautious men of his day who had saved their money, denying themselves all frivolity and luxury, and wound up broke anyway when their investments vanished. Kearns wanted to be cut in by $5,000 out of Corbett's end of the purse and insisted that both participants agree to give Fields first crack at the winner. Corbett's manager Larry White signed up but Pop wasn't about to have his boy win the title and then find himself in the same tight spot that Corbett was in now – unable to fight anybody but Fields. If Jimmy won, he'd fight the most logical opponent and if that happened to be Fields, fine. That didn't suit Kearns and it took a cut on the gate to finally get his blessing on the Corbett-McLarnin bout. Jimmy was on a fishing trip in Alaska when negotiations were finally closed. He managed to find enough dry land to turn a couple of handsprings on hearing the news.

To guard against any accidents, Jimmy's prized automobile was shipped to Los Angeles instead of him driving through on the Coast Highway. Carstens Ltd of Seattle was to supply all the beef and mutton that Jimmy would have on his training table and Chief Steward A.S. Agnew of the *Emma Alexander* carried half a cow and a whole sheep in the ship's icebox as a starter. Tom Doyle, manager of the Olympic Auditorium in Los Angeles, turned the place into a gymnasium for Jimmy's exclusive use. Clark Gable was among the welcome guests taking both movies and stills with the challenger. Pop wanted Jimmy to do his public boxing at the Olympic and secret boxing out at Westwood Hills where they also took living quarters. Jimmy's roadwork was done along the bridle paths flanked with fragrant California roses where Gable and Greta Garbo passed by as they took their morning horseback canters. The last time Jimmy fought in Los Angeles he and Pop lived in a shabby, tumbledown store building out on Echo Park Lake. In those days as he did his road work around the picturesque little lake he only met the swans – and the early morning worshippers at Aimee Semple McPherson's tabernacle. But Pop was still thrifty; Andy Lytle of the *Toronto Star* dined with Jimmy and Pop one evening in Westwood Village where they employed a Japanese cook. 'We were late, as it happened, and as they set places for us, I noticed the portion of steak Pop hadn't finished being carried off by the Jap. Pop followed him into the kitchen, and when our meat appeared I recognised Pop's unfinished steak on my plate.'

Jimmy's brother Robert joined the training camp and he was soon followed by Sam McLarnin, who was now seventy, and was coming down from Vancouver to see his son box professionally for the first time. Sam McLarnin last saw Jimmy fight seventeen years previously when he called over the back fence and made his 'baby' stop lickin' the neighbour's kid in a vacant lot. 'I've got to win for his sake,' said Jimmy. 'Winning a championship and winning for him are two thrills I've never experienced. I know Corbett is a good fighter, but I've got to beat him.'

Corbett was a southpaw. Jimmy had only fought one southpaw before, a good one named Lou Brouillard; Brouillard had beaten the Irishman. The scribes at Jimmy's Los Angeles training camp were as bemused with Pop's methods as their counterparts had been for years in the East. Boxing a southpaw is like trying to read by a mirror, everything goes from right to left instead of from left to right. One of the time-honoured rules is to keep moving to the left to try and render the side-winding fighters' most dangerous weapon impotent. But in his public workouts against southpaw sparring partners Jimmy disregarded the old adage. When he tired of walking straight in he moved to the right and only then if he still felt the urge, would he do a little fancy stepping to the left. Old-timers declared it the reason why his sparring mate Billy Yallowitz had been clipping Jimmy so frequently. But Pop and Jimmy were not worried, working on the theory that left-handed fighters had become so used to having an opponent move to the left that the best thing to do was step forward or to the right and surprise them.

The champion was a big, strong welterweight with long arms and heavy shoulders.

'If you can make him open up, you'll win.' Pop told Jimmy the day they signed for Corbett. 'If you can't he may hug you to death.'

The first few minutes of the fight would be particularly critical and Pop decided to make Corbett mad. Way back from his days fighting in the fairground booth he had learned the value of upsetting an opponent. He was serious about the business and so Pop and Jimmy insulted the champion at every opportunity and the usual pre-fight platitudes were set aside. To make sure the tickets sold well nearly all managers predicted a great fight between two great fighters. Pop said it would probably be a stinker. 'Corbett's not much of a fighter,' he would say, sadly.

'I winced slightly for my reputation as a modest, unassuming boy as I nodded in agreement and told the sportswriters that I expected Corbett to run away from me but also expected to catch up with him and knock him out inside six rounds,' Jimmy recalled.

California State laws allowed boxers weighing less than 145 pounds to wear five ounce gloves, and fighters weighing above that mark were obliged to wear gloves not lighter than six ounces. A welterweight championship match was made at 147 pounds and both the Commission and Corbett expected that six-ounce gloves would be worn by both champion and challenger on the basis that in fighting for the welterweight title, Jimmy theoretically became a 147-pounder. But Pop contended that inasmuch as Jimmy would weigh less than 145 pounds for the bout he would be within the rules by wearing five-ounce gloves for the title scrap. Pop told the press that if White and Corbett had their way they'd be fighting with pillows. He claimed that in the presence of witnesses, when the match was made, Larry White, Corbett's manager, agreed to let Jimmy use the lighter gloves. A compromise on the gloves of five and a half ounces was reached.

Then Pop got into a public spat with White, calling Corbett's manager a 'dirty spy'. White retaliated by saying the challenger's handler was 'nothing but a dumb one-eyed lunk'. It happened during one of Jimmy's training sessions at the Olympic on a particularly hot afternoon. White called in to see Matchmaker Hayden Wadhams to sign a contract for a preliminary fighter who was to appear on the championship bill. Pop learned White was in the building and just as Jimmy was about to start boxing he edged through the ropes, got into the ring and made a speech, demanding that White leave. Pop waited a few minutes, and then made another speech. This time he said there would be no workout until the 'spies' left. Pop had White chased off the premises. Somebody hollered 'he's gone' and Jimmy started boxing. 'Jimmy's fighting for the world's championship; 'e must be in perfect condition, and 'e's learning how to handle south-paws,' said Pop. 'We don't want any spies around. I don't think Jimmy will have any trouble with Young Corbett, but we don't want anybody from the other camp watching our training.' White said it didn't make any difference to him, that he couldn't learn anything from Jimmy's workouts anyhow. After hanging a few vocal kayoes on Pop's chin out of earshot he sent a message to Foster inviting him to come down and see Corbett workout at Santa Monica.

'While Foster has been rated a tough cuss, in business deals he has been misrepresented as unfair,' wrote Paul Lowry in the *Los Angeles Times*. 'He may have been wrong sometimes, but he was at least 50 per cent right all of the time. That's a good average, and you have to give him credit for carrying Jimmy to the top. The old man and the babyfaced kid have made one the most interesting teams in the history of the fight game. From the old clam-digging days to riches is a long step, but they both took it in stride. Neither has been affected by wealth. They are just plain folks with quick, keen minds.'

Pop and White then argued about the referee, about the methods of bandaging their fighters' hands and about the movie rights. Corbett turned twenty-five two days before the fight so Jimmy sent him a patronising wire: 'Birthday greetings and best wishes for your future success.' They stirred up a pleasant amount of unpleasantness all around, not that they were sure of accomplishing anything. As Pop assessed it, the best they could do was to get Corbett and White mad and the worst they could do was get them guessing. The night of the fight they sent

Jimmy's brother Bob to Corbett's dressing room to check the bandaging of his hands. Jimmy was just starting his walk to ring when he saw Bob coming down the runway. There was a crowd outside the dressing room and Bob had trouble fighting his way through. Half on his feet and half on his elbows, he got to the room and pulled Jimmy back inside and slammed the door.

'James,' Bob panted, 'He's gonna come out punching!'

'We still didn't have a written guarantee, but it looked good,' Jimmy recalled. 'I floated down the aisle to the ring feeling as smug and light-headed as a bride.'

The advance sale of seats wasn't up to snuff, but Promoter Jack Doyle was consoling himself with the theory that Los Angeles was a last minute fight town and that the customers would show up late as they had done in other record houses at Wrigley Field. Doyle put 10,000 one-dollar tickets on sale the afternoon of the fight and plans for a radio broadcast were cancelled to try and make the difference between staying away or sending the stragglers into the baseball park and spending a dollar or so. The proposed movies of the fight were called off during the afternoon; a cash guarantee from the film company was not forthcoming so the stands were turned over to the newspaper cameramen for their stills. The crowd began to arrive early and the bugs back in the $1 section kept yowling about something. Nobody seemed to know what. Then there was a terrific hubbub at 9 o'clock when the outfield crowd broke through police lines and dashed into the grandstand. The cops were powerless to stop the rush of humanity until several hundred had poured into the higher-priced seats. At ringside, Charley Murray, the actor, was an early arrival. He wasn't happy because there were five rows of press seats in front of him. Thought he was going to be right up under the gun. Bill Guthrie of Warner Brothers had a ringside seat and said he'd liked to have had the movie rights. James J. Jeffries, former heavyweight champion, showed up soon after 8 o'clock and took a press row seat as a special writer for a Los Angeles newspaper. George Raft and Marjorie King were right up in the front row. Georgie Stone was right behind them. Timekeeper Bill Coe's head hat loomed up like a 'wart on a debutante's olfactory organ'. Both dads were ringside, as were two brothers – one of Jimmy's and Corbett's younger brother.

'In a fight it's the first hundred seconds that are the hardest,' said Jimmy. 'You're cold physically. Your muscles are a little stiff and your reactions are a little slow. You're unsettled mentally. There is always a moment, just before the first bell rings, when you stare through the floodlights hanging above the ring, trying to pick out the people who are for you and the people who are against you. On some faces you see more faith in you than is reasonable and on some you see more hostility than is called for. You look back across the ring at the man you're going to be fighting and try to remember how you're going to fight him and how you have figured he's going to fight you. For an instant you draw nothing but a blank. You're nervous and a little scared and the feeling doesn't usually pass until the fight has started and somebody has been hit.'

As the pair entered the ring to pose for pictures, the champion appeared the more nervous of the two. Jimmy sat forward on his stool and looked across at the champion. 'When I caught his eyes he stared back for a moment and then looked away,' Jimmy recalled. 'Some of the writers who saw this exchange said afterward that Corbett's nerve was running out on him, but I wasn't nearly so optimistic. In that last minute – no matter how confident I'd been a few minutes before I began to feel, as always, a little shaky myself. If I'd been trying to psychoanalyse Corbett, all I'd have said was that he quit looking at me because he didn't like me.'

Corbett rushed out aggressively. They sparred a little and the champion landed the first punch, a left to the jaw, and followed it up with two more sharp lefts to the same spot. Jimmy then shipped a few more rights and lefts to the body. Still Jimmy waited. On the night they watched him win the title from Jackie Fields, Pop and Jimmy had noticed that Corbett had picked up a bad habit when he hit to the body. As he threw his left he dropped his right a little. So Jimmy kept his hands a little high, showing his ribs to lure Corbett in again for the body. And just as Jimmy hoped Corbett threw the left, his right came down and a piece of his jaw was suddenly open above the right glove, less than a foot from the Irishman's left hand. Jimmy rolled towards the champion, ready to throw the left or hold it, depending on whether or not he saw a target. He let it go. To the amazement of the crowd Corbett tumbled to the canvas. He had never been on the floor in any fight before.

It was a punch Pop and Jimmy had worked on for nearly fifteen years. Its arc started upward but at the last instant he turned his elbow and the fist corkscrewed and came in slightly downward. Corbett fell like a hinge on a spring. His pants hit the floor first. Then his shoulders thumped back and he rolled over on his side. The champion wasn't badly hurt and followed the count intently. He was on one knee at four, blinking and shaking his head and he shoved himself upright at nine. Jimmy charged in from a neutral corner, feinted with a right and as Corbett lifted his hands, a looping left slipped through. As Corbett staggered, two more left hooks followed with lightning speed. The champion went down again, near the ropes. He grabbed the lower strand and dragged himself to his feet one strand at a time. He threw one arm over the top rope and turned his back on Jimmy. Corbett wasn't following the count this time but working on instinct. He got up at eight but was out on his feet. As Jimmy moved past George Blake, the referee, he said,

'You'd better stop it Mr Blake.'

Blake shook his head. Jimmy spun Corbett away from the ropes and hit him two more lefts on the head and the champion was sprawled through the ropes, half out of the ring. There was no count this time. None was needed.

Just two minutes and thirty-seven seconds – the shortest championship fight in the history of the welterweight division – was all it took. Blake pushed Jimmy aside and with the same motion of his hand lifted his glove in victory.

When old Pop Foster, limping from wounds that he received in the Great War as a member of the Princess Pats, and the wispy little 'baby faced' fellow first showed up in California, the boxing people laughed at them. Now they'd returned and taken the championship of the world. 'It was a happy moment for both of us, and there had been many, many happy moments in the fourteen years that came between,' wrote Jimmy of the night he won the title. 'But no one but Pop and I can know how long those years were.'

'And thus the story of Corbett's defeat was a tragic one,' commented *The Ring*. 'For he lay helpless and writhing, but open-eyed and conscious throughout the whole time that the referee was tolling off the count which was costing him the championship of the world ... His helplessness was pitiful, while his manliness in attempting to get up and back into the fight with legs and arms that would not, could not answer the call supplied a splendid exhibition of gameness. A few seconds after the count he was on his feet, the shock over, strong as a bull and so enraged that he had to be held back from an attempt to carry on the fight against his conqueror.' It turned into a very bad month for Young Corbett III. Just a few weeks after he lost his title the former champion and his wife were abducted whilst driving through Chicago. Corbett's car was forced to the curb by the robber's automobile, the leader of the hold-up men, brandishing a sawed off shotgun, forced his way into the back seat while his accomplice took the wheel. After taking $225 in cash from Corbett and two diamond rings from his wife, the gunman abandoned the couple in their car, throwing away the keys.

'I maintained from 1924 that he [McLarnin] is the greatest fighting machine of modern times, weight and inches considered,' wrote Ed Frayne in the *New York American*. 'The real reason he waited three years for a crack at the welterweight title was that the gentlemen who controlled the title would not let their puppets fight him. Fields was offered $75,000 to meet him and turned it down. Jack Thompson refused $60,000. Tommy Freeman, who was champion for a minute or so, would not even discuss a McLarnin match. Now the whole world can realise why Jack Kearns and Ray Alvis sidestepped McLarnin. Corbett was better than both of their champions on the record, yet he could not last three full minutes with McLarnin.'

Jimmy's dressing room, high up in the stadium, was jammed with people all trying to shake hands and talk with the new champion. He was easily the calmest person in the room. In one corner Pop was scribbling cheques to pay off the hands, the help and the various hangers-on.

'I tried to get Jimmy vainly,' wrote Andy Lytle. 'I had a sheaf of congratulatory messages for him from the home town folks fired excitedly over our own wire as the news was flashed north of Jimmy's spectacular triumph.'

'There's one from the mayor,' Lytle told Pop. 'I'd like to give it to Jimmy personally. There are others, too. I think he'd like to have them.'

'From Vancouver!' snorted Pop. 'Jimmy won't care. Vancouver never done nothing for us. Give them to me. I'll see he gets 'em.' Pop handed them over two days later. 'Foster does not readily forgive slights, real or fancied,' commented Lytle.

Back from the throng that was milling, pulling and hauling about his son, Sam McLarnin beamed happily. Bobby McLarnin was gathering up the champion's ring togs, thrusting them into grips. They wanted to get away. But the crowd hemmed Jimmy in. Larry White burst excitedly into the room, rushed up to Pop.

'You'll have to fight us again. We demand a re-match.'

Pop, laboriously filling in another cheque, did not look up:

'If Jack Doyle, or somebody who's all right, puts up enough money we'll fight Corbett any time. The money end, that's what we care about.'

The crowd tried to hustle Jimmy off his feet and urged him to go to the Ambassador Hotel and celebrate. Jimmy shook his head. He and Pop spent the following day at their Westwood apartment receiving friends and reading scores of congratulatory telegrams from all parts of the country. One read: 'What were you doing the first two minutes?' Mayor Taylor of Vancouver sent Jimmy the 'keys of the city'. A similar message came from Victoria. A number of golf clubs in the Northwest sent their congratulations. Jimmy secreted three telegrams into his coat pocket and refused to reveal their contents. He neither admitted or denied that one or more were from Miss Lillian Cupit, who in a dispatch from Vancouver the night of the fight was alleged to have said she would marry Jimmy in the near future.

'I don't believe fighting and matrimony mix,' said Jimmy. 'Not unless both parties are very level headed. It's possible that I might marry, but the way I feel now I expect to keep on fighting. I believe that only boxing a couple of times a year I can keep going for five years. I haven't been beaten up in the ring, and until I feel I'm slipping I won't stop.'

Lillian, meanwhile, had graduated at the University of British Columbia and had been a schoolteacher in Vancouver while Jimmy was fighting.

Arriving a day too late to see the fight, Sammy McLarnin Jr reached Los Angeles to hold a real family celebration with the three McLarnins already on the scene – the champion, his father, and brother Bob. Mrs Mary McLarnin, mother of the new welterweight champion told Vancouver scribes that 'he won because it couldn't happen any other way'. Just a few days later she joined the rest of the family in Hollywood.

'You're a fine boxer, James,' she said. 'Whether she knew what she was talking about or not, those five words … and the pride and happiness she took in saying them meant more to me than a million words of clippings,' Jimmy recalled. 'My mother had never seen a fight and she didn't know a left hook from a ring-post, but to me that was still the last word in critical acclaim. It was just a little more than nine years earlier – less than a month after my sixteenth birthday – that I'd packed my second shirt and my second and third pairs of socks and told her I was going away to be a fighter. She couldn't have been more horrified and worried if I'd told her I was going away to rob a bank or cross Niagara Falls in a barrel. But despite her disapproval of boxing and her distrust of every boxer in the world except me, she'd sent me a wire wishing me good luck before every fight.'

Jimmy won the title, but it was the one and only occasion in his career that he fought for no money. The show didn't draw much over the champion's guarantee, so there were no net receipts to pay Jimmy his 22 ½ per cent. In fact there was no net anything, promoter Jack Doyle took a bath for something like $20,000. The show took in just $39,400 at the gate. Federal and State taxes took the total down to $33,687 or $1,313 short of the cash guarantee to the defending champion. Pop had turned down several title matches for the challenger's 12 ½ per cent with champions who would probably have drawn enough to give Jimmy a very neat bundle of dough. He couldn't have missed at least $25,000 in any number of bouts that he turned down. For Damon Runyon it was tough justice that Jimmy had to fight for nothing to win the title.

'And the retribution lies herein,' wrote Runyon. 'McLarnin,

through his tight old manager, Pop Foster, has been squeezing promoters for all they could possibly stand for years on the ground that he was the big drawing card and was entitled to the lion's share of the take. And now it turns out that McLarnin couldn't draw the price of an old wool hat for himself in California where he made his greatest battles, and where he was fighting as a California boy. And I always contended there was never a time when McLarnin's manager was turning these bouts down that Jimmy couldn't have whipped the title holder, although I confess I thought he had finally made up his mind to win the title a little too late.'

Jimmy stayed in Los Angeles for a few weeks. He lunched with Jean Harlow and Joan Crawford and played golf with stars and the big studio executives. Some said he was looking to land a movie contract. At this point Pop took charge of matters.

'My Jimmy isn't going to go making no motion pictures. You see, boxing is boxing and making motion pictures is something else. Most of the fight pictures have been flops and we don't want to be connected to anything like that. If we could make an instructive series on boxing that might be different, say something like Bobby Jones did in golf, but I doubt if the Hollywood people would be interested in this type of picture.'

Pop and Jimmy were soon back on the *SS Alexander* bound for Seattle for a fishing and hunting trip in Washington State and Canada.

'That's a great country,' said Jimmy. 'I just hopped on a boat in Vancouver, relaxed as we steamed along to Alaska and then had a week of hunting and fishing that was all anybody could ask. When I'm in the Northwest I think it's the greatest spot in the world. Then when I'm down here [California] I have a hard time deciding ever to leave.'

'Well, what's this about you planning to buy a home here and settle down?' asked one scribe.

'Gee, all you fellows want to get me married off, or so it seems,' chuckled Jimmy. 'I honestly don't know whether I'll live here or in Berkeley. You see, I have a sister up there at Thousand Oaks and it's a pretty fine place. Then again you can't beat Los Angeles for good golf weather, so I'm kind of stumped.'

'Is it true that you're going to be married here soon?' asked another reporter.

'No, I don't think so, and the young lady you refer to is still up in Vancouver.' Jimmy smiled rather broadly all the time and the writer had an idea the great English indoor sport, pulling one's leg, was in full swing.

Jimmy returned to Vancouver a few weeks later. Accompanied by his mother and sister, a cavalcade of motor cars escorted him to the McLarnin home at 1466 William Street. Grinning, he held out his hand to his dad.

'Hello Dad,' said Jimmy, 'it's sure good to be home.'

Then he turned and kissed four of his sisters, who were just leaving for school where they were sitting an examination that afternoon, even though their world champion brother was home. The neighbours flocked around him, and two pipers from the Police Pipe Band played 'Wearing O' The Green'. The summer went by, as did the winter and Jimmy did no more than play golf and travel between Vancouver and California. He appeared at charity shows and learned to acquit himself as an impromptu speaker. He developed a passion for good clothes and according to one scribe he 'patronised stores that catered to men of means and his purchases occasionally ran into four figures'. His suits were tailored and fitted him beautifully. He wore only the finest of material in shirts, underwear, and pyjamas. He had a dozen scarves and nearly as many sportily-cut overcoats. Jimmy paid twenty-five and thirty for his hats and his shoes were of 'exclusive style'.

'He has excellent taste in dress and is never gaudy nowadays,' wrote one scribe. Jimmy even had a car built to order that had 'every known gadget, including radio'. He was champion of the world after all.

'To make the change complete Jimmy now affects long hair,' commented another. 'When he made his last local appearance two years ago he kept his hair clipped, a stubble pompadour. New York has put a new cast on the kid that got his start here five years ago.'

As the saying goes among old fighters and actors, Jimmy went big in New York. For most of the time he went real big in New York and becoming champion of the world seemed to confirm Jimmy McLarnin's transformation into the slick, street-smart Irishman, the eponymous hero of Peter Quinn's *Looking For Jimmy*. Quinn's 'Jimmy' was named after Jimmy Walker and Jimmy Cagney, the two men who came to define the newly-acquired style of the urban Irish in America. 'In tandem, debonair Jimmy Walker, songwriter and politician, and Jimmy Cagney, the actor-hoofer with the looks of a handsome prizefighter lucky enough never to have had his face smashed in, expressed the style of the urban Irish in its definitive form,' wrote Quinn. 'You can see it in the newsreels of Walker and in

Cagney's films, in their gait, fast and loose, halfway between a stroll and a dance step, an evanescent strut, an electric edginess, as if they find it difficult to stand still, their ears permanently cocked to the syncopation of the streets.'

On 27 October 1933 Jimmy McLarnin and Charles Foster became naturalised citizens of the United States.

'Jimmy has made all his money here in America and it is no more than right that he should become an American citizen,' said Pop. 'He owns considerable property around Oakland and we just came to the conclusion that it would be better for him to be a real American. As for myself, it doesn't matter. I've been here twenty-five years and don't feel any different now than I ever did.'

According to Andy Lytle, the Canadian reaction was distinctly unfavourable. To Jimmy it was simply a question of business expediency.

'The Irish of New York are calling for Jimmy McLarnin,' reported the *Los Angeles Times*, 'and they want him to fight in a neighbourhood where an Orangeman has to tread in fear of his life. Hibernian societies say McLarnin must defend his championship in the Yankee Stadium.' But Pop's propensity for picking chaps smaller than Jimmy had reduced his standing as a tremendous favourite in New York to a mediocre draw. Now he'd won the title when there wasn't a welterweight in the country worth a dime as an opposing card. There was a lot of luck in winning a championship in this respect; at a time when there were other title contenders to help the champion draw money. A title wasn't worth much under any circumstances at this time, and it was worth still less when there were no outstanding contenders.

East or West, there were no welterweights worthy of a match with Jimmy on a championship basis. A few favourite sons, like Andy Callahan of Boston, made bids for a match, but none of them would attract the customers. Johnny Buckley, Callahan's manager, offered Jimmy a guarantee of $25,000 to meet his man but Pop turned it down with a laugh.

'Boston's a one-man town,' he said. 'We're not going back there where they rob you blind.'

Several welterweight champions of the past had taken a crack at the title-holder above him. Madison Square Garden match-maker James J. Johnston telegraphed Foster with an offer of a shot at Vince Dundee's world middleweight championship, but Pop was never keen on matching Jimmy with anyone heavier than his boy. Old Pop took, but he never gave in the matter of weight. In many ways the middleweight division was even worse off than the welter. It didn't have a real drawing card in it, and the title was in so much dispute that the champion was according to where you lived.

Pop put fifty thousand dollars as the smallest sum for which Jimmy would defend his title and, as a result, Jack Doyle, who lost some $20,000 giving the Irishman the chance to win the crown, found himself holding the bag without an opportunity to regain some of his losses. There would be no money in California for a return match with Corbett or a match with Jackie Fields. Although Jimmy's popularity had waned in New York few begrudged him the 147-pound championship largely because in over eleven years of fighting his name had never been linked with a shady deal. Jack Dempsey was after first call on the new welter-weight champion. Foster favoured Dempsey because of his friendship with the old Manassa Mauler, and he promised to hold off other negotiators until he had talked personally to Dempsey. The former heavyweight champion tried to make a match between Jimmy and the current lightweight ruler Tony Canzoneri, for one of the ballparks later that summer. Canzoneri's manager suggested the bout. Knowing there were few real contenders in the welterweight class, Sammy Goldman believed the two would draw big money.

'Any promoter who can get McLarnin can have Canzoneri,' said Goldman. 'Let him guarantee McLarnin $50,000, or whatever he would want to fight Tony and we'll go on a percentage basis. It's the only attractive fight for McLarnin. He'll not get any real money fighting Corbett back in California or Jackie Fields.'

As 1933 gave way to 1934 the New York State Athletic Commission started to pressure Jimmy into defending his title. He was given thirty days to accept a challenge by Bep Van Klaveren or forfeit his title. There was never any chance of a Van Klaveren fight attracting the sort of money that Pop was looking for but then along came Dov-Ber Rasofsky, the son of a rabbi, and an aspiring Talmudic scholar turned lightweight champion of the world. In the many months since Jimmy had won the title, Rasofsky, known as Barney Ross, had emerged as the obvious contender. And, of course, he was Jewish and the numbers were big enough even to interest Pop.

'Foster still wants the Empire State Building, three national banks and half of Harlem, not to mention a twelve-pound weight advantage to fight Ross,' snorted Art Winch, Ross' manager.

Ross was the best lightweight since Benny Leonard and a fight with the 'Jew Killer' couldn't miss in New York. The fight was made for the Garden Bowl on 28 May 1934.

'And what will draw you and me and our neighbours into the arena that night, among other things, will be to see whether the Irishman named Baby Face and who is now all of twenty-eight years old, is beginning to stiffen a little in the joints,' wrote Paul Gallico, 'he hasn't laced on a glove since he knocked out Young Corbett in Frisco a year or so ago, and also whether the Hex he seems to lay on the little Jewish boys who used to ply their trade hereabouts has run out.'

'IF I'D LOST IT, I'D HAVE DIED'

The first thing an opponent noticed about Jimmy McLarnin when the bell rang was the glitter that came into his eyes. Otherwise, except for the slight drawing of the lips back from the teeth, he still looked the pleasant little choirboy. Then he stepped in, with never a change of expression, but as though something had welled up in his throat and cut loose with the absolute savagery of a wild animal.

'From what deep wells of the past this strange young man draws the rancour and bitterness and viciousness that rides on any single punch, I would like to know,' remarked one boxing scribe. So would Tex 'Kid' Wallace. Tex was a $5-a-day human punching bag, otherwise known as one of Jimmy's sparring partners. A looping left to the ribs sent Tex to the canvas. A whiff of smelling salts got him upright again, but in the third session Jimmy flattened Tex again with a right on the jaw. Next up was Tony Scarpati, a former Golden Glover who earned his five bucks by stopping a few rights with his stomach. Scarpati was doubled up and Jimmy caught him on his way to the canvas. Meanwhile another sparring partner, Frankie Cinque, was in an Atlantic City hospital being x-rayed for broken ribs.

'Pop Foster's first charge as he leads his homicidal ward to Atlantic City for training will be to recruit a few sparring partners,' wrote John Lardner in the *New York Post*. 'This is not the easiest task in the world. Some time ago James was sued for $50,000 by one, Hjalmer Mogren, who explained that his jaw had been broken by the McLarnin duke during a sparring session. The jaw of a sparring partner sells for a good deal less than $50,000 these days, but you can see Hjalmer's point. No one likes to have his jaw broken, even in fun. The plight of Hjalmer Mogren made a profound impression on other sparring partners around the town. They read about the case, or had it read to them. They reflected. Jimmy McLarnin was a nice person and a fine broth of a boy, but would it be worth a fractured mandible to enjoy his society?'

The training camp was conducted with the usual parsimony and informality. Pop, Jimmy and the trainer had a couple of rooms at the Madison. When they got ready to do some boxing they wandered down to the auditorium where somebody unlocked the upstairs ballroom, tightened up the ring ropes, opened a dressing room and some forty or fifty people sauntered in at fifty cents a head. A couple of fighters appeared from nowhere and Jimmy sparred four or five rounds with them, shadow boxed a round with his bathrobe on to keep near the weight, and they all went away again. If there were newsmen around both Pop and Jimmy stayed and answered questions as long as they were required, after which they vanished again. 'My hands are in great shape. They were brittle but they're tough as rawhide now!' said Jimmy. It was all very desultory and very different to the rival camp up in the Catskills.

Barney Ross was the lightweight champion of the world with big gambling debts to settle. If you needed money badly the man to fight was Jimmy McLarnin and even though Barney was eight pounds lighter he told his men to go make the fight. His managers, Art Winch and Sam Pian, opposed the match; it was Ross who chose to ignore the difference in weights. 'Call it a hunch,' said Barney. His managers were afraid that the weight advantage would be too great while Pop Foster was demanding a guarantee of $50,000 before letting his boy step into the ring with anybody. Several promoters tried to make the match but gave up after hearing the rival demands. Then William S. Farnsworth, representing Mrs William Randolph Hearst's Free Milk Fund for Babies charity, sent for Pian and Winch to come to New York. They told Farnsworth there was no point journeying from Chicago as they were determined not to let their man fight McLarnin. Farnsworth persuaded them to make the trip but they left Chicago still determined to turn down any offer. When they arrived at Farnsworth's office Ross was waiting there to greet them. He had flown from Chicago after their train had left.

'I want to fight McLarnin. I've never interfered before, but this time I would like to ask you to let me have a word. I can beat McLarnin. I know it, and I want that bout. You can make any arrangements you want regarding the percentage and the weights, but close the match.'

It had been a year since Jimmy won the welterweight title by knocking out Young Corbett on the Coast, there were no high class welters to challenge him and he was faced with inactivity. 'You needn't wonder longer why Jimmy McLarnin, welterweight champion, waits so long between bouts,' joked Arch

Ward in the *Chicago Tribune*. 'He and his manager, Pop Foster, have cut their expenses to such a point a layoff doesn't seriously reduce the old bankroll ... Pop does all the cooking when they are in training and prefers amateurs for sparring partners... He is said to have paid off a pair of them in New York with medals, telling them if they accepted expense money they would be pros ... They have given up trying to beat Dutch Lonborg, Northwestern basketball coach, at ping-pong ... Too much spin on the ball, they say...'

Ross had taken the lightweight title from Tony Canzoneri, and after beating the Italian in a return, there was no one left in his class with whom to match him. Pop made the concession of taking 40 percent of the gate receipts instead of a $50,000 guarantee and also signed an agreement for Jimmy to weigh 145 pounds or less at noon on the day of the fight, two pounds under the welterweight limit. It would be the third time in the course of thirty-five years that the welterweight champion and lightweight champion would fight each other for the bigger man's title. The welterweight won the first two. Back in 1899, Mysterious Billy Smith beat Kid Lavigne in San Francisco and a quarter of a century later came the much-discussed Jack Britton – Benny Leonard match. Lightweight champion Leonard missed the chance to become the first man to hold two world titles by being disqualified in the thirteenth round for hitting a hopelessly battered Britton while he was on his knees.

According to Ross' biographer Douglas Century, for Barney the fight 'meant something more than a fifteen-rounder for the welterweight championship, that for Jews around the globe the glowing white square of the canvas had been transformed into something larger.' When Barney was fourteen years old, the dairy that his dad, Isadore, a rabbi, kept on Chicago's West Side was robbed. There were only nickels and dimes in the cash register and for this Barney's father was shot and killed. His mother suffered a nervous breakdown, Barney and his older brother moved in with a cousin and the three younger siblings were sent to an orphanage. He became almost pathologically obsessed with reuniting his scattered family and turned to racketeering to turn a buck. Barney was busted for running illegal crap games and went to work for various gangsters including Al Capone. Boxing was a profitable sideline and Barney punched his way to the lightweight title. If he could beat Jimmy and take the welter-weight championship he'd be the first man to hold two world titles.

High up in the Catskills Barney got angry. It had been suggested in the newspapers that the reason so many Jewish boxers had lost to Jimmy was because, as Jews, they lacked heart and that some of Jimmy's Jewish victims, especially Al Singer, had lost before the first bell tolled, paralysed by fear of Jimmy's straight right. Damon Runyon wrote that some of Jimmy's Jewish opponents 'died in the dressing room' and 'all the fight in them oozed out before they got in the ring' and that 'they were licked before they put up their hands'. And then there was the news from Europe.

'One thing that cast a cloud over my training was the head-lines from Germany which reported new pogroms by the Nazis against the Jews,' Barney recalled. 'To make matters worse, some two-bit sports writer from an out-of town paper said that the Jewish fighters who had fought McLarnin in the past lacked the fighting spirit and that I'd probably fold up the way they had. The item burned me up and the last days of my training period I was irritable and tense ... During the last few weeks of training, I "lived" with McLarnin. Every time I punched the bag, I saw him taking the punch. When I ran on the road, he ran with me. My sparring partners all of a sudden took on his face. I fell asleep thinking of McLarnin and woke up thinking of him. I had never been so keyed up and so tense before a fight. The news from Germany made me feel I was fighting for my people.'

The Roaring Twenties seemed to have roared by the Irish of New York and the decade of decadence served as a reminder that their sense of inclusion as Americans was an illusion. During the 1920s the Irish had suffered the anti-Catholicism of the Ku Klux Klan and Al Smith had lost the presidential election of 1928 largely because he was Irish. As the Great Depression took hold the Irish viewed themselves as a threatened people. The economic collapse had stopped their advancement into the American middle class and in New York, in particular, political power shifted as the Jewish and Italian communities made inroads into traditionally Irish spheres of influence. Father Charles E. Coughlin, the 'celebrated radio speaker from Detroit' reached over thirty million people with his weekly broadcasts. His messages had a populist, New Deal slant, but he developed a strong, anti-Semitic stance regarding the nefarious power of the 'International Jew'. Coughlin suggested that 'a man must be up in his Greek, mathematics, zoology, astronomy, and Hebrew before he can be a good cop'.

The Great Depression had hit all creeds and colours; one of

three men gainfully employed in New York in 1930 was unemployed by the time of the fight. There was intense Irish-Jewish competition for white collar and civil service jobs. It fostered resentment and with money and power in short supply, New York's Irish and Jews fought. In neighbourhoods where the two groups lived close to each other there were street brawls and, occasionally, organised violence. The rise of Hitler and Mussolini had prompted a mixed response among the people of New York. Black-shirted Fascists met in East Harlem, Brown-shirted Nazis marched in Yorkville, Communists organised throughout the Five Boroughs. The largely Irish 'Christian Front' was both anti-Semitic and violent. Its members considered the Front as a group to defend them against what they saw as anti-Catholic forces. It worked against Jewish influence with the trade unions, local government and society in general. Mobs roamed the streets of South Bronx and Washington Heights, vandalising homes, shops and synagogues, attacking children.

It really was the perfect time for this prizefight. Boxing was a stripped down, one-on-one battle in which the metaphors of struggle, of racial struggle most of all, came easily. Ross and McLarnin embodied the struggles of their respective peoples. 'The narrative of boxing,' wrote David Remnick, 'requires an opposition as broad as slapstick.' A fight between two members of the same ethnic group has always required a level of differentiation. When John L. Sullivan, the first modern heavyweight champion, defended his bareknuckle title in 1889 against Jack Kilrain, Sullivan was required to play the bad Irish immigrant who drank and took lots of women to bed while Kilrain was the good immigrant, the virtuous worker. Jimmy McLarnin became *the* totemic Irishman in America during the Depression. This was a time when the idea of a 'celebrity' was in its infancy and Jimmy, as the 'Hebrew Scourge', became the unwitting symbol of anti-Semitism on the streets of New York. 'They point to the Ghetto graveyard of McLarnin victims,' commented one newspaper, 'and declare that Jimmy is too big and strong and Irish to lose.'

Jimmy had been very hard on Jewish boxing prodigies and they never managed to travel very far with the Irishman. True, he out-weighed most of them, but then they didn't have to fight Jimmy; usually it was their idea. Whenever a Jewish lightweight or even a 140-pounder shared a ring with Jimmy they invariably got well knocked out. Jackie Fields, Joey Sangor, Louis 'Kid' Kaplan, Sid Terris, Joe Glick, Ruby Goldstein, Al Singer and Benny Leonard. Jimmy took them all, one by one, herded them over into the ropes and laid his left or right glove upon them and the bodies of the victims were borne from there. A few of them came to in the ring, but more often they found out what had happened in the dressing room or from watching the motion pictures. 'Don't you think that Barney Ross is too fast and too young for Jimmy McLarnin?' one of the customers asked Grant-land Rice. 'He should be,' replied the scribe, 'unless McLarnin happens to clip him. When the clipping episode takes place upon either chin or stomach, it is amazing how quickly the main fundamentals become unimportant. This is one reason the fight game is entirely different from all other competitions.'

Such was the importance of winning over the Irish fight crowd in America that many Jewish boxers adopted Irish names to get more fights. World middleweight champion Al McCoy, for example, was born Alexander Rudolph. 'I don't care a darn for fighting' said Jimmy, 'this fight game is just a business proposition with me.' And he was a good businessman. Even in the teeth of an unprecedented economic crisis Jimmy had drawn $1,240,000 of custom through the turnstiles. The fight with Barney Ross promised to be his biggest gate yet. Eleven days beforehand advance sales of $40,000 were reported.

Harold Ribalow, author of *The Jew in American Sports*, lived in a neighbourhood of ultra-Orthodox *yeshiva* students. 'These boys knew little about boxing, but they could not miss the excitement throughout the city,' wrote Ribalow. 'And the fact that McLarnin had beaten so many Jewish fighters made the event more important to them. It was odd, watching these boys, with skullcaps on their heads, taking time out from their Talmudic studies to listen to a fight on the radio. And no matter how long I shall remember the famous trio of Ross-McLarnin fights, I shall recall the intense faces of the Jewish students who listened to each blow-by-blow account as though it were the most significant thing in the world.'

Barney had taken four hard fights in the previous year against one round for Jimmy. Ross had been busy at his trade – Jimmy hadn't. And the older Jimmy got, the long vacations led to more and more trouble when it came to accuracy, timing and judging distance. The boxing scribes all agreed that Ross looked great in training, that he was getting the kind of work he needed, that he would be fast as a streak and that, on the contrary, Jimmy was working against cheap, broken-down sparring partners, was having poor workouts and didn't look so hot. Foster still made the New York hacks mad. He was unreasonable to their way of thinking. He never spent money on sparring partners, entertainment, trying to be a good fellow or in any other way. He just didn't spend – especially on them. He had Jimmy working against a lot of broken-down pugs because he wouldn't spend over $15 a day for sparring partners. So, largely because of their dislike of Pop, the New York slickers wanted to see Ross whip Jimmy.

The Irishman was in high spirits at the end of his last sparring session and when Harry B. Smith, the sports editor of the *San Francisco Chronicle*, walked in, Jimmy chipped:

'Mr Smith, won't you please recite that little ditty of yours I so admire.'

And the big fellow from the Coast crooned:

Here lies the body of William O'Day.
Who died maintaining the right of way.
William was right as he speeded along.
But he's just as dead as if he'd been wrong.

Jimmy laid back his head and tore off a good, hearty laugh. His work was over.

In the weeks leading up to the big fight people sensed that this match mattered. The golden age of boxing had been swept away by the Crash, fixed fights and hapless heavyweights. But now there was evidence of recovery and for the first time since the days of the gold rush on lower Broadway there was some genuine interest in the outcome of a boxing match. 'The citizens are no longer going about with that sort of glassy film over their eyes, shaking their heads and inquiring what hit them,' wrote Paul

Gallico. 'It is true that in the past two or three years a number of them have been going to prizefights in just that state, but I think more from force of habit than anything else. They had acquired the prizefight habit during the Golden Days and when the bally-hoo began, shell-shocked though they were by the catastrophe, they wandered through the turnstiles, sat down on their four inches of pine bench, and failed to see much of the fight, as they had been accustomed to doing. But their hearts weren't in it. It was all purely mechanical. Now, for the first time, I believe I detect something of the old zest returning.'

There were editorials condemning the price of tickets once more. Preachers thundered from the pulpit again against the brutal spectacle of man pitted against man for Mammon's sake, there were strange rulings by the Boxing Commission, arguments about the officials, counterfeit tickets, all of the old beloved ballyhoo once more. The biggest row in the build-up was caused, as usual, by Pop. He told reporters that his fighter's welterweight title would not be at stake against Ross because of the concession they'd had to make on the weight. Winch and Pian had insisted that Jimmy weigh no more than 145 pounds on the day of the bout and the Irishman had to post a forfeit of $10,000 to bind the deal. If Jimmy stepped on the scales an ounce over 145 the ten grand went to Barney.

Fighters and managers were called to the offices of the New York State Athletic Commission to settle the matter. Jimmy and Barney had never met until the signing of the contract on 10 April, but they were very friendly and cordial with each other. There was a marked difference in their manner however. Ross was gregarious and smiling, he laughed and joked until he became bored with all the delays after which he settled down to read the cartoons in an evening newspaper. Jimmy was quiet and 'grim lipped' throughout. During one of the many delays in the proceedings he slipped surreptitiously down to the basement where the Commission scales were kept and weighed himself. It was a precautionary measure to check the commission's scales against those he was using in Atlantic City.

Four pairs of gloves were tossed on the table and the fighters were invited to choose a pair. Pop let Ross take first choice and his manager Sam Pian became suspicious.

'Where did these gloves come from anyway?' he demanded. 'Who gave orders for them to be brought up here? I believe they were all made to McLarnin's measurements.'

This was vigorously denied by Pop and Ross was persuaded to try them on. He found one that fitted his right hand but the left ones were all too big, too loose or too stiff. Four more pairs were sent for, causing an hour's delay. This irritated Pop and he accused Pian of stalling so that Jimmy couldn't get back to Atlantic City in time to work as he'd planned. Finally a new batch arrived but this time Ross couldn't find a glove that fitted his right hand.

'They feel like sparring gloves,' Ross said. 'They feel heavier than the ones I use in training. Here put this on, Jim,' and he handed one to his opponent. Someone then thought to look at the box in which they had been packed and it was discovered that they were six-ounce not five-ounce gloves. So another trip had to be made to the base of supply and another hour passed in waiting. Ross wasn't any more satisfied with the third consignment than he had been with the previous two. These were too big around the wrists. Jimmy found a pair he liked and before Ross could get his hands on these Pop asked the commission to put them aside for his man.

'What about Ross? Is he going to fight with bare knuckles?' Pop asked.

'No,' a Commission official said, now annoyed by the delays. 'Ross will have his measurements taken and gloves made to fit him. We will order two pairs and he will have to use one of them whether they satisfy him or not. There's been enough of this.'

Now that Ross was going to have his gloves made to measure Pop decided that maybe the gloves Jimmy had selected weren't satisfactory after all. So a tape measure was called for and both men were measured.

'I'd like to have mine double breasted with two pair of pants,' cracked Ross while the 'tailor' jotted down the figures. During the intermission Jimmy told reporters that he planned to holiday in Ireland after the fight and that he was going to take his father and mother with him.

'Well, so long, Jimmy. Take care of yourself,' Ross said shaking Jimmy's hand in parting.

'Thanks, I will. See you Monday,' Jimmy smiled in reply.

Jimmy had posted a private agreement backed by a stiff forfeit, to weigh less than 145 pounds. He trained so hard and worried so much over the possibility of losing his forfeit that he shaded the agreed mark by three pounds. At the weigh-in over at the Commission offices, Jimmy tipped the beam at 142 pounds, the lowest he had weighed in five years, five pounds below the welterweight limit and three below the private arrangement. Foster tried to brazen it out that Jimmy's best weight was 140.

They both knew better. Had the fear of missing the 145 preyed on his mind and dropped him far below that limit? Had he worried off the weight?

'It was poor sportsmanship on the part of Ross and his managers to force Jimmy into this trick weight agreement,' said Pop, 'and if we should lose, we'll still claim the welterweight title.' The idea that Jimmy was much heavier and bigger than Ross wasn't true. The Irishman only had a few pounds in weight and Ross was taller.

The minute the day dawned clear, bright, warm and sunny a last minute rush for tickets was assured. A special train was laid on for Ross' supporters in Chicago to arrive in New York and the first reservation was made by Ross himself. It was a present from the lightweight champion to a former school chum who hadn't been doing so well. As an inducement to prospective customers 5,000 seats at $1.15 were put on sale. The lower prices for a major championship fight and the fact that there was no radio broadcast swelled the eventual crowd. Vendors selling bags of peanuts, chewing gum, cigarettes and rubber mats for the hard wooden bleachers had set up stall in the afternoon. In the course of the next few hours over 60,000 people gathered at Madison Square Garden's outdoor abattoir out at Long Island City. The gate was staggering in such desperate times. It wouldn't have been big news in the golden days of Tex Rickard but it was exciting news in the battered world of Depression-era boxing. The Milk Fund was taking 10 per cent off the top, before the fighters and landlord got a cent and $20,000 bought a lot of milk. Jimmy, as defending champion was on 40 per cent and Ross 25 per cent. The remaining share went to the Madison Square Garden

Corporation for renting the park, fully staffed.

The early comers began roosting on their perches before the evening sun went down. The ermine and boiled shirt gentry barged in just before Jimmy and Barney went on. 'A good many of our best people and some of our worst – depending on your point of view – crowded into Madison Square Garden Bowl,' reported the *New York Daily News*. 'The elite rubbed elbows with pickpockets; the gold spoon scions swapped opinions with the gamblers; Harvard '29 gabbed with Elmira '32; a good time was had by all and there wasn't a watch stolen in the crowd.'

Sitting at ringside were Mayor La Guardia, the three baseball magnates – Charles Stoneham, Colonel Jake Ruppert, Judge Stephen McKeever – the owners of the Giants, Yankees and Dodgers respectively, the Marx Brothers, Jack Dempsey, Gene Tunney, Benny Leonard, Theodore Roosevelt Jr and Ralph Pulitzer. Just a few feet from the press row sat Father Charles E. Coughlin.

'And soo,' shrilled Ed Wynn, the fire chief, to Graham McNamee, who sat beside him. 'McLarnin will win by a knockout – I'll betcha, Graham!'

'I've got ten grand on Jim,' confessed Leo Fitzgerald, Broadway booking agent.

'I like McLarnin,' admitted Mayor Frank Hague of Jersey City.

The accepted wisdom in boxing is that a good 'big un' will always beat a good 'little un', but there was a lot of money going on Ross to win this one. Al Jolson tried to bet at least five grand on Ross but he got down less than a thousand. Betting was brisk and set a new post-Depression record. Ross was the slight favourite and according to the *New York Herald Tribune* there was a 'widespread snapping of rubber leashes on bank rolls panting for action on Rasofsky to give McLarnin a beating.' Jimmy had struggled badly against Brouillard after a year of idleness. He'd fought just a single round in eighteen months before this match and as one scribe remarked, 'it still takes fights to make fighters'.

The iron bars supporting the lights were bent into the shape of a clenched fist. Sixty lamps burned over the ring. People crammed onto nearby roofs. It was a perfect night for a prizefight. Jimmy was in the ring first, sporting a new pair of boots and his old green robe, and there was a long delay before Ross made his way in a tattered terrycloth gown that Ma Rasofsky had stitched and patched together. 'Sentimentalists will be glad to know that the moon rose over dreary Queens just at the moment when Ross entered the ring,' wrote one ringside scribe. 'The omen didn't shift the betting however and they remained at 13 to 10 McLarnin at the opening bell.' Ross sprinted through the crowd and his trainer Art Winch had to slow him down, wave to the fans and told him the referee wouldn't start without him. According to one ringside scribe he was 'fierce as a dog lapping for action, cunning as a savage pitted against the wilderness'.

'When McLarnin came into the ring and sat down, Pop Foster and his seconds were in front of him, blocking him, and I couldn't see his face,' Barney recalled. 'Then for a moment, they moved out of the way and I saw Mac looking straight at me with those cold blue eyes of his. Boy, did they freeze me! They called McLarnin "Baby Face", and maybe his face did have the look of a cherub, but his eyes were another story.'

'McLarnin looks like the kind of opponent you would pick for yourself out of a gang in a street fight,' wrote Paul Gallico. 'If trouble started you would give the mob a quick look-over, spot the medium sized, timid-looking, calm-faced little fellow standing on the fringe with his hands in his pockets and say, "I will take that one over there." If you were still conscious after the meek-looking little man hit you once, you would be able to realise your mistake immediately. Otherwise you would find out about it in hospital.'

As the bell rang Ross kept backing away, staring at Jimmy. The champion smashed two long lefts to Barney's head and then hooked him to the side of the head with the right. Barney's eyes widened, but he didn't flinch. According to Century, 'Barney's strategy was one of naked psychological warfare: to stand and trade with Babyface; to show he wasn't afraid of the big right hand.'

'Keep going, Jimmy,' Pop called during the first two rounds when his boy seemed to have the edge.

Jimmy outboxed Ross in the second and chased him around the ring. 'The Irish were out in force; so were the Jews,' commented the *New York Herald Tribune*. 'To an unskilled judge of sound, McLarnin seemed to get a shade the better of the opening ovation. He drew a roar of approval with his left to Ross' face in the first, but the lightweight champion was accorded a noisy acclaim when he countered with a lightning jab.' But just before the bell Ross sent a right onto Jimmy's mouth. It set the pattern for the next few rounds. Ross got faster and was making Jimmy miss. Barney backed off for the first half of the round, refusing to lead and then he'd suddenly open up.

He started taunting Jimmy in the third. 'Hit me with that right, go ahead, go ahead.'

'The right hand came, cutting through the air with a loud swish,' Ross said. 'But I was already inside him, my left slashing his face, so his punch went cockeyed and bounced off my shoulder … He was mad now, he threw the right again, but I was too quick and it brushed the side of my head. His left counterpunch came at me fast, but I blocked it and landed a right hand of my own that rattled his teeth. McLarnin looked dumbfounded. I tore into him, completely unafraid. My punches splattered him like rain on the roof, and he fell back. Then the blood came … from his nose and his mouth and his head. But as we swung toe to toe, his own Sunday punch finally clobbered me and I cried out in pain.'

Ross had figured out Jimmy's right hand. He hung his body on a swivel, leant away from the champion and turned smoothly so that every time Jimmy threw a right he would turn slightly and the punch would land on his shoulder or whizz over his head. One ringside scribe likened Ross to a wasp on the ear of a horse. He put his left hand in Jimmy's face in the first round and kept it there, drawing blood from his nostrils and worrying him so much that 'he forgot he was the greatest fighter of his pounds in the world.' Jimmy's nose bled from the fifth round to the final bell.

'Keep your hands up, Jim,' Pop pleaded when Ross began to set the pace.

The ninth was the best of the fight. Jimmy landed a short left hook that sent Ross to the canvas but he got up before the time-keeper's gavel struck one. 'No one had ever counted over me in a prize ring and I wasn't about to let them start now,' said Ross. Just twenty seconds later Jimmy took a right hook and was down but he also got back, with a sheepish grin, to his feet before a count could begin. Ross' teeth were grouted in crimson from some left smashes in the ninth and his mouth bled from then onwards.

'Keep your head down and your hands up,' Pop shouted between the ninth and the tenth. He was anxious now, the fight was close. Jimmy landed his best shot in the tenth, a right. But by this time Barney had sampled the worst and he sailed in with a two fisted attack. It was, according to the *New York Times*, a fight 'bitterly, systematically and, at times, savagely waged'. Jimmy outboxed Barney in the eleventh but lost the round because of a low blow.

'Keep crowding and punching,' called Pop in the eleventh. He sounded happier, Jimmy was looking stronger than at any other time in the fight. He won the twelfth and thirteenth. Ross answered the bell for the fourteenth and opened up with both fists. He fought in sudden bursts, usually after a clinch or after he'd been hit. He cut Jimmy's face and slugged him around.

'Keep going,' shouted Pop. 'Walk right up and hit him.' Barney was coming back.

'There was a timid, wide-eyed, black-haired boy who backed away from McLarnin throughout the battle, refused to lead until stung and played the game sweet and safe up to the last round, when he battered a tired McLarnin for three full minutes,' reported Paul Gallico.

'Keep fighting, Jim. It's pretty close.' This was the fifteenth and Pop's voice rose to a fervent plea. 'Keep going Jimmy, keep going. Fight like hell.'

At the final bell both men were bloodied but still standing and now the two judges and the referee would decide their fate. Tom O'Rourke, veteran fight manager and promoter, gave it to Jimmy. Harold Barnes gave it to Ross and it was up to old Eddie Forbes, the referee, to settle it. The microphone was lowered and Joe Humphreys shouted, 'the judges have disagreed and Referee Forbes declares …'

The huge crowd, largely rooting for Ross, seemed to think that their man had lost the fight and when the decision was gargled into the microphone there was a brief silence. Jimmy looked more like a harmless old man than a 'Baby Faced Killer'. The smile was gone and his lips were drawn across his teeth. The hands that had knocked out so many men hung weary.

'The first one in was my brother Georgie,' Ross recalled. 'He found me bawling like a baby.

"Barney, Barney, what the hell are you cryin' about?" he shouted.

"I don't know," I mumbled through my tears.

'This fight meant so much to me. If I'd lost it, I'd have died.' Ross' mother never listened to his fights on the radio, but listened that night. 'Barney is fighting for the good name of his people. *This* kind of fight I must listen to. After the fight was over she asked: 'Was this fight broadcast all over the world? Someone nodded. 'Hitler will know about it then. Maybe he'll learn something from it about our people. He should know that he can kill millions of us but he can't ever defeat us.'

Tom O'Rourke, an Irishman, apparently only saw an Irishman in the ring, and gave Ross but one round. Judge Harold

Barnes scored just two rounds for Jimmy while Referee Eddie Forbes, scored only one round to Jimmy. The scoring was a mess. Jimmy was warned for low punching on at least four occasions and even though the low blows were unintentional, if a referee issued a warning, that boxer lost the round. After the fight Forbes denied taking any rounds away from Jimmy for low hitting yet General Phelan, chairman of the Commission, admitted that Forbes' card showed that he had penalised Jimmy in four rounds. Forbes also seemed to keep the fouls something of a secret from the judges. Later, Forbes explained that they were so obvious he thought anyone could see them and didn't feel it necessary to get up and shout about something so apparent. O'Rourke failed to credit Ross with any of the contentious four sessions and Harold Barnes awarded one of them to Jimmy in spite of the official forfeit. Pop accused the Ross camp of planting ringside stooges to bellow 'foul, foul' so loudly that they confused Forbes into taking the rounds away from Jimmy. The old man refused to shake hands with Eddie Forbes when the two met again the following evening while Jimmy showed the veteran referee a 'prompt courtesy'.

Ross did little fighting in the first minute or two of the rounds and Jimmy piled up the points with left jabs and hooks. Then towards the end of each session, the challenger opened up with eye-catching flurries of punches that would blast the champion clear out of his path. But were those bursts enough to take Jimmy's title away? 'If he ever fights McLarnin again with judges who can remember anything but the last thirty seconds of the round he's likely to find the decision against him,' wrote Bill Henry of the *Los Angeles Times*. 'But do they have fight judges who can remember that far?'

'Inasmuch as McLarnin was champion and Ross challenger, I felt that McLarnin should have been scored higher for being aggressive and chasing Ross,' wrote Paul Gallico. 'I am still waiting to see a champion stop dead in his pursuit of a back-away, counter-fighting challenger and say, "All right, sonny, you want my title, come and get it!" The newspapermen voted along geographical lines. The Pacific Coast writers thought Jimmy should have retained the crown while the Gothamites generally approved of the verdict. 'The only way I can dope it out is that Referee Eddie Forbes, a doddering old gentleman, who looked as if he'd fall down from the breeze created by the swings that missed connections, must have been looking at some other fight than the one I saw,' wrote Bill Henry. 'I want to go on record with regard to just one thing; the only thing rotten about the fight was the decision.'

Three rows of cops joined hands and cordoned off Jimmy's tin-plated dressing room. No one was getting into the sanctum of the fallen champion and the newspapermen, photographers and hangers-on were made to wait. 'At last he appeared, woeful, looking rather small, huddled between gargantuan bluecoats,' wrote Caswell Adams in the *New York Herald Tribune*. A flying wedge of policemen rushed Jimmy along the ramps, along the three-quarters of the edge of the cavernous bowl and out to a far exit to a waiting car. Pop trailed along behind, unnoticed. Jimmy didn't utter a word, and all Pop would say was 'Yeah, Jimmy's in fine shape.'

'Jimmy fought a good fight. He fought a smart fight. He made no mistakes. He did all the leading, all the forcing. I don't understand the decision. I don't understand it at all. Jimmy won nine rounds,' said Pop, sitting, shirt-sleeved, on the side of the bed in his apartment at Bretton Hall, way up Broadway, unburdening himself to Damon Runyon.

It was just a couple of hours after Jimmy had lost his title. 'In the living room of the apartment many sad-faced gentlemen are quaffing beverages of different kinds and wagging their heads dutifully at every quaff,' wrote Runyon. 'Mr Marcus Griffin, brilliant young Broadway columnist, is observed in the distance, doing some special head wagging. Mr Griffin's usually buoyant heart is heavy over the McLarnin defeat.'

Pop was 'saying some things in great ire' that he wasn't likely to repeat when he cooled out. 'If you understand how Pop loves Jimmy McLarnin, and how he hates to see him defeated, you excuse the old gentleman's show of displeasure, his intimations of suspected shenanigans and all,' wrote Runyon. Jimmy was bruised and swollen from the pitter-patter of Ross' left. He offered no comment on the decision, but proudly introduced his father, 'greatly depressed by his son's downfall'.

'I'm taking Dad on a trip to Ireland,' Jimmy said.

'How much was in the house?' Pop asked.

Runyon told what he had heard of the first count, and it was close to $200,000.

'It's a lot of money,' Pop says. 'After all, that's all there is to fighting – money.'

Pop looked over at Jimmy, but Jimmy offered no reply. 'You can see, however, that he is not altogether in accord with Pop's view,' wrote Runyon. 'You can see that this boy feels keenly the loss of his title in his first defence of it.'

'I don't understand the decision,' Pop remarked.

Jimmy said nothing.

'What did you think of the decision?' The various quaffing gentlemen asked Runyon. He was too wary to reply. There was a certain truculence in their asking that suggested argument unless he said the decision was awful. But to Jimmy, Runyon said:

'I think you were away short. You were ring rusty. A man can't lay off fighting for a year, and then expect to start right in where he left off.'

Jimmy nodded.

'He fought a good fight,' said Pop. 'A smart fight. I don't understand the decision.'

'It's a great return match,' Runyon ventured to Pop. 'Never has there been such difference of opinion on a decision.'

'Well,' Pop said slowly, 'Ross is the champion now. Maybe he won't want to fight Jimmy again. Maybe Jimmy won't want to fight anybody again. He has plenty of money. He feels pretty bad about the decision. He fought a smart fight. Ross kept backing away and covering up and bolting. He wouldn't make a fight of it.'

Nobody was going to tell Pop that Ross made quite a fight of it. 'A manager who loves his fighter as Pop loves McLarnin is not apt to see anyone in a fight but his boy,' remarked Runyon. 'He is bound to discount everything the other fellow does.'

Pop made no excuses. He thought Jimmy won, and that is all there was to the matter.

'Jimmy is a better fighter than Ross,' said Pop. 'He is a better boxer. He fought a good fight tonight in every way.'

'He was missing a lot with his right hand,' Runyon suggested.

'And Ross made him do a lot of things, pulling him into leads and all that.'

'No,' said Pop, sharply. 'Jimmy made Ross fight to suit himself. It's hard to hit Ross with a right hand the way he blocks and covers. Jimmy did everything right. I don't understand the decision.'

Pop brooded a moment, sitting there on the bed, then, according to Runyon, 'the spirit of sportsmanship that never dies in a man like Pop' asserted itself as the old man leant forward and said:

'But I'll tell you one thing – Ross is a better fighter than I thought.'

'THE FOUR IRISHMEN
& THE JEW'

When the cash boxes were emptied they showed a total paid attendance of 39,968 with gate receipts of $194,721.71. With taxes cut there was $163,721.71 left of which Jimmy got $58,936. A return match was a natural, but would Jimmy, with his pockets lined and his timing gone, really want it? His long service in the ring, the mental hazard of making weight, his brittle hands and his twenty-seven years were all against him. He had been fighting over ten years while Ross had been going half that time and the length of ring service determined a fighter's age more than his actual years. 'Tunney was perfectly right in quitting when he was at the top,' Jimmy had once said. 'Only those in the fight game realise the danger of continuing in it and taking unnecessary head punishment after making enough to retire.' He abandoned those ideas after the Ross fight, and once more, the old man and the kid returned to the Coast to prepare for a prizefight. But just before they left there was a football match to attend.

With New York ahead at 9 to 6, two opposing players started to exchange punches and almost immediately fights broke out across Yankee Stadium. Special policemen and officials rushed onto the field but could do nothing to check the hostilities. Before long, some of the bandsmen and a few spectators, at least one of whom was equipped with a hurling stick, were among the one hundred people involved in the scrap. Mounted policemen eventually quelled the riot while Ireland's best fighter sat and watched in the stands. New York went on to defeat Cavan, the All Ireland champions, to win the World's Gaelic Football Championship and the Jimmy McLarnin Trophy. Jimmy was on hand to present his trophy to the New York captain after the match.

Mrs William Randolph Hearst's Christmas Fund representatives clinched the inevitable return match for 6 September 1934 at the Garden Bowl, Long Island City, and the talk of New York once more was of the Hebrew and the Irishman. Thousands of men who just a few years earlier would have been queuing for tickets were now lining the streets waiting to be fed at a Christmas and Relief Fund lunch wagon. Some of the wise ones on Broadway were suggesting that they should just take the motion pictures of the last fight out to the Garden Bowl and run them off again and save a lot of money. Jimmy began training, very gently, in Vancouver. He took a long run every morning in the loose sands of Crescent Beach to strengthen the legs and played baseball to sharpen the eye. Then he worked for three weeks, boxing with his two brothers and got his weight down to 150 pounds. With the rematch just over a month away Jimmy set sail on the SS Alexander to San Francisco and on to Los Angeles. After a few days in California he flew to New York. Pop was already there to greet him. 'And you know,' wrote John Lardner, 'when you see his placid countenance in your town, that McLarnin, revenge, and September are just around the corner.'

Jimmy claimed not to be superstitious, but he returned to Orangeburg for this match because he had never lost a fight after conditioning himself there. 'I never felt so young in all my life,' said Jimmy, as he relaxed in his cottage half a mile from Gus Wilson's training camp. He clenched his right hand and rubbed it with his left.

'Is your right hand sore?' he was asked.

'No, sir,' Jimmy shot back, 'I'm just thinking about Barney Ross. I missed him with it three months ago, but it'll be a different story next week. Barney is a great fighter, make no mistake about that, but I'm going to prove that I won the last fight.'

Three months on and Pop still blamed Referee Forbes for the decision against his boy in the first fight. He claimed Forbes' error in judgement cost Jimmy his title and $20,000, the difference between the champion's and challenger's share in the rematch. The commissioners carefully explained to both fighters and their managers what constituted a foul, especially low blows. General Phelan explained the referee would be instructed to inform both judges definitely when a foul was called.

'I thought the worst I deserved with Barney before was a draw, so I'll try to leave no room for doubt this time,' said Jimmy. 'That "foul" yelling stuff of Winch's is the bunk – he knows I'm a clean fighter and so does Ross.' Jimmy also claimed that he was at a great disadvantage in the first fight because of the private agreement that he was not to weigh more than 145 pounds. The responsibility of complying with the weight requirement preyed heavily on his mind, and he weighed in 2 ½ pounds under the limit. 'I wasn't overconfident in my last fight,' he declared. 'The trouble was having to make 145 pounds. We have no such agreement this time, and I'll be at least 145 pounds when we meet next Thursday night. I'll be stronger. I'll be a much faster fighter, too.'

Pop ordered Jimmy to keep away from the gymnasium a few days before the fight. He wanted his boy to stay at 146 pounds so on the eve of the fight he fed him a big dinner; steak, string beans and tea. After a short walk they went to a movie in Nyack and spent the night at the Blue Hill Country Club. They broke camp on the morning of the big fight and motored down to the city with an escort of State Troopers and rain showers. It fell slowly at first and then in increasing sheets until it sluiced around the Garden Bowl just beyond the banks of the East River. The ushers were all slicked up in their circus uniforms, the ticket takers were at the gates and in the box office cubbyholes the cashiers were sitting patiently waiting for the dollars to slide across the wooden stills. The showers started early in the afternoon just when the average customer was trying to decide whether to go home after work or phone the missus to keep his pork chop in the ice box. There was nearly $130,000 in cash in the box offices when the fight had to be postponed to the following night. A bright tomorrow was expected and gate receipts would be up to around $175,000. But when a big, bad rainstorm blew up from the sunny South and waterlogged the timbers of the Garden Bowl the fight was put back a further twenty-four hours.

Ross' friends feared that a wet canvas might hamper the shifty champion. He depended on leg speed; jumping and skipping away from trouble. Pools of water, dripping showers, wet ropes, soggy gloves slowed up a Fancy Dan type of fighter. But the deluge continued and whatever edge Jimmy appeared to hold seemed to vanish with a third postponement. When his light-weight championship with Sammy Mandell in 1928 was post-poned for several days he finished a sorry second. Jimmy was making weight for that fight as he was for the welterweight title fight with Ross. And just like he was having trouble doing 135 pounds in 1928, he was struggling to stay at 147 for Ross. He would have to spend most of the time in the steam room of some Turkish bath, trying to keep his tonnage to the required limit. The fight was put off until the following week. It was just a few days before the Jewish holiday, Rosh Hashanah, and Ross' relig-ion prevented him from fighting. Faced with a week's inactivity the boys decided not to return to their training camps but to work out in local gymnasiums. Jimmy took his sparring partners to the Pioneer Club, while Barney, after observing the holiday, set up camp at Stillman's. Following one drill at the Pioneer, Jimmy was introduced to Marco Apicello, a former Brooklyn middleweight and one of the survivors of the ill-fated *Morro Castle,* the ship that caught fire en route from Havana to New York, killing 137 passengers and crew members on 8 September 1934.

'I'm glad to see you,' said Jimmy.

'I'm glad to be here,' replied Apicello, who was seven hours in the water before a rescue party picked him up. His head ban-daged, Apicello was satisfied just to be around.

The weekend's inactivity did a restless, fretful Jimmy McLarnin no good and Pop was worried about keeping his

Left: Jimmy squares off with a picture of Barney Ross after turning up in Mike Jacobs' office, 7 May 1935.

Right: Barney Ross scores a knockdown in the ninth round of the first fight with Jimmy

Above: Jimmy regains the title from Ross at Long Island City, 17 September 1934
Left: A battered Jimmy after beating Barney Ross in the second fight

Above: Jimmy (with Pop Foster as best man) marries Lillian Cupit
Left: The honeymoon in Hawaii

Above: Jimmy and Pop set sail for Ireland on the *S.S. Washington*, 26 September 1934

Below: Jimmy taking the beating of his life from Tony Canzoneri

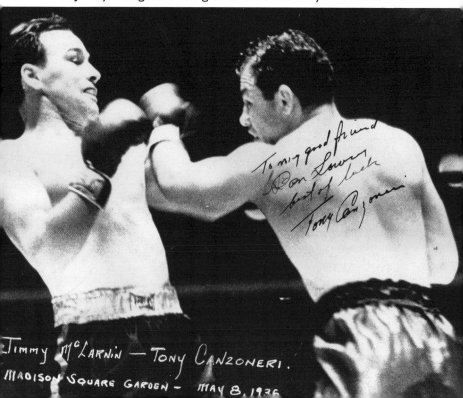

JIMMY McLARNIN — TONY CANZONERI.
MADISON SQUARE GARDEN — MAY 8, 1936

Left: Jimmy and Lillian
Below: Jimmy is declared the winner against light-weight title-holder Lou Ambers at Madison Square Garden, 20 November 1936. He would never fight again

Above: Sam McLarnin and Pop Foster
Below: Babyface in Hollywood; Jimmy with Humphrey Bogart

Above: Jimmy leaps a bench after making a hole-in-one on the Atlantic City golf course.
Below: Lillian, Grace Ellen, Nancy, Jean, and Jimmy

Above: Jimmy working in an airplane specialties plant in Los Angeles in 1944
Left: The McLarnins with latest addition, Jimmy Jr

charge within the 147-pound mark. Jimmy seemed irked by the decision not to get the whole affair over with. He was quiet and introspective by nature and spent much of the time looking out of windows and watching the rain, asking what time he was due in the gym that day. 'No-one knows McLarnin. They may know Pop Foster. They may know the McLarnin Pop Foster unfolds for them,' wrote Pat Rosa in the *New York Post*. 'Few, if any, know the little Irish lad, virtually the adopted son of the gruff, callous, deceptive Foster. Foster has done all the thinking and talking for his boxer since McLarnin was fifteen. Who knows just what's behind that aging Baby Face?' So it was with particular concern that Jimmy arose to find that on the morning of Monday 17 September the rain wasn't falling. Garden officials would have been hard pressed to find another date that week had there been another delay. Yom Kippur, the Day of Atonement, started at sundown the following night and all orthodox Jews would inaugurate a twenty-four-hour fast. Jimmy, who had already made three futile trips to the boxing commission office in taxicabs to be weighed, implied that if he never stepped on another scale again it would be too soon.

It rained a little in the afternoon but the skies cleared at 6pm in downtown New York. It rained for another hour out toward Long Island and when inquiries brought the surprising reply that 'the fight is positively on' a lot of people didn't believe it. The start was delayed and what there was of a crowd came late. Though there was no concerted rush to fill the spaces, the stream of travel was steady, and slowly the throng mounted until the nearest patches of pinewood were covered with spectators and the ones further back were hidden in darkness. It was the usual fight crowd, recruited from all the avenues and sidewalks of New York, New Jersey and nearby stations, with bankers and brokers, publishers and politicians sprinkled among the butchers and bakers, tailors and taxi drivers. The New Dealers dominated, but the old were also represented at the Garden Bowl. Mayor Fiorello La Guardia, Tammany Hall leader Jim Dooling, Postmaster General James A. Farley and Senator Robert Wagner were all present.

Jimmy and Barney arrived at ringside at the same time. As they shook hands Jimmy asked: 'How are you, Barney boy?' Ross just grinned. He was still grinning just over an hour later as the two fighters embraced after another fast and furious fight. Jimmy looked in a pretty bad way. His left eye was a mere slit – he was bleeding at the nose and mouth, and, in the two final rounds, he had tired badly. There was a short delay. Just like the last fight, the judges disagreed. Tommy Shortell gave it to Jimmy, Charlie Lynch voted for Ross. It was up to referee Arthur Donovan, who, in accordance with commission rules, had marked his slip before the judges. On it Joe Humphreys found the name of Jimmy McLarnin, and Jimmy, with just one good eye, turned two handsprings, did a high kick and was swept away by his admirers. Before 23,777 people who paid $138,902.62 for the privilege, Jimmy had won back his welterweight championship and the jinx of the Garden Bowl remained intact. A champion had yet to defend his title successfully there. It had been very close. Shortell gave Jimmy six rounds, Ross five and called four even. Lynch gave Ross seven, Jimmy six and called two even. Referee Donovan saw a decisive margin giving the challenger ten rounds, and the champion five.

'If McLarnin chases Ross in this second fight, then he is a bigger sucker than anyone has the right to suspect him to be,' predicted Paul Gallico. 'He didn't get anywhere with those tactics the first time, and he will probably be bright enough not to fight the same losing fight twice or to think that he can win with a system that lost the first time.' Both fighters had adjusted their strategies and seemed to reverse their tactics. Jimmy relied more on short left hooks and jabs to the head and body. Ross was prepared to trade shots. The fight opened with the champion aggressive and standing up straight instead of fighting from the hanging crouch he adopted in the first meeting. Ross as champion was more confident and aggressive and in the second round he punched Jimmy around the ring. But Jimmy was also much improved and in the third round he gave Ross a beating with overhand rights to the head, cutting his mouth and his eye. Jimmy looked stronger and defter and outboxed as well as outhit Ross and he won the fourth, fifth, sixth and seventh rounds in a row, although judges and reporters at ringside were told that Ross had been given the fifth round because of Jimmy's low foul left early in that session.

Then the fight changed. Ross began to push the Irishman backwards with a series of crashing rights. One landed below Jimmy's left eye and started a swelling that grew until, in the final rounds, it was completely shut. The champion reverted to the hanging crouch that he used for the first fight and Jimmy could no longer reach him with big rights. Ross took the eighth and ninth but the tenth was an even bloodbath. 'It was something of a crimson carnival,' wrote Grantland Rice. 'McLarnin's left eye was shut closer than a locked door in a picketed textile mill. McLarnin wore a bump on his forehead and his nose was flowing the old claret again … Ross was bleeding badly at the mouth and there was a gash over his right eye.'

The first few rows at a big fight were usually occupied by the ex-millionaires who could still afford the car fare to the arena, retired alcohol vendors and other leading members of the smart set. But the outer reaches of the ballpark were a different story. 'Big fights usually attract heterogeneous crowds and when you buy your ticket you don't know whether you will be rubbing elbows with Marion Davies, the mayor of New York or the guy who is wanted for the murder of that bank clerk in the Bronx,' reported *Collier's*. 'On a clear day you could just get a glimpse of the ring with the naked eye. The customers out here couldn't see the fight very well but they were in a grand spot to yell about it. In the eighth round one leather-lunged nitwit rose to his feet to shout encouragement to Ross.

"Kill the Mick!" he bellowed and several of his colleagues took up the cry.

'A round or two later McLarnin made a bid and for a time he was all over Barney like a swarm of bees. The leather-lunged nitwit shifted his verbal affections.

"Murder the Jew!" he roared. The leather-lunged nitwit looked like the kind of person who would enter even his own home by means of a window out of force of habit and there were thousands like him there that night yelling homicidal encouragement either to Barney or Jimmy or both. It was then that the bright (well, fairly bright) thought came to me that the chief trouble with boxing was not the boxers but the audience.'

Jimmy landed a short right chop that hurt Barney badly in the tenth and the momentum of the fight changed once more. Jimmy won the eleventh, but in the twelfth Ross again nailed the challenger with overhand rights and punched him all around the ring, buckling his knees with the hardest blow of the fight, a right to the temple. The last three rounds could have been scored either way. They didn't stop brawling and they fought over every inch of the canvas. Jimmy's left eye closed tighter and blood squirted from a cut over Ross' right eye. They fought on every rope, in every corner and out in the middle until the final bell stopped them and nobody in the park knew who had won. 'The battle was desperate and both lads suffered heavy damages,' wrote Nat Fleischer in *The Ring*. 'It was a stand-up, cruel mill, the kind that fans enjoy.'

'The Jews said it was Ross, the Irish said it was McLarnin and the Italians said they didn't know,' wrote Paul Gallico. 'There was a dead silence in the park when Humphreys said the judges had disagreed, but also a great cheer when he announced that McLarnin had re-won the title.'

'I knew I'd do it, Pops; I knew I'd do it.'

Half laughing, half crying, Jimmy danced his way to his dressing room. 'Whew, but that Ross was tough tonight,' said the new champion. 'He had everything, but there was never a minute's doubt in my mind that I'd take him this trip.' Jimmy's left eye was completely closed now and there was a bump the size of a doorknob in the middle of his forehead as he stretched on a rubbing table in his little tin dressing room after the battle.

'My right hand did it,' he grinned. 'I might as well have left it in the hotel the last time we fought, but this time I regained my title by clipping Ross with my money fin.'

'I didn't knock him out, to be sure,' Jimmy continued, as old Pop clucked around his protégé like a mother hen, 'but I larruped the daylights out of him with it and that's how I beat him.'

'Then why didn't you knock him out?' one scribe asked.

'Because he is a very tough guy.'

'Will you give Ross a return match?' Jimmy was asked and Pop replied:

'It's a bit early to talk of that.'

'Sure I will,' interrupted Jimmy. 'He gave me one didn't he, after he took my title on what I thought was a questionable decision? Well, I'll return the favour. He can have a shot at me any time a responsible promoter wants to stage the bout. But in the meanwhile I want to take that trip to Ireland that Barney made me postpone because of the result of the last fight. I guess I can go there now with a clear conscience.'

'Quit fighting?' Jimmy concluded. 'I shouldn't say I won't – not after tonight. Why, I must be good for a couple more years, don't you think so?'

Pop and Jimmy climbed into a car and started for his hotel, where he called up Lillian.

'I won – and he didn't hurt me a bit.'

'The big question along Broadway and cauliflower row today was who really won the Jimmy McLarnin-Barney Ross welterweight championship fight,' reported the *Associated Press*. 'In pubs, cigar stores, and poolrooms the fight faithful gathered to agree or disagree with the decision that cost Ross his title at the end of fifteen rounds. The payoff was on McLarnin, but a majority of fight writers at ringside, backed by a considerably larger number of spectators, thought that Ross should have had a draw at the worst and kept his title.'

Barney Ross thought he won the fight. When the scribes wrestled their way into the stuffy wooden shanty of a dressing room they were surprised to find Eddie Forbes there ahead of them, murmuring into Ross' ear and patting his kneecap as he spoke. Forbes was the referee who had given Ross the casting vote and the title in the first bout. 'With his arm placed caressingly around the drooping shoulders of the young Jewish lad,' wrote one scribe, 'Forbes kept whispering, "I think you won, boy." Forbes had been sitting in the back of Ross's corner and throughout the fight he kept advising Sam Pian and Art Winch on a plan of battle, devised from his score sheet. At least once he was heard to say, "Let him coast, Sam, he's way ahead."'

'The fact that McLarnin, both judges, and the referee were all of Irish descent wasn't lost on many in the crowd,' wrote Ross' biographer, Doug Century, 'and a joke began to circulate even as the crowd was streaming out of the Bowl: *Did you hear the one about the four Irishmen and the Jew?*'

Ross admitted that a return match appeared doubtful. 'I guess the public is tired of hearing of Ross and McLarnin,' he said. 'I know there were moments in the ring when I was mighty tired of Jimmy and I felt there were other times when he was mighty fed up with me.'

'Old Pop Foster will probably ask for the house and all its furnishings,' said Art Winch, Ross' manager. There would certainly be no return meeting of McLarnin-Ross that year. Pop wouldn't even consider a rematch until the following spring. There were several reasons, chief among them the tax situation. 'This gets more complicated the longer you are associated with it, and it gets discouraging as well,' explained Pop. 'The more you make the more you have to pay. Jimmy has about paid the limit for this year, at least.' Meanwhile Jimmy's father was announcing his son's retirement.

'Jimmy had definitely made up his mind to retire from the ring whether he won back the title or not,' revealed Sam McLarnin. 'I believe he has fought his last fight.'

After the fight Jimmy said, 'Pop, you've given me everything you promised except one thing. Once upon a time you said you'd take me to Ireland. How about it?'

'We'll go to Ireland, my boy, as soon as a boat is sailing. I mean a boat that doesn't charge too much.'

Barney Ross' victory in the previous fight cost Jimmy more than the welterweight crown. It postponed indefinitely his marriage to Lillian; it postponed a trip to Ireland with his family and his prospective bride and it prevented his retirement from the ring as undefeated champion. He and his fiancée had planned their wedding to be celebrated shortly after his first successful title defence. That had to wait, along with the honeymoon in Ireland, until he regained the crown. That was to have been a triumphal visit. An Irish world champion going home to Ireland. Jimmy expected to have a lot of fun, and Ross spoiled it. 'Everything was arranged for that trip,' Jimmy explained. 'My father was in town, and my mother was coming east after the fight. We had a brand new automobile fixed up to take to Europe with us. I was that sure of beating Ross.'

But now Pop and Jimmy set sail for Europe and stayed for two months. Pop went to England to track down friends and relatives, while Jimmy spent most of his time in Ireland. As he stepped on board the *Ile De France* to return to the United States Jimmy scaled 154, seven pounds over the welterweight limit. He had gained more than a pound for every week of his vacation and blamed it on the kindness of friends in Ireland, England and France.

'What can a fellow do?' asked Jimmy. 'Everywhere I went in England or Ireland I was asked to tea. I am not accustomed to eating over two meals a day, but over there I could not get out of less than five. It's their magnificent hospitality.'

A LAST REEL FADEOUT

The New York train pulled out of Chicago on time. A man shook his head and said to his companion, 'Isn't that too bad? He was a nice boy and a good fighter, too.' He folded the evening newspaper over to reveal the headline, 'McLarnin Reported Dead in Crash.' Jimmy was sitting directly behind the two men listening intently. 'I pinched myself, found everything all right, and immediately wired to my manager Pop Foster that the report was somewhat exaggerated,' Jimmy recalled. Jimmy had planned to fly from Los Angeles to New York four weeks before the fight. It was a far cry from the day that he and Pop climbed into a rickety old car to invade the East and prove to a doubting world that a youth with such a baby face could fight. Jimmy arrived at the airport in Los Angeles on the night of Sunday 5 May 1935, and bought seat 13 on Plane No. 13, first section of a TWA Sky Chief heading points east. Stops were scheduled for Albuquerque, Kansas City and Pittsburgh. He got to the airport early and boarded the plane, which was to be followed by a second section flying the same route. Everything was fine until Jimmy's plane approached Kansas City, where it ran into a dense fog. While the passengers slept the pilot looked for a hole in the fog and at one point the plane suddenly shot upward at a precipitous angle. A woman screamed and for the first time the passengers realised they were in danger. Someone joked about there being thirteen on board and suggested that one passenger get out for the general good of the rest. After lengthy manoeuvring, the pilot found the opening he had been seeking and managed to land with a couple of hard bumps. The passengers were taken to a hotel and the following morning they continued by air to Chicago. Having encountered more fog, the trip to Chicago was a cautious one and when they arrived TWA officials decided it was too risky to continue and cancelled the remainder of the flight.

The second airplane, trailing Jimmy's flight by only half an hour was hitting denser patches of fog. It circled over Kansas City airport, but smoke and fog prevented its landing and the pilot was instructed to proceed to a field at Kirksville, 120 miles north east. 'It seemed we merely went on and on through that heavy curtain of fog that enshrouded the earth,' said one passenger. 'Then suddenly, without warning, came the crash. I believe we must have hit the ground as though in landing and then turned over.' Out of a foggy sky, United States Senator Bronson Cutting of New Mexico, a young woman and two pilots plunged to a swift death in a giant air liner, its five gasoline tanks nearly dry, its cabin echoing the shout, 'Buckle your belts tight.' The Sky Chief crashed with terrific force in a mud-soaked farm near Atlanta, Mo., fifteen miles from the emergency landing field in Kirksville. 'I consider myself a very fortunate young man,' said Jimmy. 'If I had been delayed or arrived at the Los Angeles airport late, I would have been in that section. But my faith in air travel is still unshaken. It's too bad that this terrible accident had to happen.' Jimmy told reporters that he wasn't superstitious, but he did remark that there were thirteen passengers on his plane and the serial number began with the figure thirteen. He continued to New York on the railroads to start training for his third match with Barney Ross still feeling 'a bit shaky'. Jimmy was met at Grand Central Station by Pop Foster, promoter Mike Jacobs and Barney O'Connor, a friend.

'It will not surprise me if I travel by air again,' said McLarnin.

'Not if I know it,' growled Pop, who had several uncomfortable hours when Jimmy was flying somewhere over the Middle West.

'Why Pop, that was the first major accident in a year,' Jimmy explained. Pop turned his attention to the fight.

'Money is secondary in this fight. This Ross can't fight and he's been around too long for a fellow who can't do that. Why Jimmy is a greater champion than Tommy Ryan.'

Jimmy smiled at this outburst and moved off to a waiting automobile.

The inevitable Ross-McLarnin rematch was made for 28 May 1935 almost a year to the day since their first encounter. Ross had fought three times since the second fight with Jimmy. He met Bobby Pacho in Cleveland, Frankie Klick in Miami and Henry Woods in Seattle. Jimmy, meanwhile, hadn't drawn on a boxing glove, but contented himself with daily golf and a few weeks of gym work in California before coming East. Both fighters set up camp in the Catskills and the mountains were crawling with 'cauliflowers' that year. The delicate fragrance of the mountain blooms was intermingled with sharp whiffs of liniment and iodoform and the locals were talking of left hooks, right uppercuts and kidney clouts. The spot where the stolid Dutch burghers helped develop America back in the sixteenth century looked like a busy day in Stillman's. 'There's a pugilist peering from behind each pine,' wrote Jack Miley in the *New York Daily News*. 'The winding wooded highways are cluttered with jogging jolters. And the ploppety plop of padded pokes against punching bags – both inanimate and human – swells a swat symphony that kayoes the cacophony of the crickets up in the hills where old Rip Van Winkle sneaked his twenty-year snooze.'

'The feeling is prevalent in this parcel of the Catskills that Ross will win,' reported John Lardner. 'This parcel of the Cat-skills is not strictly neutral. Most of it is occupied by members of the chosen people, and Barney is their chosen guy. James Archibald McLarnin, an Irishman of Scotch ancestry, seems as lonely and out of place up here as a square of butter on a Catskill dinner table. Butter is bootleg stuff.'

Jimmy's name was not James Archibald. It was merely James. He thought up the Archibald as a joke on a Press Agent one afternoon, and the agent took him seriously. From then on he was known the world over as James Archibald McLarnin. But whatever his name, Jimmy was now written of as a veteran fighter, nearing the end of his fistic tether. But when his years of service and number of fights were compared with his predecessors as welterweight champion, he was little more than a Johnny-come-lately. Of all the welterweights since the start of the division only Mickey Walker had made anything like the money that Jimmy had collected during his career, and the

Irishman had most of it laid away, so he didn't enter the ring spurred by necessity. History told of many colourful and attractive welterweights, but none had ever equalled Jimmy McLarnin as a drawing card. When he defended his 147-pound title for the first time against Barney Ross, he drew the biggest house – close to $200,000 – that any welterweight had ever drawn. It more than doubled that which saw Jack Britton defend his title against Benny Leonard a few years previously. Hundred thousand dollar gates, or the approach to that sum, had been common for the Irishman. No fighter, other than the leading heavyweights, could rival Jimmy at the box office. 'I would like to give Barney another chance at the crown if he wants it,' Jimmy told the *Los Angeles Times*. 'He's the only man whom I know will draw any money and that's the object of my affection at present. I've made a study of fighting and I'll know when I'm losing my grip. That time hasn't arrived. I've never really been hurt. In two fights I have learned that Ross can't hurt me. And in what business can I make as much money as in boxing?'

Joe Gould, the manager and booking agent of James J. Braddock, the Cinderella Man, said it would be a good thing for boxing if Barney Ross scored a decisive victory over Jimmy and advanced a number of reasons in support of his theory. One of them was that Jimmy's career had been a curious one. He had remained like a great dangerous spider in his lair in Vancouver and Los Angeles, waiting for cards to be built up in New York, preferably Jewish cards. When they were ready he would come to town, stroke them once or twice with his left or right, knock them twitching and then retire once more to the Coast. In the meantime, the kids he knocked out would be practically ruined for service in the East.

No manager had been criticised more than Pop Foster for his penny-an-ounce splitting management of his fighter, for his care in picking opponents, for his training methods, and for everything else he did in handling his charge. Yet the old fellow made Jimmy a drawing card from the very beginning of his career, and his boy never had to go through the desperate grind of preliminary fighting that fell to most prizefighters. He went right to the top and remained there. Pop made sure Jimmy had plenty of time between fights to rest and play. He nearly always had money in the bank. The title came relatively late on in his career but it was all the sweeter to win it then than earlier on and to spend years fighting on as an ex-champion. There was nothing in the fight game that Jimmy had not tasted under the management of the gnarled old fellow who had been his manager since he was a little boy. Pop was careful, frugal and difficult, but once Pop committed his word, a promoter had nothing more to worry about. Neither did he have to trouble himself about honesty or gameness of performance. Jimmy was always levelling, and rarely had he turned in a poor display in eleven years of fighting. But to the New York scribes Pop was the same old lonesome guy who was mostly suspicious of everyone in the world save 'his Jimmy'. McLarnin's crusty old counsellor was the 'fellow who taught Lauder how to be thrifty'. A boxing scribe once described Pop's handling of his fighter the '5-and-10-cent-store method of training'. His camps always seemed to be a haphazard sort of affair. There were never very brilliant sparring partners around and all hands seemed to wander through the workouts with a sort of detached air. A sparring partner would appear and Jimmy would knock him down. Then he would muss around with a couple of others and that would be that.

'It might interest you to know that Jimmy McLarnin, whose theme song is, "She Swallowed A Spoon and Now She Can't Stir!" is waiting for a good offer from the YMCA before he picks a training site for Barney Ross,' reported the *New York Daily News*. 'Pop Foster, the Mick's penurious pilot, sent a hurry call to the AAU [Amateur Athletic Union] for sparring partners. Pop will pay off in neckties!'

Pop eventually chose a country club, on the banks of Swan Lake in upstate New York for a training camp. The club Commodore was Jewish, as were most of the other residents, but they had watched the pleasant-faced, pleasant-mannered Irishman so long that they had formed an attachment for him, and were going around hoping that Jimmy was going to beat Ross. It seemed to be some kind of achievement for Jimmy, who worked clad in a dark green shirt and emerald green fighting trunks, with a yellow shamrock stitched in one leg of the trunks. He and Pop were probably the only Irishmen in Sullivan County. Looking out over the expanse of water, Pop said:

'Now this is a beautiful place. Isn't it Jimmy?'

'We'll lick him, Pop,' replied a smiling Jimmy.

'You don't need me,' growled Pop, angry for the first time. 'You're the greatest fighter since Tommy Ryan.'

'All right, Pop. I'll lick him myself if I have to,' said the champion with a laugh.

'He had something on his mind last year,' said Pop. 'I don't know what it was, but he is only thinking about knocking out Ross. He'll do it too.'

Jimmy had been fighting from the age of twelve and by this stage he could no longer improve. After all those years, was there anything more Pop could teach him? He was hitting as hard as he ever would and Ross had tasted his best punches; Jimmy hit him and he took them. It was hard to tell when a fighter was on the downgrade. Physically, Jimmy looked great and was under the weight limit before the real training began. But somehow he seemed tired of the whole business. He worked hard, but, when he climbed out of the ring, he talked in a wistful way about loafing and going to shows. Like most boxers, for Jimmy training was the worst part of the business and he wasn't really happy about Pop's choice of training camp. 'It's terrible when you get up in the country all by yourself,' said Jimmy. 'I believe I could train better in a city. I like to see the shows. Two or three hours at a show after the workout and I'm all relaxed, loosened up.' Pop and the training crew began to argue about this but Jimmy paid no attention to them. When someone made a suggestion about new gloves or the danger of getting overheated or the value of one of the sparring partners, Jimmy just nodded and said: 'Yeah, all right, here's what we'll do.' In a nervous, absent-minded way, Jimmy was running the works. Lounging in a canvas chair, on the club's rambling veranda while the setting sun made a fiery mirror of Swan Lake, Jimmy talked of settling down. 'Win, lose or draw with Ross I'm going to get married. That is if it's OK with Lillian.' And the grin on his face indicated that he already knew it would be OK. 'I never had but one girl friend in all my life. This is one aspect of my lost boyhood, at least, that I can look back on with no trace of regret because she's still my girl,' said Jimmy.

There wasn't much left for Jimmy to get out of the business of boxing. He had experienced all the excitement, glamour, glory, pain and punishment that prizefighting produced. They called him an old man and the urge to fight just wasn't as great as it was before. On the other hand, Ross had known nothing but poverty until he won the lightweight title from Tony Canzoneri just two years previously and only then did he begin to make real money out of fighting. Making money, winning fights, being a champion, were all exciting to him. In his time away from New York Jimmy seemed to have aged suddenly, the way fighters often do. He had been fighting for a long time and the youthfulness had gone out of his face, which was more rounded and puffy. They didn't call him 'Baby Face' any more. He wasn't marked up, his ears weren't cauliflowered, his nose was still straight, and the lips were still thin. But age catches up with fighters with amazing rapidity, and almost overnight. He was no more than twenty-eight years old, but had suddenly acquired the features of a man of thirty-six or thirty-seven. 'Now I realise you do not fight with your face, but, to me, that certain settling and puffiness in a fighter's countenance always gives away changes that have taken place on the inside,' wrote Paul Gallico. 'That age and puffiness will tell against him in the fight. I'll wager that he won't shake off punches as easily as he used to do. I'm still out on my dear old limb. I think Ross will knock him out.'

One interested spectator at the camp was a new heavyweight sensation from Lafayette, Alabama, named Joe Louis. 'That McLarnin is a picture boxer and he gives me a tremendous thrill with his hokus pokus,' said Louis. 'I'd never seen McLarnin before and I must admit he's just as good as they say he is. Jim is the smartest kid I ever looked at, and if I could box like him, I'd be happy!' A reporter asked Jimmy about former heavyweight champion Jack Dempsey who had picked Ross to win in a syndicated newspaper article. 'I'm glad he did,' Jimmy said. 'If Jack had picked me I would have been afraid that something would happen. Now I know I'm sure to win.' Pop said nothing about Dempsey to the reporters but for many years he had known a couple of New York detectives who took care of him and Jimmy when they were in the city for a fight. Before this match they told Pop that a friend of Dempsey's had been betting a lot of money on Ross. So Pop had gone to promoter Mike Jacobs demanding that Dempsey not be selected as referee. The old man also kept the scribes happy by goading Ross and dismissing him as a 'boxing boon doggler who tin-cans like a panicky pup' whenever Jimmy tossed a punch at him. 'He always runs away from my Jimmy,' harangued Pop. 'He's afraid to stand up and take it.'

'I'll stake Pop a pair of spectacles, if he won't buy 'em himself – for he certainly needs his eyesight fixed,' Ross snapped back from the foothills of the Catskills. 'That old gaffer is walking on his heels if he says I'm yellow! I banged his Mick all over the lot the last time we fought and I'll drop him in Pop's lap next time. Jimmy is a nice kid, but he's in bad company with that crackpot Foster!'

Ross elected to do his training at what became affectionately known as the Kosher Kountry Club, a holiday spot for orthodox Jewish people run by the Grossinger family. Barring the odd jibe at old Pop most of the noise coming from the Ross camp also concerned the referee. Charging Arthur Donovan, who had refereed the second fight, with incompetence and racial prejudice,

Sam Pian, Ross' manager notified the State Boxing Commission that his charge would refuse to fight if Donovan was selected as referee again. Donovan had scored ten rounds for Jimmy and five for Ross the previous September. Soon after that fight Donovan spoke at a boy's club in Brooklyn and his remarks were far from flattering toward Ross. 'We didn't get a square deal from Donovan the last time Ross fought McLarnin and there is no reason to believe we'll get one again,' claimed Pian. 'If Donovan steps through the ropes I'll not let Barney box. We'll return to our dressing room and there'll be no show!' This was the usual pre-fight fare served up for the boxing writers trickling into training camp. The ballyhoo was on. The fight itself was never enough; reams and reams of newsprint were needed to crank up the heat. Those who had been holding off now headed for the ticket offices.

'Where do those young pups get the idea of talking through the newspapers about whom they want to referee?' snarled Pop. 'I thought that the referee was not supposed to be named until the men were about ready to get into the ring. Why doesn't somebody tell these people from Chicago, who are trying to run boxing, where they belong? Reliable businessmen like Bill Brown, General Phelan and Colonel Wear, who are giving their services for nothing, are quite capable of selecting a referee and judges with New York licences without being insulted through the newspapers by young managers.'

It was the first big outdoor show of the New York Summer boxing season. Although Ross was a favourite in early betting, money for Jimmy had started to show. The betting rule in New York was to make the champion favourite; on the theory that you had to string with a champ until he lost. And for this fight Pop had bet his own dough on his man, and this alone was enough to shake the confidence of the stoutest believer in Ross. It was said of Pop that he wouldn't bet the sun would rise tomorrow, so if he was laying real cash on the line he had to feel that he had an absolute cinch. Pop visited a commission broker's office on Forty-Second Street and bet $400 against $800 on Jimmy to beat Barney. So confident was Pop that he accepted the 2-to-1 odds offered without holding out for the 12-to-5 price prevailing along Broadway.

'As for the prizefight this evening, I expect it to develop pathos and much drama,' predicted Paul Gallico. 'McLarnin has been a brave, a well-loved ringman and a fine performer. He will not quit, which means that if Ross wins the fight, as he expects to do, Barney will have to slug McLarnin into complete oblivion, or hurt him so badly that emotions of fear and mercy will make themselves felt in the breast of the referee, and he will stop the fight.' Nobody expected a sudden, dramatic knockout by Ross because he was not that kind of puncher. But from what the boys had seen of Jimmy in training there was a suspicion that he was past the time when he could soak up the kind of hard, steady punishment that Ross would deal out for fifteen rounds. Surely, at some point, Ross would catch Jimmy with one, vicious, damaging punch from which he would never recover and from that time on he would take more and more until finally flesh, bone and heart would accept no more and he would collapse from a punch. That was the way old champions usually went.

Jimmy scaled 144 ¾ and Ross 141 when they were examined at the State Athletic Commission offices. The champion looked

drawn and haggard after drying out in the steam rooms to get
down to weight the previous night, but Barney was glowing and
peppy and explained he had eaten a big steak, with trimmings,
just before he reported for scrutiny. The physical condition of
both boxers was perfect but the commission's doctor reported,
'McLarnin seems under a strain, but Ross is composed and cool
as an ice cube!'

The fight did not draw quite up to expectations, but
$141,000 gross was still a lot of money in 1935 – one in five
men was still unemployed – and this was the third time around
for Jimmy and Barney in New York in just a year. Nearly six
thousand ringside seats were sold at $10 and the falling off was
in the cheaper seats. The boys who had always bought the high-
est priced seats were still able to buy them, but the lads who used
to be able to purchase the $1 and $2 perches no longer had those
bobs. There were the usual altercations among the customers
during the semi-final bouts while the Commissioners met at
ringside to select a referee for the title fight. The usual procedure
was to order ten officials to the ringside ready for work and among
these men it was within the jurisdiction of General Phelan, as
chairman of the New York State Athletic Commission, to name
the referee. Until a few minutes before the main event was
ready to begin nobody but Phelan, not even the referee to
work, was aware of the arbiter's name. Prizefights had always
been larcenous to some degree but they were not quite as
brazen and mischievous as these days when a large percentage of
the fighters were owned and operated by purveyors of booze,
narcotics, and other characters who practiced larceny as their
daily trade. The identity of the referee was hidden until the very

last to keep the racketeers guessing.

A sweltering and shirt-sleeved throng of 31,000 had gathered within the cavernous confines of the Polo Grounds. It was very humid, the most uncomfortably warm day of the year so far, and the night was the same. Those at ringside shed their coats; those in the faraway open bleacher seats came without them. Most of them were old Ross-McLarnin followers, having seen both bouts the previous year. Politicians and actors, the judiciary and clergy, blue and white collar were gathered around. The flags atop the double-deck stand flapped in a light breeze but down at the bottom of the arena barely a breath stirred. The powerful arc lights only added to the heat. Ross, now in the role of challenger was in the ring first; Jimmy wasn't far behind. But then Pop glanced over to the large bow-tied figure perched in a neutral corner. The Commissioners had chosen Jack Dempsey to referee. The old man was enraged. He ignored Jimmy and strode straight over to General John J. Phelan, shouting at the Commission chairman: 'It looks as if the works are in!'

'We can't have this fella,' demanded Pop. 'He's a Ross guy. Strictly we want a square deal.'

'Go on, Pop,' said the General sternly, 'Dempsey is as square as a dime.'

'Yeah, and how square is that?'

Foster objected to the judges and the referee. 'He was certain Judge Abe Goldberg was a Hebrew, Jack Dempsey himself has boasted of his Semite strain and the other judge, George Le Cron, might be masquerading under a phoney moniker, so far as Pop was concerned,' wrote one ringside scribe. 'But poor Pop's wails fell on deaf ears. He was cast in the tragedian's part and he limped dismally back to McLarnin's corner, registering resignation and despair through every strand of his tattered grey sweater.' Pop was still arguing with the commissioners as Jimmy shed his bright green bathrobe. 'A routine matter at all prizefights was varied slightly at the Ross-McLarnin show,' wrote Paul Gallico. 'Instead of waiting to insult General Phelan after the fight, as is customary, the manager, in this instance Pop Foster, insulted the General BEFORE the match began, and the good General was quite purple before the first punch was struck. I thought that Pop Foster made rather an ass of himself with his blistering protests against Dempsey as referee.'

For the first few rounds it looked like the choice of referee was completely irrelevant. Ross won them by wide margins and it seemed as though he was going to knock the champion out. He carried the fight to Jimmy, peppering him with series of left jabs that reddened the Irishman's left eye and occasionally crossing smashing rights to the chin. Jimmy was off balance and retreating. Then Barney stopped doing it and in the middle part of the fight Jimmy took control. He wasn't landing any big rights but he was sharper 'than the crease in Grover Whalen's pants' and he boxed like a master. Jimmy won the seventh, eighth and ninth rounds in a row. Ross was on the receiving end of numberless jabs and hooks. He was retreating, crouching and occasionally pecking with a faint left. Then Ross fought back. The tenth was close, the eleventh undoubtedly Barney's. Jimmy took a wild right-handed swipe at the back of Ross's head in the twelfth and something snapped with the retort of a pistol. A crimson stream had started from Barney's nose in the second round and it continued for the rest of the fight. By the twelfth Jimmy was seeping blood from slight cuts over each eye. Norman Mailer once wrote that two great fighters in a great fight 'travel down subterranean rivers of exhaustion and cross mountain peaks of agony, stare at the light of their own death in the eye of the man they are fighting, travel into the crossroads of the most excruciating choice of karma as they get up from the floor against all the appeal of the sweet swooning catacombs of oblivion.' So it was with Jimmy and Barney. The last four or five rounds were a real grim battle for something that Jimmy was trying to hang onto and something that Ross was trying to take away from him. The customers roared with delight.

'I have often wondered what thoughts, if any, pass through the minds of two good fighters who have fought each other twice before, just before they are to go to it again,' wrote Paul Gallico. 'Does each remember the pain the other caused him at some time or other in former battles? Have they a mental picture of the other's style? Do they remember their own mistakes and resolve not to make them again? It has always seemed to me that the more two men fought, the duller their contests should become, unless one grew to outclass the other on the way up or down. McLarnin and Ross can have few surprises for each other. Fighters never change their styles. They merely become more set in their ways, and perhaps more adept at delivering their goods.'

Their last three minutes in a ring together was a slam-bang finale with both fighters trying to dump each other for a convincing finish. But it was Jimmy who hogged the camera and copped more footage than Barney to take the nod for the round. When the last bell sounded both were still standing, their eyes glazed, their faces pink, and their bodies raw. They had been through three great fights together, forty-five rounds, and as one scribe remarked, they were 'closer than Clark Gable and Claudette Colbert in a last reel fadeout'.

Jimmy thought he'd won it, comfortably. Before waiting for the verdict he was handspringing his way back to Pop. The verdict was unanimous. The cards of the officials showed Dempsey gave Ross 5, McLarnin 3 and 7 even. Goldberg gave Ross 8, McLarnin 6 and 1 even. Le Cron handed Ross 9, McLarnin 4 and 2 even. A loud majority of the fans booed and, unusually, six of the sixteen New York boxing writers thought Jimmy won. 'I have been watching fights and reporting fights for thirty years,' wrote Nat Fleischer of *The Ring*. 'I cannot permit myself to fall in line with my colleagues ... Jimmy was less bruised than his opponent, finished fresher, stronger, and more full of fight than did Barney.'

'Al Jolson was hatless, Lou Holtz was tieless, and some of the boys that took the short end on McLarnin are shirtless,' remarked one scribe. New York Commissioner 'Bill' Brown, a famous referee in his day, and Lewis E. Lawes, warden of Sing Sing, went in for a bit of joshing over the telegraph wires after the decision.

Wired Lawes:

'Have three cells empty for officials who made that decision.'

Flashed Brown:

'Better clear out another cell stop felt same as officials did about it stop.'

Jimmy just stood still for a while. There was no mother to comfort him, but there was Pop, the ruddy-faced, iron-haired old fellow who took him off the streets and made a world's champion out of him. Pop who had stood by him, seen him rise and fall and rise again, and now had seen him beaten back again. Jimmy turned to the old man, flung his arms about his shoulders and buried his chin in his chest. But Pop needed more consoling than the beaten champion. 'Jimmy won nine of the fifteen rounds,' he declared. 'Look at him. There's nothing the matter with him. He's through fighting after tonight. I have the contract and after this I won't match him with anybody.'

'Now, Pop,' put in Jimmy, 'we'll go right along.'

'No,' he insisted. 'Why, Dempsey was in Ross's camp during the preparations. He picked Ross in the papers.'

Back in the dressing room, a dejected group of handlers surrounded the beaten champion and wondered how it all happened. 'It was a plain case of robbery,' stormed the red-faced Foster. 'I don't remember when we've had a rawer deal. You say the decision was unanimous? Well, if that's so I don't think I'll ever match the boy in New York again. What did they mean putting Dempsey in there to start with? He's been friendly with the Ross camp ever since Barney started train-ing. Mike Jacobs, the promoter, assured me Dempsey would not referee. I never would have let Jimmy go into the fight if he hadn't had his gloves on.'

'I think I won nine of the fifteen rounds tonight and had an even break in several others,' said Jimmy. 'Ross may have looked better than before, but he certainly didn't worry me as much as last September. I think we had better get out of here as soon as possible, go back to the Coast, and let Pop cool down a bit.'

Pop was pretty hot at everybody that night. He was bawling out the Boxing Commission, the judges, Jack Dempsey, and the big town in general. He said there was no justice for Jimmy in New York, though he would have to admit there was plenty of money. 'But Pop Foster can be excused to some extent because the old gentleman is so wrapped up in Jimmy that he can only see Jimmy's side of the argument – his James can do no wrong,' wrote Damon Runyon. 'The irascible Pop's temper had cooled by the time he got around to collecting his money, he was not so drastic in his declamations.' Jimmy's share was 40 per cent of the net gate of $118,894.21, which came to $42,526.52. Nursing a big purple shiner under his left eye and a small cut on his right brow, Jimmy said he would demand a fourth fight with Ross and he agreed with Pop that he was 'given the works'. 'I thought I beat Barney by a wide margin. I was amazed at the decision. It was the worst in my career.'

It was the familiar cry of 'We Was Robbed' emanating from a prizefighter's manager, but at least Pop was consistent. He stoutly maintained before the fight that he was going to be gypped and he remained in character when it was over by bawling that he had been. Branding referee Jack Dempsey as 'incompetent' and promoter Mike Jacobs as a 'double-crosser,' Pop spent the following morning storming about the curbstones of Broadway. 'I don't say the fight was crooked. There wasn't any big bank rolls about. The mobs weren't betting, so there was none of that old fixing in. I merely charge that Jack Dempsey had gone to Ross' camp, that he had been photographed with his arms around Barney, that he had drank with his pals and that he had picked Ross as the winner months in advance. Then he steps in the ring and tries his best to be neutral. It's against human nature. His seven rounds – BLANKS, mind you – speak for

themselves. Here is a world's championship fight and the referee can't make up his mind how half the battle came out. The
two judges did their best, but they are appointments of political stuffed shirts. They can't help but be influenced by the fact
that a popular Jewish idol is fighting before a stadium full of
Jewish people in the greatest Jewish city in the world against a
"foreigner" from Vancouver,' explained Pop.

Dempsey was reported to be very upset, especially with his old
rival Gene Tunney who gave a statement to the papers that Jimmy
should have got the decision. 'Dempsey doesn't say so but from
his attitude you can tell that he feels this was a bit unethical,'
reported one scribe. Dempsey was also furious with Pop. Sitting
in his restaurant the following day the old champion told reporters, 'Foster and I have been friends, but I draw the line when he
presumes to make me look bad in front of 30,000 people, just to
get an alibi. He knew our friendship could have no bearing in
the ring. He knew very well how I felt about McLarnin; he's one
of the finest boys I've ever known, a credit to boxing. Yet Foster
got up there in front of a lot of people and suggested in every way
possible that I was liable to be biased in favour of the other side.
Why, there just is no price on my prejudice. But I would have
cheerfully given a thousand dollars not to be in there at all. I
didn't want the job.'

Pop was hauled in front of the New York State Athletic
Commission to substantiate his claims. The old man was in an
unrepentant mood and used the hearing to make public his
suspicions on Dempsey's motives. He was taking on the newspapers, the promoters, the New York State Athletic Commission and the most popular man in America. 'Abe Lyman, the

orchestra leader, had a cash bet of $10,000 on Ross to win,' Pop told the commission. 'Dempsey is Lyman's best friend. All of Broadway knew that Lyman was trying to get the money down on Ross and Lyman, himself, bragged about his wager and his loyalty to Barney in Dempsey's own restaurant. Many other night club characters had heavy wagers on Ross but these others, although they, too, are friends of Dempsey, made bets of which I had no certain knowledge. I did know of Lyman's, however, and so when Dempsey went into the ring and raised Ross's hand he made a nice piece of money for at least one of his pals.'

Commissioner Phelan shut off Pop as he started to speak of the political connections of official Judge Abe Goldberg.

'Confine yourself to the facts please,' came the sharp order.

But Pop wasn't finished.

'I charge that Dempsey has had operations on his eyes in the past because of ring injuries. I charge that he did not undergo the regulation eye test required of all officials. His own card sets a record in scoring seven rounds blank.'

There was an embarrassed silence. It was then discovered that Pop was correct.

'However,' said Phelan, 'we will see that Dempsey takes the examination soon.'

Pop still wasn't finished.

'I have here clippings of syndicate articles signed by Dempsey and for which he was paid calling McLarnin "fat" and "old" and ridiculing him in various ways. These appeared in leading newspapers throughout the country as well as in New York. I have other clippings in which Dempsey acts as an expert and predicts McLarnin's loss with a guess that Jimmy might be knocked out.'

There was another embarrassed silence.

'I charge then that Dempsey could not humanly be neutral or score the fight without prejudice,' Pop concluded. 'I ask the verdict be reversed.'

He then turned on the promoter. Pointing his finger squarely at Mike Jacobs, Pop shouted:

'He told me Dempsey would not referee. He said, "Pop, Dempsey would charge me $1200 to work the fight and I won't pay it."'

Orchestra leader and friend of Dempsey's Abe Lyman was incandescent with rage. He offered to wager Pop $10,000 to $7,500 that Ross would beat his boy again – he was even prepared to let Pop referee. There was no McLarnin-Ross rematch in sight so Lyman sought retribution through the courts and he sued Pop for $500,000 in damages. Lyman's suit charged the old man with 'embracery and fraud'. The case was eventually settled out of court but the basis of the settlement was not disclosed. Pop told the press that Jimmy McLarnin would never contribute a dime toward Lyman's cash fortune. Willing or no, Jimmy did make a $1,200 deposit in Lyman's bank account.

And so the Jimmy McLarnin-Barney Ross story, one of the great trilogies in boxing came to an end. They'd made a huge amount of money together and their fights had assured both of them a place in any all-time great list. Some thought Ross had won all three fights, others were convinced that Jimmy deserved a trio of decisions where he got only one. And after forty-five rounds they were getting no nearer to the establishment of superiority. With their ring partnership safely and profitably dissolved Jimmy and Barney became close friends; sending each other postcards and birthday cards. Barney made several trips to the Coast where he and Jimmy would go drinking together. Jimmy had always hated the tags of 'Hebrew Scourge' and 'Jew Beater' anyway.

'I've done all the fighting I want to do and I don't think there's any special Valhalla to which old fighters go when they die,' Jimmy reflected in later years. 'But if there is Valhalla, and they've got boxing gloves there, there's one more fight I'd like to have. Barney Ross will be in the other corner. I hope he'll be right at his best and if I don't win, I'll gladly take the elevator down.'

CANZONERI IN THE GUEST ROOM

O ver a decade since they first met on a tennis court Lillian Cupit and Jimmy McLarnin were married at the home of the bride's parents at 1606 McLean Drive in Vancouver. It was a quiet ceremony with only members of their respective families present and, of course, Pop, who was Jimmy's best man. 'I've had more than my share of bally-hoo,' said Jimmy. 'I want to avoid all this rice and shoe-throwing. It is no occasion for a charivari. Just two people getting married.' Before leaving on the night boat for Victoria, the first leg of a honeymoon tour that would take them to Hawaii, Jimmy said that he would continue to fight.

'Why shouldn't I? It's my business. I should be a better man now because there's two of us.'

He managed to turn a deaf ear to a Honolulu promoter's attempt to arrange a fight for him during the honeymoon. Jimmy was offered $2,500 to fight with Kid Moro, a Filipino lightweight.

'I couldn't fight this trip for $25,000 plus $2,500. If you want to get up a series of fights, I'll be glad to come back later. But no fighting now. I'm on my honeymoon.'

The fight game had been good to Jimmy. He was wealthy almost beyond his hopes and he'd taken his family from the slums of Vancouver to a life of comfort. He'd assumed the role of provider as a boy and every month he sent $300 home to make sure they went for nothing. Pop moved in with Jimmy and Lillian at their new, beautiful Beverley Hills estate. They had the clothes, the cars and cash in the bank. Jimmy had become completely 'housebroken' since his marriage. He mowed the lawn, washed the dishes and tinkered with the family car. Jimmy occasionally trudged over to the Beverly Hills Athletic Club for a brisk workout where he punched the bags, skipped rope, sparred and shadow boxed. He and Pop also had a new interest, the management of Lee Ramage, a San Diego heavyweight who was on a comeback trail after having the misfortune to fight Joe Louis twice. Jimmy had all the money he needed, a new wife, a new home and old Pop living with him; yet he just couldn't walk away from boxing. Jimmy had everything except, it seemed, an inoculation against the germ, the virus, of the boxing business. It was too strong, too overpowering to resist. 'McLarnin has made enough money to be a comparatively wealthy man,' wrote Damon Runyon. 'However, it is only human nature to want a little more, even at the risk of ring damage.' Half a million dollars was always a lot of funds, even in sports, when the boom was roaring. But the trouble with half a million is that it shrinks and has to be constantly recharged like a battery.

'Like the rest of the mitten tossers, Jimmy can't stay retired,' wrote Braven Dyer in the *Los Angeles Times*. 'He's a pleasant-mannered, intelligent young man of twenty-nine and why he should wish to continue fighting is a puzzler. First thing he knows Jimmy will fool around too long, get a thumb stuck in his eye and lose the sight of an optic. Fidel La Barba, one-time champion, had hardly a mark on his face until some palookas jabbed him in the eye and today the local boy can't see out of one peeper. McLarnin has been exceedingly fortunate in his career and there is no reason for him to continue now that he has financial security for himself and his family.'

Jimmy had fought four times after a layoff of seven months or more, and lost every one of those fights – almost as many as he lost during all his other fights put together. A fourth McLarnin-Ross fight was discussed, but New York had seen this particular show three times already. It would be a great fight for any crowd that hadn't seen it, but as it was now taking Pop about a year to fully cool out and decide on Jimmy's next step, all talk of the match fizzled out. However there was another ethnic rivalry to exploit. Matches between Irish and Italian fighters were great draws in New York and the lightweight champion of the world happened to be Tony Canzoneri, and he was one of the greatest fighters around. He had been a titleholder three times in his career and he never failed to give the customers a run for their money. Canzoneri had been on Jimmy's trail for the last five years. When the Irishman was in his prime, and was knocking everybody dead in New York, Canzoneri clamoured for a match. 'Tony was obsessed with the idea he could whip him,' said Tom McArdle, the Garden matchmaker, 'and he still has that notion in his noggin. Frankly, I was afraid to match 'em, and I used to tell Canzoneri: "You're too nice a boy to get messed up by that Irish murderer. He'd kill you kid, so stay away from him." I still think so, but maybe Canzoneri knows more than the rest of us. Who can tell – until that bell rings?'

Canzoneri's battle-scarred kisser had haunted poster gazers for more than a decade and Jimmy had been fighting even longer. Now they'd fight for the first time as the two grand old men of the prizering in a ten round bout at Madison Square Garden. Both were past their prime and each was financially independent; they were worth about a million dollars in cash between them. Canzoneri owned a large farm near Marlboro, New York, and a haberdashery business near Broadway. Jimmy still held title to the soap factory in Oakland, real estate in various parts of the country and valuable fishing grounds in Alaska. 'Perhaps the old man with the limp and the little boy with the baby face will find the peace and the contentment they are seeking so zealously when and if Jimmy regains the title he lost to Ross last year,' mused one boxing writer. But even if Jimmy beat Canzoneri, the future held little for him in the welterweight division. Another match with Ross, even if Jimmy could get it, which was doubtful, wouldn't draw in New York, and there were no other welterweights who could pull in Jimmy's fee. Jimmy's star as the ring's glamour boy was on the wane. A young heavyweight sensation from Detroit was knocking over everybody who shared a ring with him, and Mike Jacobs who had taken over at the Garden after the death of Tex Rickard, sensed a new idol. That boy, of course, was Joe Louis. 'There's never room for two glamour boys,' said Pop, 'and when Louis came along, Jacobs forgot about Jimmy.'

The McLarnin-Canzoneri fracas was a Jim J. Johnston production. Johnston, like Pop, was Liverpool-Irish and along with the old man was one of the few who, even in that time, had the courage to resist the mob guys. 'Both boys [McLarnin and Canzoneri] are stout fellows, strong-hearted, not easy to defeat. But a tougher figure than either is the waxy Liverpudlian, James J. Johnston, the "boy bandit" of cauliflorida, for Jimmy has been down and bounced up again more often than the combined records of Phil Scott and Joe Beckett,' wrote Andy Lytle. 'This is Jimmy's promotion … The ageless little man with the derby cocked over an ear is forever being removed from his Garden job yet always he hangs in there doing the best he can.'

Pop and Jimmy, just as they had for the best part of a decade, set off for New York, but this time there was another person in the party. Lillian was going to watch Jimmy fight for the first time even though she didn't want her husband to fight and she heartily disliked fights and fighters. 'Lillian worried about me almost as much as my mother did and I'd been telling her for eleven years, ever since she was thirteen and I was seventeen, that the only difference between being a boxer and being a taxi driver or an insurance salesman was that the boxer earned his money a lot easier,' Jimmy recalled. 'I didn't believe this myself and don't believe it now, but the night I fought Canzoneri I was hoping to make it look that way to Lillian.'

Reports reached New York from California that Jimmy was a bum, all washed-up and hog fat, that his recent marriage had caused him to lose all interest in boxing, and that he was taking on Tony for one last soft touch before settling into permanent retirement. A year of quiet domesticity, far from the frontline trenches had done him no good, and in practice tilts against inferior opposition Jimmy displayed none of the old skills. 'Hard training as a fighter gets older seems to speak of the dull deaths of the brightest cells in all the favourite organs,' wrote Norman Mailer, 'old fighters react to training like beautiful women to washing floors.' Jimmy took several powerful lefts and one smashing right hand on the kisser from sparring partner Paris Apice at the Pioneer Gymnasium. 'If a fair-to-middlin' pug like Apice can reach the McLarnin pan, they reason such a sharp-shooter as the lightweight czar can certainly do the same thing,' commented one scribe.

'Where have I heard those things before?' asked Barney Ross when asked about Jimmy looking bad in the gymnasium. 'Oh, yeah. I remember now – that's just what they used to say about Jimmy before each of my three fights with him! Well, don't be misled by such rumours. That McLarnin is pretty cute and his manager, Pop Foster spends his spare time wising up coyotes. Jimmy will probably come bouncing into that ring full of zing and zip and look like Bold Venture did coming down that home stretch. That's what he used to do with me. He's a miracle man, that Mick. I don't know how he does it, but he can lay off a year at a clip and still keep his stuff. I can't and I know few other fighters that can, either, except McLarnin.'

Jimmy tilted back on a battered stool, rested his rumpled head against a wall and breathed heavily as Pop rubbed his aching leg muscles and tugged at the laces of his ring shoes. He used the thick thumb of a ruby-red boxing glove to stop the perspiration trickling down between his eyes. Jimmy had always been one of those 'yes and no, but don't quote me' guys in the past but now he was different. 'I shall not only whip Tony Canzoneri, but I hope to knock him out – probably in five or six rounds. I have never been so sure of anything in my life. A lot of folks around New York, I understand, are betting on Tony to beat me. They'd better save their money. I am very fond of Tony. He is a grand little fellow and has been a great credit to boxing. He'll go down in ring history, along with Benny Leonard, as one of the greatest lightweight champions who ever lived. But he'll find out that he overmatched himself when he signed to fight me!'

'As for that old myth about matrimony ruining a fighter, they'll have to show me. My domestic life has been very quiet. Mrs McLarnin and I don't care for the gaiety and whoopee stuff. I know plenty of unwed boxers who play the cabarets and night-clubs – the Maxie Rosenblooms, the Harry Grebs, and the rest of 'em. Do you mean to say I'm worse off than them?'

Tony Canzoneri had passed the previous year in a maze of ring encounters and he'd belted over all who crossed his path. He looked good in his training skirmishes and the unexpected dash of the gnarled Italian caused the odds against him to 'dip like a Coney Island shoot-the-shoot'. When he heard that Jimmy had invited his schoolma'am bride to attend the fight, he sat right down and wrote a letter to young Mrs Mac, which read:

I understand you've never seen a prizefight. Well, you won't see one when your husband fights me. It'll be a massacre and you'll see the hired hands scrape your sweetie pie off the canvas after a few rounds – if he lasts that long! I also under-stand that when Jimmy married you he told you he was a fighter. Well, I do not wish to destroy this illusion, so you'd better stay home with a good book. I shall try to maim Jimmy as painlessly as possible and I will do my best not to disfigure

his handsome features, for your sake.
Sincerely, T. Canzoneri.

Jimmy dashed off a telegram to Canzoneri at his Marlboro,
New York farm:

I am taking my wife to her first fight because she has never
seen one before, and I want to break her in gently. I assured
her it wouldn't be much of a fight, that we'd get away early
and be able to catch a movie. I hear that your father expects to
sit in your corner. He is a fine old gentleman and I am very
fond of him, but I understand he has a weak heart and is
easily excited. I would advise you to keep him away, lest the
shock of seeing his son knocked out affect his uncertain
health.
Sincerely, J. McLarnin.

Jimmy and Tony had always been perfect little gentlemen in
the past and neither of them had ever resorted to cheap shots to
sell a fight. 'They've never been wounded by cap pistols in radio
stations, they've never rescued beautiful dolls from drowning,
and they've never sung those phoney hymns of hate on the eve of
battle,' wrote Jack Miley in the *New York Daily News*. 'Hovering
in the background during this "acrimonious" exchange between
the fighters was the derby-hatted, pouter-pigeon named James J.
Johnston, the Garden's matchmaker. "Tony says you're a
tramp," Jimmy whispered in McLarnin's ear; then he dashed off
to a long-distance phone call to tell Canzoneri that "The Irishman says he never saw a Wop he couldn't snap like a stick of

spaghetti!" His good-will work done, Mr Johnston rubbed his hands in Puckish glee and chortled, "I hope those guys are good and mad at each other!" Could it be that this dove of peace had been purposely stirring up the gladiators? I wouldn't know.'

Although the boys had been speaking of the match as a 'battle of the wooden soldiers' as they termed a contest between old timers, the fight was like a return to the days of the fistic gold rush. The whole town hopped up over the prospects of a Pier Sixer. Even though they were two ring relics meeting in the faded lustre of their glittering careers, the scrap generated such feverish agitation and interest in the 'Big Burg' that a capacity crowd of 18,000 jammed its way into the Garden. Except for the Joe Louis-Paulino Uzcudun heavyweight bout, Canzoneri and McLarnin drew the biggest indoor gate the Garden had enjoyed since Jimmy stopped Benny Leonard in 1932. Every Irish and Italian boxing fan with the price was there, not to mention the Jewish ringworms who had never stopped hoping for the day when they would see Jimmy, despoiler of Leonard, Goldstein and Terris, grovel on the Garden canvas. The fight also saw the return of former Mayor Jimmy Walker to the Garden to see his first fight since his return from Europe where he fled to after being forced from office on corruption charges.

Tony Canzoneri wanted his 'lucky' corner – on the Fiftieth Street side of the Garden. Pop, even though Jimmy cared not for either corner, insisted that he, too, wanted that corner, so a coin was flipped. Canzoneri won the toss. A new bride took her ringside seat and prayed that her Jimmy might land one of those blows that had crushed Singer and Terris. Then the two men stepped under the arc lights for the best fight that had been seen in the Garden in years. Barney Ross paused to talk a minute with Jimmy after being introduced to the crowd. Canzoneri turned towards his corner after the fighters had taken their instructions and smacked into the microphone hanging down over the centre of the ring, cutting him over one eye. It was quite a bang and Sammy Goldman, Canzoneri's manager, said after the fight that it caused his charge to forget his corner instructions and to go out and fight Jimmy in just the way to get nailed. And Jimmy duly obliged.

Canzoneri was nearly stiffened in the first frame and the customers were reaching for their hats and heading for the exits. Jimmy slugged the iron-jawed Italian with enough lethal blows to stop a dozen ordinary guys and the fight looked pitifully one-sided, just as the experts had suggested it would be. A left cut an oozing red ridge into the bridge of his flat nose and Tony was sent staggering to his corner at the end of the session and it didn't seem possible that he could go another three minutes with Jimmy. But the blood was swabbed off, the split patched up, he was doused with water and his seconds talked to him. Tony came out of his corner at the bell for the second just as if he'd bounced off a chopping block. 'He caught me coming in with a terrific left hook in the first round,' said Canzoneri. 'For a few seconds I didn't think I could stand up under such a vicious shower of blows. When I was able to walk to my corner unaided, however, I figured I could win.'

Over in the other corner Pop was patting Jimmy's back.

'That was wonderful,' Lillian remarked. 'Isn't Jimmy marvellous? I feel so sorry for poor Tony.'

Jimmy sent another sledgehammer left for Canzoneri's open

jaw in the second. But as he did the Italian stepped inside and caught him with a short hook right on the temple. Lillian leaped up from her seat, hand to mouth, terror in her eyes. 'I can't tell you how this punch felt,' Jimmy tried to explain. 'It's the only punch that ever hit me so hard I didn't feel it. The next thing of which I have personal knowledge is not easy to describe. It was less an event than a sensation. I had a vague feeling of far-off pounding and darkness, not particularly unpleasant but baffling, something like coming half awake in a dark Pullman berth and going to sleep again because it's too much effort to remember where you are. I remember too that I was thinking vaguely of Lillian and reminding myself that we were either going to get married or were already married. This is my total recollection of the last half of the second round and of the five rounds after that. Then Pop was leaning over me in the corner. When he told me I was going into the eighth I asked him how many times I'd been on the floor.

'None,' Pop said.

'Can I still win?' I asked him.

'If you take the last three,' he said.

As he sat in his corner at the end of the seventh Jimmy was oblivious to the veteran reporters in the press row who were shouting for the referee to stop it along with the others who had paid $85,763.50 to see the battle. He was unaware that he was taking the beating of his life. Jimmy was an open target but Tony couldn't finish him. 'He was in a daze,' said Foster. 'He was fighting entirely by instinct. I knew Jimmy was tough, but I didn't know he was that tough. I never saw him take so many punches on the jaw.'

Somehow or other Jimmy managed to win the eighth but it was a temporary reprise and he was beaten 'from hell to breakfast all the rest of the way'. They came out for the ninth and it seemed that Jimmy was stronger and fresher and he was piling up points just as he had in the eighth. But Canzoneri had been coasting, saving up for a final effort and the pounding that Jimmy took had everyone in the Garden marvelling at his durability. They were both very tired and were measuring each other for a knockout blow in the last minute of the round when Canzoneri cut loose with a left hook to the jaw that dazed Jimmy. The lightweight champion leaped through the air with a sizzling right cross that caught Jimmy flush on the jaw and sent him staggering across the ring and into the ropes. Jimmy bounced back like an acrobat and Canzoneri flew at him with both hands. The Irishman dropped his gloves limply to his sides. Canzoneri slugged him with lefts, rights, lefts and rights that had Jimmy reeling around like a drunk. He was out on his feet and Tony knew it well, as did Lillian sitting just a few feet away. Canzoneri threw everything he had and pegged away at a helpless target. Lillian turned away, Jimmy's eyes closed and his head snapped back so often it seemed his neck would break. Canzoneri never quit swinging and the crowd went wild. The bell saved Jimmy; another punch would have nailed him to the canvas for keeps.

'Not since the Eighth Avenue abattoir opened its doors for plain and fancy skull-busting a decade ago have the clients got such a run for their money as Tony and Jim gave them,' wrote Jack Miley in the *New York Daily News*. 'The frenzied ringsiders spent half of their time standing on their chairs, women screamed hysterically and several of 'em fainted dead away. Men threw hats in the smoke-filled air and pummelled their neighbours excitedly as the Broadway Wop and the Vancouver Harp ploughed through their Pier Sixer.'

The fight ended with two fighting men still on their feet and swinging. They were both badly battered. Jimmy's face was so swollen around the left eye that at first the doctors thought his jaw was broken. As was usually the case when two game veterans who couldn't remember all the things they used to know, got together, both men finished well busted up. They had cuts and contusions to mend. Canzoneri looked the worse and Jimmy felt the worse. In their younger days, they wouldn't have bruised so easily. But Tony and Jimmy each drew down $22,658.12 for beating the other up in a fight that brought good times back to the 'House that Tex' built.

'Fighting once a year is tough going,' said Jimmy and he conceded he 'ought to quit' but he wasn't as convincing about it as Pop. 'I will insist Jimmy quit the ring. He should never have taken this fight. I was against it.'

Pop shook his head dejectedly. 'What's the use of talking. It's all over now.'

It was very close to a sell-out, a distinct novelty in those days for the Garden that had taken to asking the public to tell it how to fill it up. One answer seemed to be a McLarnin-Canzoneri fight and the management need have no worry about what to do with their air-cooled Garden on any summer evening they cared to name. It only took a few hours for Foster-McLarnin Inc to put all thoughts of retirement away once more. 'A saddened, lonely old man with a limp, Pop Foster, slipped quietly from

New York yesterday where he painfully watched "his boy" Jimmy McLarnin, accept one of the most brutal beatings of his long and illustrious career in clout from truculent Tony Canzoneri,' reported Jack Singer in the *Los Angeles Times*. 'The old man with the limp scoffed at reports that "his boy" – who had whipped eleven world's champions, more than any boxer that ever fought – would never again lace on a glove for ring combat.'

'Jimmy's not through fighting,' croaked Pop in a husky voice. His tired eyes flashed. 'Jimmy's only twenty-eight and he's too great a fighter to pass out and leave behind the memory of such a bad fight as he made against Canzoneri.'

'I never felt precisely like cheering when I lost a fight, but after I read the newspaper accounts of this one, I figured it was some-thing, at least, to be still breathing,' wrote Jimmy. He was still a month on the right side of his twenty-ninth birthday and this beating was the best of all reasons for quitting. He'd always promised himself that when he started losing he'd quit. But then Jimmy remembered the times he'd thought, either seriously or idly, of quitting before. Once, way back in Los Angeles, when he'd started to grow too fast and gone sour. Once, after a bad beating by Petrolle. Again after losing the second decision to Ross. And now the beating from Canzoneri. Each of those times he'd wrestled it out with himself and decided that, no – he had to give the crowds something better than that to remember him by. Lillian wanted him to quit right there and then.

'What?' replied Jimmy, 'and have Canzoneri living in our guest room for the rest of our lives?'

AT THE GARDEN
WITHOUT POP

'**M**r McLarnin's killer instinct has been detected and interpreted in various ways,' wrote John Lardner. 'Some of the boys see it in his blazing blue eye, alight with the thirst for blood. Others note its existence in "his strong right arm, sudden as a flash of lightning and dangerous as the bite of a cobra." A third school of thought reads the killer instinct in "every move of Jimmy's body as he stalks his prey in the ring."

'"Killer instinct" is a fancy phrase in his case, as it is with most professional or amateur pugilists. Mr McLarnin fights strongly, gamely, and sometimes with a good deal of abandon, but he admits himself that he never exercises the homicidal impulse upon anything larger than a Hudson River Valley mosquito.

'"I'm not exactly a killer," said Mr McLarnin the other day. "I just like to fight."

'This may be an accurate diagnosis, but there are times when you doubt very much whether Mr McLarnin is even deriving enjoyment from his profession.'

There were no blaring bands, no batteries of photographers when Mr and Mrs McLarnin dropped out of the azure, sunny Southern California skies. Jimmy was not returning in the familiar role of a conquering hero. Pop was there, rising at 6am and nervously waiting two hours for the giant TWA Sky Chief carrying his precious boy to descend from the vaults of the heavens. 'Sure I'm going to fight again,' said Jimmy in a quiet, self-assured voice. 'I'd like to meet Tony in a return fight. I think I deserve another chance. I know more about Tony's style now and I'm sure I'll know how to handle him next time out.' They hustled to a waiting automobile and Jimmy and Lillian spent the afternoon shopping for a new home. Jimmy had laid off too long Pop admitted. 'You have to keep boxing to be a boxer. Jimmy didn't like to do ring work after he got in the money. He softened up. But I believe he can whip Canzoneri if he's willing to dig in and really work in the gymnasium.'

'For one, I hope the rematch never comes off,' wrote Paul Lowry in the *Los Angeles Times*. 'Jimmy McLarnin is too nice a kid to get his brains addled by being made a punching block. He has made good money from the ring, saved it and should never fight again. It was a stunning blow for his young wife to see her husband cruelly hacked and cut about the face by Tony Canzoneri's butcher blows. It was her first fight and her last, she says. After the bout Jimmy locked himself in an apartment and refused to see anybody for two days, even his wife. It was that bad.'

Pop and Jimmy spent the summer of 1935 preparing for Canzoneri and managing their heavyweight prospect, Lee Ramage. It had been a frustrating time for Ramage and a proposed fight with Frank Rowsey was postponed several times, prompting Pop to claim a $250 appearance forfeit from Rowsey as stipulated in the contract. When they eventually met in the ring Ramage gave Rowsey a whipping. Pop crossed the ring, his face wreathed in smiles, and walked over to Braven Dyer of the *Los Angeles Times*. 'What about that $250 forfeit money you collected from Rowsey?' Dyer asked. Pop squinted and burst out: 'Rowsey's a nice boy and I'll come up to your office with a cheque for him. He can have his share of the money back. But not his manager. We had a perfect right to the money. We lost eleven weeks waiting for this fight. But I understand Rowsey is broke and he can have the money back if he comes up to your office.' True to his word Pop dropped in with the money and an extra fifty bucks on top as a present from Jimmy. Dyer held the cheque for Rowsey, who read about his windfall in the newspaper. Could this be the meanest man in boxing? Parsimonious Pop was largely a creation of the boxing writers who expected to be paid for publicising a fighter. The old man wasn't about to give a cent of his boy's money to a scribe and as Jimmy would say, he was a very generous man, but he wasn't a fool.

On the strength of the severe drubbing he gave Jimmy just five months previously, Canzoneri was a 6 to 5 favourite to repeat. But even though he was given the decision, the fight with the Irishman had damaged Canzoneri. He lost his lightweight title to Lou Ambers in his next fight and the boys believed the gruelling scrap with Jimmy had put Tony on the downward path. Jimmy had battered the Italian's nose so badly that forty-eight stitches were required and Canzoneri also suffered a badly slashed lip in training that required the rematch to be post-poned. After the stitches were removed Canzoneri's doctor and handlers agreed that the three days rest that the postponement had afforded would leave the little Italian in perfect shape.

Jimmy entered the ring looking like the pink-cheeked boy who came swinging out of Vancouver ten years previously. Grantland Rice described him as 'the youngest-looking old-timer in the trade'. Canzoneri was knocked down by a right to the jaw in the second round but when Jimmy saw that Tony was not going to stay down, and that Tony would keep swinging his own big right hand, the Irishman turned cagey. He reversed his style, put the right hand in dry dock and left-hooked Canzoneri into a blood clot. Jimmy used nothing but his left and slashed it at Tony's face at will. It cut a red gash over Canzoneri's right eye and it opened the old wound on the bridge of his nose. 'At the end of five rounds Tony's face was a circular mask, the colour of burgundy wine,' reported John Lardner. Jimmy won every round but the fourth and the tenth and had the fight under control all the time. He was fast and his jab was lightning and slashed Canzoneri unmercifully, sometimes four to six in a row connected before one missed. 'In one round I counted thirty-two lefts to Tony's face,' wrote Nat Fleischer. 'No wonder poor Canzoneri's face looked like raw beef!' The former lightweight champion's nose and eyes and mouth were gashed and blood streamed down his cheeks. Jimmy's chest was blood-covered, but it was Tony's blood. Jimmy got his revenge as well as a large piece of change and won the unanimous decision of the referee and judges. 'It was a canny business fight, worth some $15,000 to the winner, and Jim fought it like a businessman closing a deal in oil,' wrote Lardner. 'That was all he needed or intended to do. The firm of McLarnin and Foster is famous for cold, commercial candour. Both partners knew Tony was not the Canzoneri of old, so they took the little fellow coolly and calmly and collected.'

His win, and the manner in which he won, had once more made Jimmy a contender for the welterweight championship and he lingered in town to await developments. 'I don't know what I'll do,' Jimmy said. 'Ross? Well I'd like to fight him again. The others? Well, we'll see.' Garden matchmaker James J. Johnston was seeking to arrange a future attraction. Jimmy's performance in beating Canzoneri had fight managers scrambling to match their fighters against the Irishman once more. A fourth meeting between Jimmy and Barney Ross for the welterweight title was one option and a fight with Lou Ambers, the lightweight king, was another. It was an old story, but it was one that never failed to catch the public fancy in New York. Jimmy McLarnin fighting the lightweight champion in an overweight match at Madison Square Garden. 'And just a few words about those critics who are continually throwing the harpoon into two fine characters in the field of fistiana, Jimmy McLarnin and his manager, Pop Foster, because of the many fights the Vancouver Irishman has had with men lighter than he is,' commented *The Ring*. 'In all fairness to McLarnin and his mentor, it must be admitted that at no time in his honourable career, has Jimmy, through Pop, gone after those fights. It was always the other way. Whenever a manager figured that the bankroll of his fighter and himself was rapidly disappearing, he sought a McLarnin fight and naturally, Pop Foster, always eager to accept any contest that would benefit his boy financially, accepted the defi. Then why blame McLarnin and Foster?'

There wasn't a huge amount of weight difference between the two men. And just as he was against Canzoneri, Jimmy was dazzling. Lou Ambers fought the Irishman off his feet in the early rounds; he weaved and bobbed and tried to circle away from his opponent's right but then Jimmy started to catch him with lefts to set him up. Ambers showed great resilience in standing up to a storm of rights that Jimmy showered on his chin. The lightweight champion fought gamely, but was behind from the sixth round and needed a knockout to win. Jimmy landed a stiff left in the sixth that started blood flowing from Ambers' nose. It was his best round. He punched Ambers groggy and almost out from a right to the chin. He followed up but couldn't land solidly and the Italian stayed on his feet. Just when the ringworms thought him about washed up after more than a decade of warring, Jimmy stepped out and gave Ambers, the young 'Herkimer Hurricane' such a battering that the 10,229 customers wondered what was holding the lightweight champion up. After Jimmy's tri-hammer blows to the head had slowed Ambers up, the 'Hurricane,' usually one of the most elusive targets in the ring, became just a blood-splattered punching bag.

Consecutive victories over Tony Canzoneri and Lou Ambers in the space of just a few months had established Jimmy as the strongest candidate and best drawing card for a welterweight title scrap with Barney Ross. Just a week after Jimmy had beaten Ambers, Ross had retained the welterweight title by beating Izzy Jannazzo in fifteen rounds. Only 8,484 customers netted $22,000 to see the battle. Ross' handlers immediately balked at an order by the New York boxing commission that Barney stake his championship in a fight against Ceferino Garcia, pointing out that Jimmy McLarnin was the next logical opponent for the champion. Once more, Jimmy was the biggest draw in town and the boys said he looked better than ever. There was talk of two more fights in the next twelve months and Jimmy told one scribe that he wouldn't consider laying away the gloves until he felt that intangible something that warns athletes they are approaching the end of the road. But while Jimmy seemed to be turning the clock back, time was catching up with Pop and his rheumatism was getting much worse. Pop was in Jimmy's corner against Ambers but he couldn't get into the ring after the final bell because his legs kept buckling pitifully. He was finding the travelling and the training grind much harder, and could Jimmy really see himself walking down the aisles of the Garden without Pop walking beside him?

Pop and Jimmy were still flirting with a return to the ring. There was an offer to meet Barney Ross in a welterweight title scrap at the Chicago Stadium but there wasn't going to be enough money outside New York to lure Jimmy. Freddie Steele, the new middleweight champion, was another option but Pop was never going to take a match against a heavier opponent. There was talk of a match with Milt Aron at one of the Chicago ball parks but was Milt Aron enough of a draw? Eventually, Jimmy nailed his gloves to the wall. He left the ring with $500,000 and there were some countries that didn't have that much money in 1936. Frugal Jimmy and his even more frugal pilot had all the dough they could ever spend and, besides, they never spent any. The tax deal was also pretty good. One year Jimmy made $105,000 and paid just $7,500 in income tax without the aid of sharpshooters to find the loopholes.

'Pop and I didn't have a penny when we started out,' said Jimmy. 'Now, Pop has more money than Fort Knox I guess ... I often think of what he told me: that, in boxing, it's not how much you make, it's how much you save.'

Though there was no fighter whose style exhibited more clearly a passion for his profession, Jimmy never enjoyed the fighting, though he did hate losing. The moments he spent inside the square of ropes were not the ones that he liked or remembered with any pleasure. It was hard work; nothing else.

'There was no sense quitting when I was winning, and to judge from my past performances I had too much pride or bullheadedness to quit when I was losing,' wrote Jimmy. 'It's on precisely that kind of logic that all those horseplayers die broke and that far too many boxers, good ones included, end up hearing noises that other people don't hear. Both Pop and I had salted away enough money in annuities to keep us for the rest of our lives. We talked it over – Pop clinched it. His reasoning was a little different from mine, but it came out at the same place. He told me that he thought my last two fights had been among the sharpest I'd ever fought and if I really wanted to fight at least once every six months I could go on without any fear of being hurt for another two or three years. But there's only two reasons why a man should fight, Pop said. One's because he likes it, and you stopped liking it a long time ago. The other's for money, and you know you don't need money.'

'A WONDERFUL THING
TO HAVE BEHIND
YOU'

On the morning of 11 May 1937 a blind peanut peddlar was up in front of a Police Court in Washington DC charged with selling his wares in a restricted area in the park behind the White House. He appeared in court with his two-year-old German shepherd dog, which he got two months previously from the Seeing Eye training school. Felix Destrito, a former flyweight champion of the Philippines, told the court he could not support his wife and eight children unless he went through the parks selling peanuts. Destrito said he had fought under the name of Young Aguinaldo against Fidel La Barba, Tony Canzoneri and Jimmy McLarnin. He lost his sight, he said, from continuous beatings. After hearing the story the judge took the man's personal bond and advised him to see the District Commissioners about getting a licence to sell in parks.

By then, Jimmy was through at the age of twenty-nine, when most men were just about beginning a long, useful career. That was the fight game and that's why Pop fought for every dime Jimmy could command. It was a rough racket, but Pop made sure Jimmy got paid. And big. A prizefighter's days were limited and if he couldn't earn sufficient to put aside when he's in the game, he'd find very little opportunity to do so after the fighting was over. A lot of people thought Pop had a deep affection for nothing but dollar bills, but those who knew the McLarnin-Foster combine knew better. Pop would have gone down into the deep regions of the damned for Jimmy. He felt every glove that hammered onto his boy in every fight he ever took. 'These Damon and Pythias combinations add a kindly touch to an unkindly game,' wrote Jack Kofoed. 'There have been none more perfect than the friendship of Pop Foster and Jimmy McLarnin.'

In those days, a manager took one-third of the purse and on a $60,000 take that was a good chunk. Then the mobsters got in the game and cornered all the champions. The honest guys couldn't buy a title fight. 'McLarnin,' wrote Damon Runyon, 'was the best-managed fighter in my experience.' Pop was a shrewd, penny-saving old fellow, who was bred in a different school. He made Jimmy take care of his money and he kept the mobsters from homing in. They pulled out of a title fight once in New York when they were warned not to win. Prizefighters from the slums suddenly made rich bet thousands of dollars on horse races or crap games because they couldn't realise that this was really money. It had come too suddenly and too easily. A man with a substantial business would have hesitated and possibly would have called in his lawyers before deciding to risk as much on a far more conservative deal.

'Just one more battle!' was the usual cry of ring veterans, especially those who had held the upper hand for so long and when

Father Time beckoned, they refused to heed the call. Jimmy hadn't gone the way of most champions. 'He's almost an advertisement for a cruel sport,' wrote Jim Murray. The smell of the resin hadn't been too alluring for him to ignore. 'Boxing's a very hazardous business and I'd always felt that anybody that goes into it for fun has to be out of their entire cotton pickin' mind,' Jimmy reflected. 'But then I started to make money: when I was nineteen I had $100,000 in the bank – so all of a sudden I realised boxing is for me and I put my entire mind into it. There was no romance in it. It was a tough, tough ordeal, but as the years went by and I got to know boxing, it wasn't as hard as I thought it would be, although it isn't the easiest game in the world. I'm glad I was a boxer now, in something like the same way that Steve Brodie must have been glad when he jumped off Brooklyn Bridge. It's a wonderful thing to have behind you.'

The only fighting Jimmy did in 1937 was in his movie debut in the Spencer Tracy picture, *Big City*. Jimmy, alongside Jack Dempsey, 'Man Mountain' Dean, Jim Jeffries, Maxie Rosenbloom and Jackie Fields, played the part of an old prizefighter who battles it out with a bunch of gangsters on a wharf. Jimmy admitted that he 'couldn't act for nuts', but he understood why so many boxers and wrestlers of his generation went into the movies. The movie people were big fight fans and every Friday night at the Hollywood Legion Stadium was celebrity night. 'You had the Marx Brothers, the Ritz Brothers, George Raft, Al Jolson, Joan Crawford, Joan Blondell and of course Mae West was a biggie. She always had a fighter or wrestler as a bodyguard,' Jimmy recalled. So the filmmakers put their heroes into the movies usually with bit parts, or as extras or stunt men. At that time most of the stunt men in Hollywood had been fighters. 'By any other names, except possibly those of Luise Rainer and Spencer Tracy, the Capitol's *Big City* would be Class B melodrama and nothing more,' wrote the *New York Times* movie reviewer. 'It is casual, superficially diverting, singularly unimportant stuff.'

But superficially diverting and singularly unimportant stuff was just what Jimmy was looking for in 1937. Pop moved into a bachelor apartment in Hollywood while Lillian and Jimmy settled about a twenty-minute drive away in Glendale. Jimmy returned to live in luxury in the city from which he and Pop were driven out by those in control of boxing who insisted the lad, still in his teens, was washed up. His biggest regret was that he missed an education. Jimmy scarcely finished grammar school but after boxing he toyed with the idea of sitting a few medical examinations. He figured that with the knowledge he gained in the ring on diet and training he could put it to valuable use. But Jimmy would be at least forty by the time he finished that so those plans were shelved. He organised a soccer team in Los Angeles and became a member of a 'Sunshine Club', a group of Hollywood socialites with season tickets for the Los Angeles Rams on the sunny side of the Coliseum. Jimmy and Bob Hope were the club's first members. And every week Pop Foster came over for Sunday dinner.

Over the next few years, Jimmy became a gentleman golfer who did all his fighting on a bridge table. He became a member at the Lakeside Club, close to Warner Brothers and Universal, and spent his days teeing off with the likes of Bob Hope, Humphrey Bogart, Fred Astaire and Bing Crosby. He joined the hole-in-one club when he shot an ace on the 180-yard twelfth. His pals were movie stars, politicians, guys who ran movie chains and guys who ran the railroads. And Jimmy never had to fold a hand to any of them. He became a regular at Crosby's annual clambake at Pebble Beach and his Hollywood pals got him a few movie roles. The only visible scar on his face was a white line across the bridge of his nose that he got playing golf with Johnny Weismuller. The Tarzan of the movies swung his putter in disgust after missing a shot – and popped Jimmy right on the nose. Jimmy played against Howard Hughes occasionally and told of a group of gorgeous Hollywood starlets known as H.H.'s Harem. One time Hughes, Jimmy and a group of others were putting for money. 'I won't say Hughes cheated to beat people, but there on Hughes's balcony above us appeared one of those girls, naked as a grape. We all six-putted,' Jimmy recalled.

During one round at the Lakeside Club Jimmy was talking boxing with Humphrey Bogart. At the seventeenth tee, he was asked about one of his early fights at the Oakland Arena in which he had knocked an opponent out with a stomach punch.

'That's impossible,' Bogart insisted. 'Nobody can knock a man out with a blow to the stomach.'

Jimmy claimed that it had been a stomach-blow. Bogart repeated that it couldn't be done and wagered Jimmy $500 that he couldn't knock him out with one to the stomach. Jimmy shrugged and agreed to the bet. Bogart braced himself. Jimmy hit him in the stomach, Bogart's knees buckled; he collapsed, and lost the $500. Jimmy always maintained that a good punch in the stomach was worth two on the snout.

One of his old adversaries was still fighting for real. Although only twenty-eight years old, Barney Ross had fought almost three hundred times by the time he stepped through the ropes to meet Henry Armstrong in May 1938. During the last three rounds, Armstrong pounded away at the exhausted Ross, and the crowd pleaded with the referee to stop the fight, but he respected Ross's wish to end his career never having failed to go the distance. As he left the ring the sportswriter Grantland Rice asked, 'Why didn't you quit?' To which Barney answered, 'A champ's got the right to choose the way he goes out.' Henry Armstrong had replaced Barney Ross as champion and it didn't take long for talk of a match with Jimmy McLarnin to surface. Rumour had it that Jimmy was seriously considering a comeback and a whack at Armstrong and the welterweight title. The ballyhoo had it that Jimmy believed he had a punch that would short-circuit the human dynamo in the apparently tireless 'Homicide' Henry. 'I was offered $50,000 to make a comeback and fight Henry Armstrong,' Jimmy recalled. 'I was playing golf with Bob Hope and I was at the tee at Lakeside when Pop brought over a telegram from Mike Jacobs for a $50,000 guarantee. And that was a lot of money in those days. But I said, "Oh Pop, I don't think I want to go through all that again." And Bob Hope looked at the telegram and said, "Are you going to turn down all that money to fight a guy? I'd fight him."'

The Armstrong story helped publicise Jimmy's latest movie, *The Crowd Roars*. The star of the picture, Robert Taylor, described Jimmy as a swell trouper, and said that he did very well both in the role he was given to play and as a technical advisor. In later years Pop admitted that he secretly wanted Jimmy to take that fight. 'Armstrong's style was just Jimmy's meat. A win over

Armstrong would have been a real ending for Jimmy. But Jimmy didn't want to fight any more. After you get mixing with that Hollywood bunch, things come a bit too easy, like.' And old Pop didn't like things that came 'a bit easy'.

When war broke out four of Jimmy's brothers were under arms at a military base in Vancouver. Jimmy did his bit by being a 'man behind the man behind the gun'. Even though he was still independently wealthy, Jimmy took a job with Aeronautical Specialties in Hollywood, a war plant making fighting equipment for Uncle Sam. 'If I can't fight I'm not going to make money supplying those who do,' said Jimmy. He refused to take a penny from war work done for the government. During the war years one generation of the McLarnins made way for another. On 2 June 1939 Jimmy became the father of an eight-pound four-ounce girl, Grace Ellen. Two more baby daughters soon followed; Jean and Nancy. But on 8 February 1940 Jimmy's mother, Mary Ferris McLarnin, died.

The McLarnins of Vancouver were once described as boister-ous, wayward, unruly and lovably mischievous. 'I drove Jimmy to his home as he returned from one of his successful eastern campaigns,' wrote Andy Lytle of the *Toronto Star*. 'I didn't go beyond the portals. When we drove up to the McLarnin home it seemed to me that a city was welcoming its hero. It was the McLarnins, deliriously happy at the sight of him. They screeched in unison as he appeared. Jimmy bounded out of the car and was in the embrace of at least half a dozen grimy-faced brothers and sisters before his mother could get half way down the steps. In another instant she was in his robust arms, both entirely oblivious to the curious stares of a gawking neighbourhood. Of all the pictures I retain of Jimmy McLarnin, I like that one best.'

He had a lifetime annuity of $1,000 per month, a $25,000 mansion in Glendale, Califonia, and a growing family. Most people who had saved the best part of half a million dollars earned in fifteen years of hard fighting in the ring would have been content to spend the rest of their lives living comfortably off the interest, but not Jimmy. Golfing and gardening and an occasional business deal were not enough. He had been out of the game a couple of years and it had been a while since the last offer for a comeback. Jimmy talked a shrewd business deal and he admitted that some of his so-called friends had clipped his pocketbook with a sneak punch or two especially on sixteen lots he bought in New York City. Then late in 1944, just as the war as drawing to a close, Jimmy embarked on his most ambitious business venture when he bought a precision tool manufacturing company from Howard Hughes.

'Jimmy McLarnin is like thousands of other American businessmen,' reported the *Vancouver Province*. 'He wakes up with the baby at about 6.30 am, watches his wife pack the older kids off to school about 8.30 and arrives at his own office promptly at 9.' Also, like many other successful businessmen, Jimmy frequently knocked off work early in the afternoon and charged out to the golf links.

'Not very exciting I guess, but I'm not very young any more either,' said Jimmy. Things had changed since he sold the old *World* newspaper at Carrall & Hastings in Vancouver, aged ten; weighing 58 pounds. 'My little girl is ten and she weighs 105, so you know I had it tough,' said Jimmy.

Business was good enough to begin with so that Jimmy, Bing Crosby, and a few other Hollywood businessmen with chips could play games where the stakes ran as high as $1,100. Once or twice a month he and Lillian attended a night club where Jimmy admitted to taking 'one or possibly two drinks of hard liquor', a trick he had learned for the first time five years previously. But Jimmy's high-rolling days were drawing to an end. He had bought about $90,000 worth of equipment to machine parts for the arms industry. He got all set up and the war was over. 'If the war had continued I would have been rich,' said Jimmy many years later. 'Pop Foster said, "What do you know about business? What are you trying prove? Now godammit Jimmy, get out, you've lost enough money, get out of this."' But undeterred Jimmy bought another business manufacturing steel titles. In three years he lost two hundred thousand bucks. 'I was a bad businessman. That was a mistake. It was hard earned money. I'd saved that money and Pop had saved that money.' The first indication that Jimmy was in trouble and may have been taking more than 'one or possibly two drinks of hard liquor' came in August 1950 when he briefly peered out at the world between iron bars after being arrested on suspicion of drunk driving. He was booked at Hollywood Division police station after crashing into another car on his way home late from a day of golfing at Lakeside Country Club.

Jimmy finally took Pop's advice and got shot of his businesses. He took a job with a Hollywood travel agency, booking trips for the stars, a lot of them his friends. One of his clients was Bing Crosby. Even Pop put some business his way when, at the age of eighty, he hopped off to visit his old home in England.

By now Jimmy was living in Glendale with Lillian, his three daughters and a new son, Jimmy Jr. 'I'll teach him to defend himself, but I hope he doesn't fight,' said Jimmy. 'I fought for only one reason: the money. I had no love for the game. I owe everything to boxing. It allowed me to help my family and build a comfortable life. But it's a hard, tough business and the money isn't worth it today.' After little Jimmy was born, they just didn't have enough room for Pop as well so he moved nearby. Pop longed to return to Vancouver and he spent a great deal of time in the city and on the Island. He preferred to stay there as long as his rheumatism could stand the climate. Once more a generation of McLarnin made way for another. Jimmy's father passed away in his ninety-third year in November 1951. At the funeral were old friends by the score, people he hadn't seen since the old fighting days, school chums, sparring partners. 'It was a wonderful thing,' Jimmy said afterwards. 'The kind of thing a fellow never forgets, no matter how cynical he may be.' He met Hec McDonald there. Hec was once a great fighter too and his connection with the McLarnin family went back a long way. When Hec's dad came over from Ireland to Vancouver, he visited the furniture shop owned by Jimmy's dad. And Jimmy himself trundled his purchases over to the McDonald home in a handcart. 'Hec weighed about fifteen pounds in those days,' Jimmy recalled. 'But what a fighter he became.'

Then came the biggest blow of all. In May 1956 Pop died in a Glendale hospital, not far from the McLarnin home after a brief illness.

'The finest man in the world has just died,' said Jimmy through the tears.

The funeral was held on 9 May 1956 by the Forest Lawn mortuary in the Little Church of the Flowers with internment at Forest Lawn Memorial park. The speaker was Jimmy McLarnin. 'I owe a lot to Pop,' Jimmy said quietly. 'He was a wonderful, wonderful man.'

When the terms of Pop's will were disclosed it showed that $1,100 was to be distributed among his friends living in Vancouver; Robert McLarnin, Mrs M. Blackburn, Alexander B. Middlemas and his wife Violet. He left $300 to another friend in England, Harold Troup. Five cousins in England were given a total of $10,000 in equal shares. The remaining $200,000 was bequeathed to Jimmy and his family. 'The old sergeant major lived frugally the rest of his days. McLarnin didn't throw his money out of attic windows, exactly, either,' wrote Jim Murray in the *Los Angeles Times*. 'But he did buy a dry hole here and there.'

'The amount was a surprise but I was aware of the contents of his will,' said Jimmy. 'Pop always saved his money. I tried to make him spend more and enjoy life, but he'd grin, "Some people like to spend. I have more fun saving."'

Many years earlier Pop had told a reporter of his intention to leave his money to Jimmy and his then fiancée. 'It represents my share of Jimmy's purses. He made it for me, so he should have it when I'm through,' Pop explained.

Pop and Jimmy never had a contract between them. They had lived and worked together for thirty-six years since Jimmy was thirteen. Pop had stood in his corner through every fight. He'd thrown every shot and taken every blow. He gloried with Jimmy in victory and groaned with him in defeat, but he turned his grim old face to the world and told it in no uncertain tones that his boy was the greatest of 'em all.

EPILOGUE

Bless us all … Bless us all…
The heavy, the light and the small,
Bless our flat noses and cauliflowered ears,
For we are the ones whom
They stood up and cheered.
Now we're saying, 'So long to us all,
The long, the short and the tall.
May God keep us busy,
We'll see you next Wednesday;
Stay cheered, guys and dolls,
Bless us all.'
The Cauliflower Alley Club

Cauliflower Alley, with its whiff of bootleg scotch and speakeasy smoke, was traditionally found behind the boxing clubs, a strip where bets were laid, fights were bought and dreams were broken. Fifty years on another 'Runyonesque collection' of former boxers, wrestlers and their actor friends gathered every week in Los Angeles under the guise of the Cauliflower Alley Club. Every Wednesday a procession of old men with bent noses, heavy scar tissue, and, of course, cauliflower ears, entered the Hollywood Plaza Hotel for lunch and a drink or three. Many of them came to Hollywood when they retired from the ring, looking to replace the arc lights for bright lights of the movies. Members were presented a giant, golden, squashed and bloated ear and a certificate that read – 'be it known evermore that X is a gladiatorial graduate of the most celebrated college of hard knocks.'

'They are schmaltzy, sentimental, remindful that their hey-days were sixty, fifty, forty years ago,' wrote Lynn Simross in the *Los Angeles Times*. 'They do not seem offended if you do not remember them, but they are glad to tell their stories. Most of them have posed for pictures for so many years, they know just the right turn of head, lift of the chin.' Jimmy McLarnin was there every week. He liked fighters did Jimmy. 'I never met a fighter who wasn't a nice fellow,' he used to say.

'A lot of them were hams, but Jimmy was a gentleman and all things considered, rather modest, but extremely confident and sure of who he was, what he was,' recalled artist Lowell Darling who filmed a video installation with this motley gang. 'Jimmy's excessive drinking is tolerated,' wrote Darling. 'He is the only member who drinks compulsively at the meetings. Some speculate that he does so because he feels guilty for having been so successful in handling his money. Others say it is because he harbours a deep-seated vendetta: he still wants a rematch with the only kid who knocked him out, over fifty years ago.'

'Sometimes he might get drunk, but he is not punch drunk. At the age of seventy, Jimmy is definitely not a man to get riled, drunk or sober. He has fists as fast as a bad idea and as strong as a good one. As he weaves toward his wife, who is waiting at the door to take him home, no one makes a wisecrack. Jimmy is the most respected boxer to walk down Cauliflower Alley,' wrote Darling.

A typical lunch was 'a little loose, a little rowdy'. Jimmy usually illustrated his stories by banging his right fist against his left hand for emphasis, sending a sharp echo bouncing off the golden velour walls. 'I never drank,' Jimmy told an interviewer in 1992 at his home in Glendale, California. 'I do a little belting now once in a while, but I never did when I was fighting. I never took a drink until I was fifty years old.'

Joe Stone, a boxing historian and World War II boxing trainer told Darling of a night when he was awoken with a phone call from a boxing student who was getting 'crocked in a gin-mill'.

'I'm here with Jimmy McLarnin,' the kid announced. 'Jimmy says to say hello. We're arguing about how to use a left hook and want you to come down and settle it. Jimmy says you taught me all wrong.'

'You never did it the way I taught you,' Stone replied. 'And I'm not getting out of bed to prove it.'

The next day the kid showed up on Joe Stone's doorstep. Joe welcomed him with a pat to his midsection. The kid flinched.

'After I called you, Joe, Jimmy and I went out to the parking lot for a boxing lesson. Each of us threw a left hook to the body. I held an arm down, but he still broke two of my ribs.'

'If you have a difference of opinion with Jimmy McLarnin, kid, don't ever take it to the parking lot.'

After the travel agency Jimmy took a job working for another ex-fighter Eddie Dyer, as contact man and salesman in a plating and metal processing company in Paramount. He also took on the role of fight promoter. When Roy M. Cohn and young Bill Fugazy of Feature Sports, Inc. wanted to stage an Archie Moore-Erich Schoeppner light heavyweight title fight at the Los Angeles Coliseum in 1960 they needed a local co-promoter since the state athletic commission frowned on outsiders marching in. 'We have had unofficial discussions with the commission and we think McLarnin, who has lived here since 1924 will be acceptable,' said Fugazy. The match never materialised. He flirted with politics and in February 1962 Jimmy was one of the 'commentators' on a series of exhibitions by professional fighters at a $50-a-plate testimonial dinner for Democrat Richard Nevins. But in September of the same year Jimmy was one of nine stars that flew out to a sportsman's barbeque in Sacramento to kick off Richard Nixon's campaign for governor. Bob Haldeman, campaign manager, said the sports stars would participate in rallies and work with a 'Celebrities for Nixon' committee.

To the end Jimmy carried just a few pounds more than his best fighting weight and there were only a few signs to betray his previous profession. It was his hands that gave him away, they looked frightening outside a pair of gloves, 'like they were soaked in molten steel'. 'Even if you met him in the dark, you'd know it was Jimmy when you shook hands,' wrote one scribe. 'His right mitt has more lumps than boarding-house pudding.' They resembled mangled claws and eventually he wasn't able to grip his golf clubs. But he kept in trim, ate very few starches and lots of fruit, vegetables, fish and chicken. 'I am fond of studying the body,' Jimmy once said. 'It gives me considerable pleasure to know just how my body is built, what foods and what exercises will keep it in proper condition and how to avoid bodily ailments. When you consider that your span of life is determined by the food you eat and how you eat it, doesn't it seem rather strange that the majority of persons abuse their body by putting things promiscuously into their stomach that with proper thought, they never would attempt to do? Doesn't it seem odd how little attention is paid to food and yet so much care is given to proper clothes? A man who takes proper care of his body physically, eats the right kind of food, digests his meals as they should be, takes the normal period of rest nightly, drinks sufficient water and lives a normal life, can live to three-score years and ten.'

Jimmy did better than that by quarter of a century. 'He was very careful with his diet, and he loved his golf,' recalled Jimmy Jr. 'He never ate bread, he chewed his meat, then spit it out and swallowed the juice. He said that was the best part of it. The entire time we were with him he always would eat that way. It was always pickle, pork or pastries. He never ate any of them. On Saturdays Jimmy would buy donuts and give them to the children. He'd watch us eat the donuts and tell us how bad they were for us.'

He became a pink-faced, scrubbed, dapper little old man with wisps of grey hair and the bright blue eyes now magnified behind bottle glasses. 'I looked at him and the years rolled back and I could see the real Jimmy McLarnin clearly,' wrote Jim Murray. 'It was in the Depression, when the bootleg era was being phased out. New York was the Great White Way. Jimmy Walker was mayor, girls were flappers and prizefighting owned our child-hood. Our heroes were not football players, unless they hap-pened to play for Notre Dame, baseball was Babe Ruth and basketball was something to do before the dance … What I see is the lithe young tiger in green trunks, the announcer holding his hand up and screaming, "The winner and still champion of the world", and it is a time when I still have his picture in my room and all is well in the old neighbourhood. When he won, we did.' Grantland Rice described him as 'one of the finest fighters and one of the nicest people the game ever knew'.

Benny Leonard had died in 1947, collapsing in the ring while refereeing a fight. Tony Canzoneri died in 1959, Barney Ross in 1967 and Lou Ambers in 1995. Jimmy outlived them all, even his old friend, Bob Hope. All the men he fought under the hot lights of Madison Square Garden were dead.

Then Lillian, his wife of more than fifty years, succumbed to cancer in 1989.

'I lost my bride,' Jimmy said. 'I didn't think I'd outlive her.'

Jimmy moved back to the Pacific Northwest after Lillian's death. Three of his children were living in the Tri-Cities and they convinced him to move to a retirement community nearby with his enormous cat named Sassy. With his golfing days over Jimmy stayed in his apartment most days, reading the paper and watching sports on the television. The walls of the apartment were adorned with black-and-white photos and newspaper clip-pings. Jimmy lunching with Jean Harlow, shaking hands with Clark Gable, and smiling, cradled in the arms of Joe Louis.

Jimmy died quietly aged ninety-six in Richland, Washington State on 28 October 2004. He had lived too long for it to be news, but the old timers knew that one of the best, the last of the great Fighting Irishmen, had passed on. There was one last journey to California and Jimmy was interred at the Forest Lawn Memorial Park Cemetery in Glendale, California. He was finally back on the same patch as Pop.

'The fight game was good to me,' reflected Jimmy in his later years. 'I was able to help my family, and we needed a little help with that big family. I sent $300 a month home for years and years and years. In those days that was big money. Then I'd go home and we'd load my father's second hand furniture store up and buy the kids all lots of clothes. So I was able to do that. Thank God for the boxing business as far as I was concerned. It's a hazardous, ruthless business but I happen to have come out of it without being beaten up too badly. Of course I lost some fights, I didn't win them all. I had a great manager, which of course is so important in boxing, and in more ways than one I was very fortunate. The Big Boss upstairs had his hand on my shoulder. Now that's taking advantage of the situation. I don't know whether He likes prizefighters or not, but He sure liked me.'

JIMMY MCLARNIN – PROFESSIONAL BOXING RECORD

1923

Dec 19	Young Fry	Vancouver, BC, Can	KO 1
Dec 28	Mickey Gill	Vancouver, BC, Can	W 7

1924

Feb 13	Frankie Sands	Oakland, Ca	W 4
Feb 22	Eddie Collin	Oakland, Ca	TKO 3
Mar 5	Joe Conde	Oakland, Ca	TKO 3
Mar 19	Frankie Sands	Oakland, Ca	W 4
Mar 26	Sammy Lee	San Francisco, Ca	W 4
Apr 2	Jimmy Griffiths	Oakland, Ca	W 4
Apr 9	Frankie Grandetta	Oakland, Ca	W 4
Apr 23	Johnny Jockey Lightner	Oakland, Ca	W 4
Apr 30	Jockey Joe Dillon	Oakland, Ca	W 4
May 2	Jimmy Griffiths	Sacramento, Ca	W 4
May 14	Abe Gordon	San Francisco, Ca	KO 2
Sep 30	Benny Diaz	Vernon, Ca	W 4
Oct 7	Frankie Dolan	Vernon, Ca	W 4
Oct 14	Young Nationalista	Vernon, Ca	W 4
Oct 28	Fidel LaBarba	Vernon, Ca	W 4

| Nov 11 | Fidel LaBarba | Vernon, Ca | D 4 |
| Dec 9 | Memphis Pal Moore | Vernon, Ca | D 4 |

1925

Jan 13	Fidel LaBarba	Los Angeles, Ca	W 10
Mar 25	Teddy Silva	Los Angeles, Ca	W 10
Apr 11	Young Farrell	Los Angeles, Ca	W 6
Apr 18	Eddie Spec Ramies	Los Angeles, Ca	W 6
Jun 2	Charles 'Bud' Taylor	Vernon, Ca	L 10
Jul 4	Pancho Villa	Emeryville, Ca	W 10
Aug 10	Mickey Gill	Oakland, Ca	W 10
Nov 12	Jackie Fields	Los Angeles, Ca	KO 2
Dec 8	Charles 'Bud' Taylor	Vernon, Ca	W DQ 2

1926

Jan 12	Charles 'Bud' Taylor	Vernon, Ca	L 10
Mar 3	Joey Sangor	Los Angeles, Ca	KO 3
Mar 17	Johnny Farr	Los Angeles, Ca	L 10
Sep 7	Joe Glick	Los Angeles, Ca	W 10
Oct 15	Doc Snell	Vernon, Ca	L 10

1927

Feb 22	Tommy Cello	San Francisco, Ca	D 10
Apr 5	Tommy Cello	Los Angeles, Ca	W 10
May 6	Freeman Black	San Diego, Ca	KO 2
May 27	Johnny LaMar	Hollywood, Ca	W 10
Jun 24	Lope Tenorio	Hollywood, Ca	W 10
Sep 9	Charlie McBride	San Diego, Ca	KO 2
Sep 23	Don Long	San Diego, Ca	KO 3
Oct 18	Louis 'Kid' Kaplan	Chicago, Il	KO 8
Nov 23	Billy Wallace	Detroit, Mi	W 10

1928

Feb 24	Sid Terris	New York, NY	KO 1
May 21	Sammy Mandell	New York, NY	L 15
	– Lightweight Championship of the World		
Jun 21	Phil McGraw	New York, NY	TKO 1
Aug 2	Stanislaus Loayza	New York, NY	KO 4
Nov 30	Ray Miller	Detroit, Mi	L RTD 8

1929

Jan 11	Joe Glick	New York, NY	W 10
Mar 1	Joe Glick	New York, NY	KO 2
Mar 22	Ray Miller	New York, NY	W 10
Oct 9	Sergeant Sammy Baker	New York, NY	KO 1
Nov 4	Sammy Mandell	New York, NY	W 10
Dec 13	Ruby Goldstein	New York, NY	KO 2

1930

Mar 1	Sammy Mandell	Chicago, Il	W 10
Mar 28	Young Jack Thompson	New York, NY	W 10
Sep 11	Al Singer	Bronx, NY	KO 3
Nov 21	Billy Petrolle	New York, NY	L 10

1931

| May 27 | Billy Petrolle | New York, NY | W 10 |
| Aug 20 | Billy Petrolle | Bronx, NY | W 10 |

1932

Aug 4	Lou Brouillard	Bronx, NY	L 10
Oct 7	Benny Leonard	New York, NY	TKO 6
Dec 16	Sammy Fuller	New York, NY	KO 8

1933

| May 29 | Young Corbett III | Los Angeles, Ca | TKO 1 |

– Welterweight Championship of the World

1934

| May 28 | Barney Ross | Long Island City, NY | L 15 |

– Welterweight Championship of the World

| Sep 17 | Barney Ross | Long Island City, NY | W 15 |

– Welterweight Championship of the World

1935

| May 28 | Barney Ross | New York, NY | L 15 |

– Welterweight Championship of the World

1936

May 8	Tony Canzoneri	New York, NY	L 10
Oct 5	Tony Canzoneri	New York, NY	W 10
Nov 20	Lou Ambers	New York, NY	W 10

INDEX

ALSO AVAILABLE FROM THE O'BRIEN PRESS

Staying the Distance
Ronnie Delany

Ireland's most famous Olympian won the 1,500 metres gold in Melbourne fifty years ago, and went on to dominate middle-distance running for years. Here is his story, in his own words and lavishly-illustrated with over a hundred photographs.

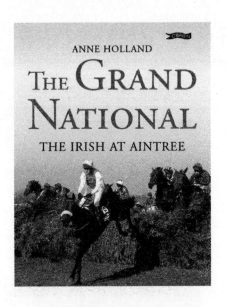

The Grand National – The Irish at Aintree
Anne Holland

This lavishly-illustrated book examines the Irish presence at Aintree from the festival's earliest years to the present day. A wide-ranging and compulsively readable account of a beloved institution.

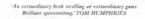

Kings of September –
The Day Offaly denied Kerry Five in a Row
Michael Foley

The award-winning, bestselling account of the classic 1982 final. An epic story of triumph and loss, joy and tragedy. *Boylesports Irish Sports Book of the Year 2007.*

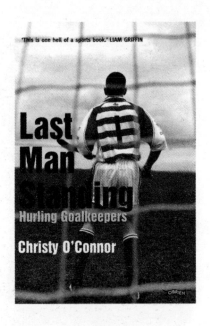

Last Man Standing – Hurling Goalkeepers
Christy O'Connor

What is it that makes a hurling goalie tick? Why would anybody be mad enough to take the loneliest position on the pitch? With unique access to many of Ireland's top players, Christy O'Connor reveals their drive, failures and triumphs.

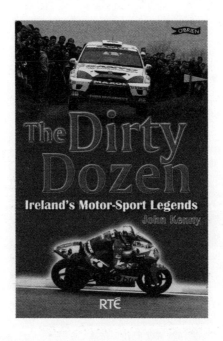

The Dirty Dozen – Ireland's Motorsport Legends
John Kenny

Celebrating Ireland's top racing drivers, from Formula One and motorbikes to rallying. All the glamour of the motor sport scene as well as its colourful characters.